desiring or feeling God's
presence   p 280

∞

SaintMaker

Michael de la Bedoyere

SaintMaker

The Remarkable Life
of Francis de Sales,
Shepherd of
Kings and Commoners,
Sinners and Saints

SOPHIA INSTITUTE PRESS®
Manchester, New Hampshire

SaintMaker: The Remarkable Life of Francis de Sales, Shepherd of Kings and Commoners, Sinners and Saints was originally published in 1960 by Harper and Brothers, New York, under the title *François de Sales*. This 1998 edition by Sophia Institute Press contains minor editorial revisions throughout the text.

Copyright © 1998 Charlotte de la Bedoyere

All rights reserved

Jacket design by Lorraine Bilodeau

The cover artwork is a detail of a window of the basilica adjacent to the monastery of the Visitation Convent in Annecy, France. The window was designed by Charles Plessard and made by Francis Chigot in the 1940s. Photograph by A. Robert McGilvray, O.S.F.S.

Sophia Institute Press®
Box 5284, Manchester, NH 03108
1-800-888-9344
www.sophiainstitute.com

Library of Congress Cataloging-in-Publication Data

De la Bedoyere, Michael, 1900-
   [François de Sales]
   Saintmaker : the remarkable life of Francis de Sales, shepherd of
      kings and commoners, sinners and saints / Michael de la Bedoyere.
      p. cm.
   Originally published: François de Sales. New York : Harper, 1960.
   Includes bibliographical references.
   ISBN 0-918477-86-7 (pbk. : alk. paper)
   1. Francis, de Sales, Saint, 1567-1622. 2. Christian saints —
      Biography. I. Title.
   BX4700.F85D37   1998
   282'.092 — dc21
   [b]   98-37647 CIP

98 99 00 01 02 10 9 8 7 6 5 4 3 2 1

To
John Carmel Heenan
Archbishop of Liverpool
of whose pastoral zeal
and gift for friendship
I was often reminded
while writing this biography

*Alas, my daughter, I am a man
and nothing if not a man.*

Francis de Sales, in a letter
to Madame de Chantal

Contents

∞

Introduction

Who would deny, however unsatisfactory their own lives, that to be a saint is the supreme expression of human life on earth? We recognize in sanctity or great holiness the closest possible relationship between a man and God, who is the supreme Reality, the supreme Truth, Goodness, and Beauty. "God is the only reality, and we are only real so far as we are in His order, and He in us," wrote Coventry Patmore.

When we reflect on the all-comprehensiveness of God, it is not surprising that the saints should vary immensely in the outward signs of their sanctity, and, in honesty, we must admit that many saints seem strange and puzzling figures. Saints, of course, are not born saints, and their sanctity has to be incarnated in the psychological and physical complex which makes them the particular human beings they are. This life-long process of growing union between one individual from among the infinite variety of human character and the supreme "isness" of God must lead to many different expressions of sanctity.

Each of us, therefore, with his own particular character and taste, will tend to find one saint more attractive and understandable than another. Similarly, people of one culture and period of history will tend to prefer certain saints, certain kinds of holiness, and be puzzled perhaps by the popularity of saints in earlier epochs.

Today it is the contemplative and the unassuming saints who seem to attract us most: St. Francis of Assisi, St. Teresa of Avila, St. John of the Cross, St. Thérèse of Lisieux, St. Thomas More, St. Philip Neri, the Curé d'Ars. St. Francis de Sales[1] would probably be included in any short list, but less perhaps is known about him by the ordinary person than about the others — in Britain and America, at any rate. Many books about his contemplative teaching have been written, and his two great works, the *Introduction to the Devout Life* and the *Treatise on the Love of God*, called by Dom John Chapman[2] "the greatest work of genius in theology since St. Thomas," are still widely read. But, strangely, no English-speaking writer has for a very long time told the fascinating story of St. Francis's life. This was one reason why I have been bold enough to attempt the task.

The second is that St. Francis de Sales is the patron of writers and journalists, and it is surprising that they have not queued up to make their patron better known. In passing, may I say that the study of his life showed him to be a most suitable patron for a great variety of occupations — of viniculture and pubs, for example (for he once performed the most charming of miracles to enable his traveling companions to drink wine rather than the excellent mountain water) and of rowing and

---

[1] This edition uses the English rather than the French spellings of some names (such as Francis de Sales and Jane Frances de Chantal), as they are more commonly known to today's English readers.

[2] John Chapman (1865-1933), Benedictine patristic scholar and spiritual writer.

university boat clubs (for he called himself a "doctor of row-ing"). A third reason is that St. Francis de Sales was indeed the greatest of all mystical theologians — the saint of the "love of God," the spiritual approach which more and more people to-day, however dimly and feebly, find to be the most rewarding.

I was encouraged to try my hand because the task did not seem to be so very difficult for a journalist-writer. There can be few saints about whom more is known, and what is known has been made easily available. The monumental Annecy edition of his works in twenty-six volumes is an inexhaustible quarry, and it is to the English Benedictine Dom Mackey that we owe this great work, completed long after his death. Two immense lives in French — the 1,300 pages of Hamon and the nearly 1,500 much better informed pages of Msgr. Trochu (published during the war)[3] — give us the facts. Bremond, of course, sets the scene.[4]

Alas, all this proved a veritable *embarras de richesses* for the writer of a short life which would be neither a mere summary of the long lives, nor an essay on the saint. One was faced with the problem, for example, of telling the story adequately and yet finding room for letters which the great lives, long as they are, omitted presumably through lack of space. For me it is in his letters that St. Francis most vividly lives today.

I must now quite simply confess that the writing of this book has left me with the conviction that Francis de Sales is

[3] André Jean Marie Hamon, *Vie de François de Sales* (1854); François Trochu, *Saint François de Sales* (Lyon: E. Vitte, 1942).

[4] Henri Bremond, *A Literary History of Religious Thought in France* (New York: Macmillan Co., 1936).

the greatest of the saints — at least for modern times. And I base this conviction on the sense I had all the time that here was the human being of our period of Western history who, naturally, instinctively, as well as supernaturally, reflected most directly the character and way of Christ our Lord. It was long after this truth had been brought home to me that I read the words of St. Vincent de Paul:[5] "Msgr. de Sales ardently wished to imitate the Son of God. So closely did he model his life on our Lord as I myself saw, that many a time I asked myself with astonishment how a mere creature could reach so high a degree of perfection, given human frailty. . . . Recalling and meditating on his words, I felt them to be so admirable that I could only see in him the person who most nearly reproduced the Son of God living on earth."

"Perfection," yes; but, in the case of Francis de Sales, it is the humanity within perfection, the love, the tenderness, as well as the tremendous strength, which make one so strongly feel how like he was to our Lord.

It has been waggishly said that Francis de Sales "invented Christian charity." We need not do more than smile at that, while at the same time finding the phrase unforgettable and by no means entirely off the point. It seems to be the paradoxical answer to the fear one has of men who are "too perfect." There will be something of the hypocrite in the "too perfect man," we feel, or else we shall come up against strains of harshness, inhumanity, resulting from lack of balance, from suppression of endearing human weaknesses. Miraculously, Francis de Sales

---

[5]   St. Vincent de Paul (c. 1580-1660), founder of the Lazarist Fathers and the Sisters of Charity.

comes out the "perfect man," not the "too perfect man." Did he not say of himself that he was "nothing if not a man"?

It was his glory that the humanity in him was always retained and rightly directed, but through the hardest and highest of spiritual disciplines: increasing detachment from his ego so that God who is Love might transform with the touch of Divinity itself the natural balance and tenderness of his character. It was in the continuous practice of giving himself up to God and to his neighbor that his own humanity became radiant and without blemish.

Love, or charity, for Francis de Sales, while reaching in the end to the heights of mystical love, also seemed inevitably to feed on the lesser natural loves for his own family, his friends, the people entrusted to his pastoral care, the great and the humble, and not least the weak and sinful. Nor did the great apostle of the Chablais, brought up in times of religious wars and trained in the harsh views of intolerance then current on both sides, see the heretic as other than his neighbor to be converted by love. "Love will shake the walls of Geneva; by love we must invade it; by love we must conquer it," he said to the chapter of his diocese when first he addressed it.

Francis de Sales is immortally linked with St. Jane Frances de Chantal, for their relationship, apart from its spiritual fruits, was unique. To the ordinary person, that relationship can only be a mystery, for it went unbelievably deep in the natural as well as in the supernatural order. It was love, even human love, free and full, in which there was no taint, no suspicion, no breath of anything but their supernatural vocations. Again one is forced back to Scriptural parallels: the love of Joseph for Mary, the love of our Lord for Martha and Mary.

Among the other women with whom Francis de Sales came into close contact through his spiritual direction and his gift for friendship were Madame Acarie (Blessed Mary of the Incarnation), one of the most interesting mystics of her time, and Angélique Arnauld, the famous Abbess of Port Royal, who might be accounted his one great failure, despite the tenderness of their relations.

Francis de Sales sought to live outside the great world of his day, asking only to minister to his "poor wife" of a diocese and to train men and women in the love of God, most of all Jane Frances de Chantal, with whom he founded the Order of the Visitation, whose beginnings make one of the most beautiful of pictures of religious life. Yet his birth, his status, his gifts, and his fame connected him in many ways with the period of history when the religious civil wars of France under Catherine de' Medici[6] ended with the pacification and renewal of the country under the convert Henry IV.[7]

To anyone who knows the decadence and immorality of those times, it is astonishing to think of the sanctity of a Francis de Sales. He was the friend of kings and princes, of semi-feudal nobles and their families, of cardinals, bishops, and clergy of every type, yet untainted in a relationship which was always personal and natural. Further, he holds his place in French literature as a writer in the formative period which led to the great days of Louis XIV.[8] For the reader, as for the biographer,

[6] Catherine de' Medici (1519-1589), queen of Henry II of France.

[7] Henry IV (1553-1610), King of France from 1589-1610; called Henry of Navarre.

[8] Louis XIV (1638-1715), King of France from 1643-1715.

these trimmings lend color and glamour to one of the most human lives lived all for God.

Had he had his own way, Francis de Sales would have been happiest as a writer and a spiritual director of souls. God willed that he should be a bishop and a public figure. It was in bearing these honors and dedicating his life to the heavy, active duties they entailed that he endured with unique zeal and never-failing cheerfulness a constant, unsung martyrdom. That, for him, was the method of detachment from self-love for the love of God.

The reader, by this time, will surely be accusing me of having lost my head over my subject. Actually, what follows is written in a detached manner, for throughout I have sought to regard my hero as a historical figure, freed from the overtones which his reputation and sanctity too easily import into a biographer's judgment. And perhaps just because I have sought only the "man" and the "human," I have been driven, as I look back, to see him only as the most wonderful and fascinating of saints.

I hope that these pages may be of interest to readers who do not belong to the Faith which unites their subject and their writer, for St. Francis has always had a wide Christian appeal, not least to members of the Anglican Faith. I have all the greater hope that this may be so in that I have long had in my possession a copy of the *Devout Life*, inscribed "A. W. Roffen," the signature at one time of my own grandfather who was successively Bishop of Rochester and Bishop of Winchester, Anthony Wilson Thorold.

∞

SaintMaker

Chapter One

Discovering the Love
That Casts Out All Fear

1567-1588

Francis de Sales, a young nobleman of then-independent Savoy, had been sent by his parents from the backwoods of the lower Alpine ranges of his native country to complete his studies in Paris, the capital of worldly culture.

The boy, we are told, had begged his father to allow him to do his Parisian studies under the Jesuits in their fashionable University College of Clermont, near the Sorbonne, so modern, so sound, so brilliantly staffed by the most brilliant of the sons of St. Ignatius.[9] They were eager to show that the very best contemporary learning could be effectively enlisted under the Standard of God and not be entirely appropriated by the Standard of Satan. Aristotle, Plato, Epictetus, Pliny, Virgil, Horace, Cicero, Seneca — those high-minded pagans could teach the good Catholic of the day a great deal worth fitting into Catholic philosophy, morals, and spiritual doctrine. A perfect acquaintance with Latin and maybe Greek would help

---

[9]   St. Ignatius (1491-1556), founder of the Jesuits.

fashion the new look and style with which to present to a sinful and brutish world the "devout humanism" that could serve
God's greater glory in an age of transition when new men, new
ideas, and new ways were quickly making themselves felt.

De Sales had been fifteen years old when in 1582 he had
set out on horseback, accompanied by his private tutor, the
testy and severe Abbot Déage, on the 250-mile journey from
the château de Sales by Thorens, a few miles north of Annecy.
The young man — for development was quicker in those
days — strong, good-looking (but for a slight cast in one eye),
secretly rather proud of his mass of wavy fair hair, had taken
lodgings with his tutor, not in the college itself, but in a manner more befitting his rank in the hostelry of the Rose Blanche
across the road from the tall Gothic buildings of Clermont.

Fashionably dressed — velvet cap, embroidered cloak, dou-
blet, padded breeches, tight hose, a sword swinging from the
hips — de Sales had not taken long to accustom himself to the
social life of the capital. He had the *entrée* to its great world,
even to the court of Henry III, whose queen was half-sister to
the Duke of Mercoeur, a cadet of the princely house of Lorraine
and cousin of the ambitious Guise who did not despair of
winning the throne for the descendants of Charlemagne, as he
claimed himself to be. The Saleses had for some generations
been pages of the Mercoeurs.

From them the young student heard highest-level talk of
the fierce wars of religion and the plans of the Catholic Holy
League to wrest the crown for the Cardinal of Lorraine and
thus save Catholic France from heresy and the disastrous succession to the throne of the Calvinist Henry Bourbon of
Navarre, first Prince of the Blood. The son of a brave soldier

and brought up in the shadow of Geneva's Calvinist aggression almost to the doors of his own Savoy home, this serious and quiet student would listen eagerly to such conversations. Knowing the Calvinists and the way they had overrun Catholic lands near his home in Savoy, he did not take scandal at the reversion to barbarism which this terrible fighting — part social, part political, and part religious — entailed.

Yet he himself was all gentleness, all courtesy, already someone shaping toward a more cultured and polite age. He did not shun the social life and elegant manners of the men and women around him, for his own sense of that which is fitting and his father's wishes demanded proper attention to the formation of a gentleman of Savoy. Gravely and with dignity, for he never did things by halves, he would join in the dance, mix with the ladies, and drink to the heroes of the day, just as he would devote the appropriate time to learn music, the art of fencing and equitation, and other accomplishments necessary to a person of his rank. His tough childhood in Savoy had afforded him plenty of natural physical strength and suppleness.

But if the young de Sales, as he matured in Paris, accepted all this side of life with such good grace and sincerity, it certainly did not represent the real person, for the real person was governed by two passions. One of them was learning; the other was God. One catalogs them together, not because they were remotely on a par in his mind, but because each counted in itself, even though the second was infinitely the more important.

Let us say that *au fond* he was a terribly serious young man; but in saying this we must not forget that his seriousness could never destroy an exceptional human and social sensitivity and delicacy. "I am nothing if not a man," he was to confess many years later, and those words were the key to his character and the quality of his ultimate sanctity. So if we call him a book-worm, we must also say that he managed to be that rare crea-ture: an attractive and popular bookworm.

Universities in those days were in any case no picnic. At Clermont daily life began at four o'clock in the morning, with the first lecture at five. After Mass and a *petit pain*, studies and lectures filled the greater part of the day and were resumed af-ter supper. But even if the daily round had been less severe, de Sales would undoubtedly have seen to it that not a minute of his day was wasted. He was avid of knowledge of every kind — and for its own sake.

The truth is that a whole new world seemed to be opening out before that generation in Paris University. "The very walls and roofs seemed to be philosophizing," de Sales was later to say when accepting his doctorate in law at Padua University. Education was passing from a mechanical memorizing of a conventionally agreed syllabus to the use of the understanding and the imagination in the appreciation of the beauty in the French language, in the application of the classical tradition to the still-unshaped flow of thinking and writing, in the fashioning of the renewed ideal of rounded, knowledgeable, measured, autonomous man: the ideal of the *honnête homme* ("gentleman"). The university seemed like a protected enclave hardly touched by the decadence of the last Valois and the fury of the civil wars which had cut off the first glories of the Renaissance and reduced France to years of lawlessness and anarchy. Knowledge, in a sense rather different from what we understand today, was felt to be the power: power to live, to observe, to think for oneself, and to shape a world in terms of reason, judgment, balance, harmony, and beauty.

De Sales, carrying about with him his neat notebooks — each page carefully filled with his close, clear script, set out on the page with a certain flourish of aesthetic satisfaction — was thus ardently absorbing and adapting the whole world of classicism and returning to Thomas Aquinas[10] (the first "devout humanist"), making himself a master of Latin, a passable Greek scholar (Greek was frowned upon by the old stagers but encouraged by the Jesuits), tackling Hebrew for the Scriptures, and, of course, improving his natural gift for writing, which was to develop into such an effective instrument for the free and flexible expression of the delicate nuances of the relation of the soul with God. All his life he would have the gift of keeping notes and references in such good order that he would always have to hand what he needed for preaching and writing on any subject.

With a mind thus formed in the spirit of the day, he could the better appreciate the poetry of a Ronsard and the style of a Montaigne[11] — Montaigne whom he readily recognized as a *"beau esprit"* but one lacking that seriousness, that sense of life's true purpose which, in the case of this one student in the university during those six years of his course, went far deeper than any love, however intense, of study and learning, any respect, however genuine, for the social graces of polite living.

---

[10] St. Thomas Aquinas (c. 1225-1274), Dominican philosopher and theologian.

[11] Pierre de Ronsard (1524-1585), French poet; Michel Eyquem de Montaigne (1533-1592), French essayist.

∞

The sense of life's true purpose — to understand something of what these words meant to this student from Savoy in his late teens, we must take a brief glance at his childhood. This is not very easy because it is the habit of biographers of future saints to write the wrong way around. They feel it necessary to allow the future sanctity to suffuse retrospectively every act and word from the cradle on. Francis de Sales, who was to die already acclaimed as a saint, has certainly been streamlined by hagiographers for that almost instantaneous flight to sanctity, but the characteristics of the little boy's precocious holiness, as too often described, simply do not square with the special and most attractive traits of his undisputed later character. Although self-centered priggishness is the caricature of God-centered sanctity, it is not always easy to distinguish the one from the other in saints' lives. But it should be possible to do so in any phase of Francis de Sales's life, for only an enemy could accuse the apostle of the Chablais or the Bishop of Geneva of the remotest touch of priggishness or sanctimoniousness. He was the freshest, freest, easiest of the great saints — and the most humanly attractive. The germ of all this must have been discernible in his childhood.

The picture is of a child living in a well-to-do — but for its station, not wealthy — household of some forty people in the uncomfortable château of Sales. Its lands and surroundings were in a thickly wooded valley where deer, wolves, and bears still roamed under the peaks of the Parmelan and the Sous-Dine. Francis was the eldest son, born when his mother was only fifteen. For some years, he was to be the only child, as subsequent children died at or near birth. Had Francis been born in the winter of 1567 instead of the summer, he, too, might well have died.[12]

This household was ruled with a rod of iron, although justly and from the highest principles, by M. de Boisy,[13] peppery old soldier and diplomat, nearly three times the age of his wife. All the decisions about this prized son and heir were to be his, and usually against the secret wishes of his very pious and submissive wife who, after a few years, must have felt far closer in age to her son than to her husband. M. de Boisy saw Francis as a soldier of fame in Savoy, and the last thing he dreamed of producing was a priest or a saint.

Mme. de Boisy, on the other hand, felt a deep spiritual kinship between herself and her unusually serious and devout little boy. The latter, as he grew up, secretly cherished the dream of one day becoming a priest, a notion whose fantastic nature can be realized by the fact that he did not dare tell his father until he was twenty-six. It does not seem clear whether he even told his beloved mother. Between them, however, mother and

[12] Interesting to us today is the fact that the Shroud of Turin, where the Duke of Savoy resided as Prince of Piedmont, was brought for veneration to Annecy at a time when Francis's young mother was hoping for a child. Not long after she had prayed before the Holy Shroud, Francis was conceived.

[13] Confusion may be caused by the fact that Francis's father and mother were called Monsieur and Madame de Boisy (not de Sales), a name taken, as was then the custom, from a *seigneurie*, or property, belonging to the family. Francis, before he became a priest, was for a short time called Monsieur de Villaroget. In a Roman Missal, I have seen him promoted to the rank of earl. In fact, the family, although ancient and noble, had no title at that period. One of Francis's brothers was to be made a baron by the Duke of Savoy.

son did manage to get into the head of the father that his eldest boy would never make the soldier of his dreams. M. de Boisy had therefore to reconcile himself to the fact that if this disappointing boy would never bring glory to the family in his father's footsteps, he had better be trained for the law so that he might shine one day in the senate and government of Savoy.

It is hard to believe that Francis could have been entirely happy in his home governed by his martinet father, and the intensely affectionate nature of the future man may well have developed from his compensating adoration of his young mother and, later, the younger children. For many edifying tales of his earliest years, the gentle testimony of his mother may stand substitute: "I often noticed that even when he was still quite young, he was possessed of the blessings of Heaven and breathed only the love of God. . . . He never did anything to cause me sorrow, and he was always a comfort to me."

The occasional story, however, possesses a special significance as a presage of the future man. One, in particular, we owe to Francis himself, who related it in a letter to a nun three years before his death. The nun suffered from fear of "the spirits," and the writer, who told her that a convent was a hospital for the spiritually ill who wanted to be cured, explained that the fear of the Divine Spirit should drive out unworthy fears of any other spirits. "When I was a boy," he explained, "I used to suffer in the same way. To overcome this I forced myself, step by step, to go forward alone, strengthening my will by relying on God, into places where my imagination would play tricks on me. In the end, I so strengthened my will that the darkness and the solitude of the night became a delight to me, making me feel the presence of God, which is more strongly realized when one is alone like that."[14] One can see the boy, perhaps in the darker corners of the great rambling house or by the black woods in the deep shadows of the valleys, gritting his teeth as he slowly forced himself to get the better of the terrifying fancies of a lively imagination. It was an early start to that courage and self-discipline which goes far to explain the determination behind the gentle ways that he showed in later life.

During those early years, the boy was hardened and made self-reliant in the bitterly cold winters and loneliness of the mountain country, acquiring the arts of a harsh country life: riding, hunting, fishing, snaring, rowing (of which, to the surprise of a cardinal many years later, he was to show himself a past master). Such a school of discipline was also one of delight. Tougher for such a boy was his father's decision, in spite of the tears of his mother, to pack him off at the age of seven to the boarding school of La Roche, some miles away. Later, when La Roche was endangered by the Duke of Savoy's threats to drive the Calvinists out of the Chablais, he was put to school in Annecy.

Two other good stories of those days indicate the delicate values he was already acquiring. On one occasion, he was riding with a groom who had been told to buy him a pair of gloves. The deal was done with the usual gesticulating and bargaining, and the price was duly brought down before the purchase was made. The glove-maker, of course, complained that he was being ruined. When they left, the boy let the

---

[14] *The Works of St. Francis De Sales*, Vol. 19, 13. All references are to the Annecy edition.

groom ride ahead so that he could slip back into the shop and ask how much the man stood to lose. He paid him the difference. On another occasion, the boy was crossing a toll bridge with a servant. The servant refused to pay the toll, presumably because it was not enforceable on a nobleman. The boy saw the unfairness of this and insisted on payment being made.

The life of the Saleses, their kinsmen, and their friends in that part of the country was always overshadowed and even threatened by the Genevese and Bernese Calvinists who had driven out the Catholic Faith from the country north of the château up to the Lake of Geneva. The stories of the Calvinists and the ever-present threat of danger to land and religion made a deep impression on the boy. There is a splendid story of him as a little boy being told that there was a Calvinist visitor in the château — no doubt a relation, for the Reformation had divided families. Furious at hearing that the enemy at the gates was actually being entertained by his father, Francis picked up a stick and drove the cackling hens up to the walls of the house, shouting at the top of his voice, "Come on! Come on! At 'em, the heretics!"

The Reformation was only half a century old, and his father had a way of telling people what he thought of these upstart reformers. "Good gracious me, I'm older myself than they are! Absurd to take their views seriously! They are just like mushrooms sprung up in the night." The boy's uncle and cousins lived in Brens, near Geneva, and there the boy could see for himself the evidence all around of the way in which the churches had been desecrated and signs of the Catholic Faith removed, bells, shrines, and crosses.

What sort of boy was being formed by country life in that harsh and lonely land, by boarding schools where he lived and worked away from his young mother, by the sense of constant threat to his security, traditions, and Faith? Can it possibly have been the priggish goody-goody who seems too often to emerge from the biographies — the "sweet angel on earth" of the French tradition? It is incredible. It is at least admitted that he had a naturally quick temper. And peccadilloes, usually illustrating stubbornness, are related. But the tremendous charm, the iron will, the strong gentleness, and the keen sense of humor — not least about himself — which characterized the later man sprang from something different.

We are told that he was popular in his boarding school at Annecy (where much later Rousseau[15] at the seminary must have heard much of the saintly hero of the town) despite his meticulous piety and uprightness. This would have been impossible if there had been anything of the priggish or soft in his make-up. Schoolboys are not deceived about these things. The simple conclusion is that from his earliest years, his willpower and faith in God, illustrated in the story of his fear of ghosts, was making him take definite, thought-out decisions of principle about how he intended to live his life. A temperament by nature pious, very affectionate, rather slow and plodding, with perhaps a natural timidity about a hard and uncertain world, was being chiseled into what would become a superb balance of strength and gentleness.

The popularity of the Paris university student and the respect for his spiritual earnestness had already made themselves

---

[15] Perhaps author Jean-Jacques Rousseau (1712-1778). — ED.

felt in the tougher surroundings of school life. As schoolboy and student, he had the courage, one feels, never to allow any false shame to stop him from fairly and squarely putting first things first, while expressing quite naturally and spontaneously in his ordinary behavior all that life had taught him in his country upbringing, sternly disciplined by his father, but secure in the deep love and companionship of his young mother. As such he was paid the most eloquent of all compliments. His school and university friends accepted him for what he really was, and behavior which in others they might have condemned and derided as priggish they appreciated as something for once to be respected, admired, and loved. Certainly no one who begins to understand the grown man and saint could ever believe that in the boy and student there could ever have been anything of the self-centered play-actor, anything of the mawkish spoilsport.

Later, in Padua University, to which he went after Paris, he had a rather dissolute friend. Of this friend de Sales was to write later: "He lived dissolutely. I did not. I used to give him some good scoldings, and he took them in very good part." This sentence is like a flash of light on his youth. It expresses, as Francis de Sales's own words were always to express, the perfect balance of a man who was determined to follow life's true purpose and help others to do so, while being nothing if not human, in doing so.

But although we can guess at the continuous self-discipline which made this strengthening of his gentleness and humanity possible, the attainment of the final balance was not to be achieved without heroic cost. The social graces and the delightful studies of his years in Paris — during which he never returned home — were not enough. It was at the end of 1586, and he nineteen, that the great testing came so that, for a critical moment, he seemed to hover near spiritual collapse.

By this date he had long left the hostelry of the Rose Blanche, too noisy, crowded, and near to the college to permit of the quiet concentration which he needed and enjoyed. With his tutor, Déage, who was himself studying for a doctorate in theology, he had taken lodgings where they would not be disturbed.

By now Francis had reached the stage in his studies when he felt that the inquiry into the nature of being, of thinking, of moral values and aesthetics could no longer be divorced from the far superior consideration of God's revelation of the divine mysteries as these affected the destiny and way of life in man. Even though he was a layman, seeing little prospect of realizing his desire to be a priest in opposition to his father's will, his deep inquiring mind, he felt, must not stop short just where learning would take on its full meaning in the sacred science of theology. In those days it was not rare for the layman to study theology, while the great majority of priests had neither the learning nor the opportunity of doing so.

"That I may see . . . that I may see theology." With these words he had answered Déage, who was asking him how he would wish to spend the carnival days of 1586. The young man's thoughts must have been far away, as he mumbled the words of the gospel of Quinquagesima Sunday,[16] which opens carnival time on the eve of Lent, with the story of the blind

---

[16] The Sunday before Ash Wednesday and beginning Quinquagesima, the fifty-day period before Easter.

man asking, "Lord, that I may see."[17] "Only theology," he insisted in the conversation that followed, "will teach me what God wants to reveal to me in my inmost soul."

One may guess that, besides his own personal spiritual need, other factors prompted the desire to deepen his understanding of Catholic doctrine and moral teaching. The work of the Reformers in his own country haunted him, and no matter how deeply he buried his head in his books within the enclave of the studious Latin Quarter, he could not but lament the results of the great Huguenot challenge which was reducing France to a state of anarchy in the mounting religious, political, social, and party passions. A dozen times the country was being fought over between the Catholic League — the heretics strong in their knowledge that their leader, Henry of Navarre, was the true heir to the throne — and the present monarch, Henry III — the last of the Valois, desperately trying to maintain authority and order in his kingdom, under the inconsistent advice of his Italian mother, the enigmatic and often sinister Catherine de' Medici, one moment tolerant and statesmanlike, the next terrified into dark deeds.

Unfortunately, in a life otherwise so fully documented by its subject's letters, only one student letter written in Paris has survived. It was written in November 1585, and in it Francis makes but a single reference to political affairs. "I would be most willing," he wrote, "to give you our news here, but our news is only college news, and, anyway, the news we get is so uncertain (the Prince de Condé[18] has died a thousand deaths)

[17] Mark 10:51.

[18] Prince de Condé (1621-1686), French general.

that for this reason alone, I feel I may be excused."[19] Rumors must indeed have been flying in the quadrangles, for the Huguenot Condé's irruption against the League had come to grief within a few days and he was already in exile in Guernsey when de Sales wrote that letter.

The second letter of his which has survived and which was written five years later from Padua refers with sorrow to the successes of Henry of Navarre. Worrying about the grave danger of the triumph of heresy in the kingdom of St. Louis must have been an important factor in prompting him to study the Catholic theological answers to heretical doctrine.

And there was more to it than that. Recalling Paris days later he was to say, "I do not know what God will do with France, for its sins are very great." All around him in Paris was evidence of those sins. Piety and devotion went hand in hand with fanaticism and savagery. Reform jostled against laxity of every kind; massacres and assassination were considered by good Catholics (and Protestants) suitable means for settling not only public and private rivalries, but of promoting God's kingdom. Politically, the situation could hardly have been more effectively symbolized than by the fantastic culmination of the religious wars: Henry III personally arranging the hacking to death of the Catholic leader Henri de Guise; Henry III in turn being murdered by the Dominican fanatic Jacques Clément; and the eventual triumph of the heretic Henry of Navarre, who thought Paris "worth a Mass" and established himself as Henry IV, "the Great," to mold the future strength of France.

[19] *The Works of St. Francis de Sales*, Vol. 11, 1-2.

Late sixteenth-century Paris itself must have seemed like a corner of Hell compared with the peace and beauty of Savoy, where every meadow, every hill, every homestead would always seem to Francis de Sales a book of nature in which God's hand had written lessons of Divine Providence and ways. Paris offered dark, arcaded, narrow, muddy, evil-smelling streets, awkwardly encumbered by the merchants' heaped-up stalls that made passage nearly impossible for the crowds that were packed into its small area. The constant chatter and shout, the endless bargaining, the swearing, the quarrels as likely as not to end in bloodshed, were an endless distraction to a man seeking the peace of God. The noblemen trying to pick their way in the sludge and spare their offended nostrils; the haughty, pushing, bourgeois lawyers and traders, thinking themselves with their new-found wealth a cut above the nobles, so often much poorer than themselves; the swaggering soldiers ogling the girls; the cutthroats, the cringing beggars, the endless sick and maimed — what a pitiful comedy of misguided humanity. Worst of all were the priests "whose very name had become shameful and infamous and hardly used save to describe an ignorant or debauched person," as Bremond quotes from Amelote, who, doubtless, was exaggerating a real enough evil; and the religious laxity, and, not rarely, vice, which existed within so many of the vast number of religious houses and nunneries.

The Counter-Reformation, it must be remembered, took effect much later in France than in Italy. We cannot be surprised if the pain of mounting heresy and the moral degradation around him should have threatened the spiritual balance of a mind tired after five solid years of concentrated work.

Yet the temptation itself was like a disastrous summer storm breaking out in a long period of beneficent weather, for neither before nor after was Francis de Sales to experience anything comparable. It seems totally uncharacteristic.

What guarantee had he — he began to ask himself — that he himself might not be caught up in the *massa damnata* of heretics and sinners of which the world seemed full? He had evidently been studying the enigma of predestination and the mysteries of God's Providence in the light especially of the teachings of the reformers. Brooding over the terrible and only too likely fate of much the greater part of mankind, and measuring his own state with the most delicate of measures where others were content with the roughest of scales, he asked himself whether, in the sight of an all-perfect God, the difference between his own feeble attempts to live well and the perversion which surrounded him could be anything but trifling. And if he could not but honestly judge that God had so far preserved him from grave sin, what security could he have in so evil a world that he would persevere in grace?

Alas, in that mood, he was not reassured when he turned from the frightening teaching of the reformers to St. Augustine[20] and St. Thomas Aquinas. These most orthodox of teachers seemed as uncompromising about God's foreknowledge and the consequent predestination of men. Those who are saved are saved through God's eternal disposition of the graces which will save them, said St. Augustine. From all eternity, God has once and for all decreed those destined for glory in Heaven, and this decree is prior even to God's foreknowledge

[20] St. Augustine (354-430), Bishop of Hippo.

of the merits of men. God has willed to show forth His mercy in those whom He predestines to salvation, His justice to those He predestines to damnation. St. Thomas was hardly more consoling even if he added that "this does not happen at the expense of human freedom, for man's will remains the master of his choices, thus gaining merit where the choice is of the good and being responsible where it is of evil." Yet this choice or free consent must be the result of God's will that His grace should be effective. There can be no element in salvation that is exclusively ours.

There is no question of the degree of spiritual and moral anguish which the nineteen-year-old student went through during those winter weeks, as 1586 passed into 1587, when, prompted by his own sense of the all-reality of God and of his own weakness and nothingness in the work of salvation, he found himself caught up, as though by a trick of the Devil, in the logic of the heretics he so much disliked and disbelieved. His tutor put the truth most graphically when he said that if this went on, his pupil would very soon be learning from personal experience whether he was predestined to Heaven or to Hell. The health of his body had collapsed with the illness of his soul.

The normal human reaction to the belief that one might have been predestined to Hell by God irrespective of how one lived one's life on earth would be a kind of indignation and despair. One's deepest sense of justice would be outraged and the path from this to revolt against God or denial of His existence as a good God would be short; or one might somehow persuade oneself that one had been chosen from all eternity to be one of the elect, caring little for the fate of the *massa damnata* around one. Not so the saint who, when he talks of the all-reality of God and the nothingness of the creature, really means it, because he has gained insight into the meaning of the word *God*. In his darkest hour, Francis de Sales wrote, "Whatever happens, Lord, may I at least love You in this life if I cannot love You in eternity, since no one may praise You in Hell. May I at least make use of every moment of my short life on earth to love You."

This reaction of wholly disinterested love, which the average sinful mortal can scarcely grasp, a reaction spontaneously expressed at the height of his anguish, shows that his danger had never been one of falling to the temptation of despair. There is no suggestion, either, that he could for a moment have entertained any temptation to seek in severe Protestant theology the answer to the lax teaching and practice which had so widely affected the Church before the Reformation, and which endured, not least in France, so long after it. His traditions and his nature instinctively recoiled from such a solution. Never weakening his conviction about the justice of God, it was the love of God which would nevertheless govern his spiritual life from beginning to end. It has been suggested that in this expression of pure, disinterested love, there was a foretaste of the "mystical night," the "cloud of unknowing," which blots out understanding and relish of the divine among those called to the highest states of prayer.

But his words appear to suggest a momentary loss of hope in God, and this would be incompatible with an authentic mystical state. The simplest explanation would seem to be the most plausible one. His very tired mind, vexed by seemingly inscrutable problems met with in the course of his studies, and overcome by the evidence of "the great sins" around him, failed temporarily to function properly. He was in such a state that he would not, it seems, trust any friend or spiritual adviser to help him out of his troubles.

If this is a correct explanation, it certainly brings out the fact that the temptation revealed the quality of this student's inner life, the infusion of his being by God, since in the darkness of his mind, he could not but instinctively express his love of God under the illusion that God might well repay that love by condemning him to Hell for all eternity. It was as though God allowed this student's terrible temptation to enable him to become fully conscious once and for all of a quality of love for God and an indifference to self which in fact were to be the key to his whole life and the foundation of his immortal spiritual teachings. Tempted by Luther,[21] he clung to God instead of indulging in self-pity.

No wonder the denouement was as dramatic as the trial. Unable to endure it any longer, he turned one evening, as he left the college, toward the neighboring little church of Saint-Etienne-des-Grès with its tall cornet-capped tower. In the Lady Chapel, he fell to his knees and prayed in his continuing mood of love despite the apparent blighting of hope:

> Whatever happens, O Lord, You hold everything in Your hands, and all Your ways are just and true. Although You have veiled my eyes before the eternal secret of predestination and reprobation — You whose judgments are unsearchable, You who are just judge and a merciful Father — I shall

---

[21] Martin Luther (1483-1546), leader of the Protestant Reformation in Germany.

love You, Lord, at least in this life, even if I am not allowed to love You in eternity. At least I shall love You here below, O my God, and I shall always hope in Your mercy. Always I shall continue to praise You, whatever the angel of Satan may do to prevent me. O Lord Jesus, You shall always be my hope and my salvation in the land of the living. And if it is inevitable that I must be damned among the damned who will never see Your gentle face, let me at least be spared from the company of those who will curse Your Holy Name.

As he finished his prayer, he noticed a prayer card on which was printed St. Bernard's[22] famous *Memorare*: "Remember, O most gracious Virgin Mary, that never was it known that anyone who fled to thy protection, implored thy help, and sought thy intercession, was left unaided . . ." As he recited the words, his being seemed to change. He felt like a leper suddenly seeing the marks of his sores vanishing before his eyes. A delicious sense of spiritual and bodily peace came over him. He was cured in soul, mind, and body. God had permitted the trial, and now He took it away.[23]

Thus was the saint of the love of God schooled in a youthful passage of terror of the all-reality, the all-fearsomeness of the Divine — a realization necessary, in some degree at least, if religion is to be more than a superficial, pious version of our own inherent self-love. "The fear of God is the beginning of

---

[22] St. Bernard (1090-1153), Abbot of Clairvaux.

[23] The above events are known through accounts given by Déage and Father Suarez, a professor at the college, as well as by what de Sales himself said to St. Jane Frances de Chantal and Jeanne de Creil, and to which the latter testified at the beatification process.

wisdom."[24] But Francis also learned from his experience the greater danger of allowing the righteous fear of God to blot out the mercy and love so clearly revealed in the life and teaching of the God-made-Man, on whom he was so closely and so instinctively to model himself. To those he was later to direct in their spiritual lives with such understanding, his advice would always be to be wary of allowing fear to overcome faith, hope, and love.

"My daughter," he wrote to the Abbess du Puits-d'Orbe, a rather tiresome regular correspondent of his, "I beg you to see to it that those meditations of man's four last ends finish up with hope and trust in God, not with fear and fright. When they finish in fear, they are dangerous. . . . God is not so terrible for those who love Him. . . . He asks little of us because He knows how little we have."

It was not sentimentality nor softness which was to make him the gentle and optimistic guide of souls, but the love that had cast out fear.

[24] Cf. Ps. 111:10.

Chapter Two

Discerning God's Call

1588-1590

Francis de Sales was just under twenty-one when, in the summer of 1588, he completed his university course in Paris and returned to his homeland and his parents. During those last months, the special quality of his spiritual outlook, discernible in his childhood and teens and patent to everyone once his priestly vocation had begun, seems to have been affected by the crisis he went through. We know, for example, that he was deeply moved by the decision of Henri de Joyeuse to become a Capuchin. "God calls us by that way," he was heard to say.

Henri de Joyeuse's career was characteristic of a period when spiritual heroism could shoot like a meteor before the eyes of men content with the superstitions, vanities, and barbarities of the age. The Joyeuses had been raised by Henry III to the highest eminence in the kingdom, sharing among themselves titles like Admiral of France, Cardinal, and Marshal. Henri himself had been appointed Master of the Royal Wardrobe at the age of seventeen. He was a close favorite of the monarch, and after a brilliant marriage, it seemed that France itself was at his feet.

Yet one day, as he was driving in Paris with the king, he noticed two Capuchins in their coarse habits trudging in the mud near their recently founded convent in the rue Saint-Honoré. This sight made the deepest impression on him, and when his wife died shortly afterward, he surprised and shocked the king when he told him that he, too, was resolved to throw over the glories of the world to join those two friars. It is touching to think of the last Valois — a decadent, spoiled child, yet by no means without courage and principle — reconciling himself to the loss of his friend by begging the Capuchin provincial to keep Frère Ange, as Joyeuse was now called, in Paris and writing to his old favorite to help him "save his soul, hate sin, and embrace virtue." Joyeuse's entry into so austere a religious life did not prevent him from leaving the order for a time, with full canonical permission, in order to take a command in the religious wars as a marshal of France.

Vice, virtue, worldliness, sanctity, the temporal, and the spiritual — these were all curiously intermingled in those *fin-du-seizième-siècle* days. The great Joyeuse, turned from one day to the next from the splendor of the court to the tonsured head, the rough habit, and the bare feet of a Capuchin, was an impressive sight for the ardent de Sales, who used to watch out for the times when Frère Ange was serving Mass in the Capuchin church.

It seems likely that at Saint-Honoré, de Sales also met two notable English Capuchins. The first was William Fitch of Canfield, to be known in history as Benet of Canfield; the second, a cadet of the Herberts, Earls of Pembroke, who became Father Archange in religion. Benet of Canfield embraced the Catholic Faith in London in 1585 and entered the Capuchins at Saint-Honoré in 1587. He was to become a leading figure in the seventeenth-century mystical revival, writing the famous and controversial book the *Rule of Perfection*. De Sales would meet Father Archange again toward the end of his life in connection with the future Jansenist Angélique Arnauld, who at that time was under the Bishop of Geneva's spiritual direction. It may have been that de Sales's life-long interest in the conversion of England was stimulated at this time by his relations with these two English friars.

Under this Capuchin influence, Francis de Sales began to undertake heavy mortifications in the way of fasting, hair shirt, and the discipline, a habit he was to continue for some time, and it is a reasonable guess that he was thus preparing himself to join Joyeuse. Possibly because he dared not face the wrath of his father at such an outrageous step, or, more probably, because he would do nothing in a hurry and could sense that his own true vocation was something very different, he had quietly returned home with Déage.

His parents were now living in the château of Brens, near Geneva, and the homecoming, after six years' exile, must have been as wonderful for him as for his father, his mother, and the flock of children — Gallois, Louis, Jean-François, and Gasparde — of whom he would have memories. Three others had been born while he was away: Bernard, Melchior, and Janus, toddlers and a baby, such as he always loved. What stories he must have had to tell them all of the distant dream world of famous Paris, of that great Day of the Barricades when Henri de Guise and his Catholic League had entered the capital in armed insurrection against the authority of the hesitant king; of the famous Joyeuse turned friar; of the Lorraines and the Mercoeurs and the fight for the Faith. He was the treasured son and heir, who had successfully climbed the first step up the ladder which would lead to a career worthy of the family, even though, regretfully, not a military one.

But if de Sales rightly judged that his vocation was not to be monk, friar, or Jesuit, we are left in some perplexity about why he did not now make known to his parents and family his secret resolution to enter the Church as a secular priest. Can we believe that it was sheer fear of his father or even a reluctance to hurt him? After all, his father, however domineering, was a perfectly good Catholic and presumably capable of understanding what a religious vocation must mean to so serious and devout a young man, now coming of age. Nor were the Saleses so grand a family as to feel, even in those times, that a priestly vocation for their son was below the family's social status. It appears more likely that he himself was not as yet certain that God really wanted him to be a priest. If so, this would make the biographers' rather *simpliste* account of his early years even less convincing.

Perhaps what finally decided him not to say anything was his father's decision that the next educational step for his clever son was a doctorate of law at Padua, a university then scarcely less famed than Paris. De Sales might well have thought that this degree would be of value if and when he became a priest, for as a priest, he would inevitably receive quick preferment because of his birth and connections.

So, in the autumn of 1588, after only a short time with his family, de Sales and Déage set off for Italy, accompanied by the young Gallois, aged twelve, who would do his studies at the Jesuit school in Padua.

The atmosphere in Padua was very different from Paris. Here it was the atmosphere of Shakespeare's comedies, with stories of picturesquely dressed young bloods roaming the streets at night to pick a quarrel, serenade a pretty girl, or rag incautious passersby. De Sales was up to all this, and we know that on one occasion, when attacked by some students, he drew his sword and gave as good as he got. We are also told that some friends of his managed by a trick to lure him into the house of a prostitute from which he decamped in double-quick time. Such stories serve to show that Frances de Sales at Padua was no hermit, no spoilsport where the sport was tolerable.

He was fortunate enough to find in the university a remarkable man, eminently fitted to guide him along the way which was to be peculiarly his own: the pursuit of a heroic personal sanctity consistent with his affectionate nature and feeling for the social graces of life and the intrinsic value of culture and learning. This was the Jesuit Antonio Possevino, who had lately been appointed to lecture on theology. De Sales, although never tempted to become a Jesuit, nor ever feeling that the Jesuit way quite squared with his own personalist and very individual outlook, immensely admired the Society of Jesus, and Possevino would become a lifelong correspondent of his. Although not so extraordinary in his religious career as Joyeuse, Possevino was nevertheless a man whose career reflected the curious nature of the times. No more than an ordinary priest, he had been appointed papal legate for the reconciliation of John III of Sweden to the Church and had been nuncio and vicar-apostolic in that country. He was then made papal legate to the Czar Ivan the Terrible with a mission of reconciliation between Russia and Poland. For these diplomatic tasks, which made him the most distinguished papal diplomat of the day, he wore secular dress.

An ardent advocate of Christian reunion, about which he wrote treatises, Possevino was generally unable to obtain the backing of Rome for his own advanced views, and Padua was doubtless something of a comedown. De Sales was also attracted to him because of his acquaintance with Savoy, where, before Ordination, he had preached in Calvinist Chablais. It is said that in Italy he preached on occasion to 14,000 people. Possevino and the young student must have talked together about reunion and the conversion of heretics, thus remotely preparing de Sales for one of the most spectacular accomplishments of his life.

Possevino was thus eminently fitted to give spiritual guidance to de Sales at this particular stage of his formation. His first advice was to ask him to forget all about his great spiritual trouble in Paris and wait until he had the opportunity of thoroughly studying these difficult questions. Meanwhile he was to see in his normal university work and life the means of spiritual progress. After careful reflection and some delay, the Jesuit approved the bodily mortifications which de Sales had been practicing. The latter was, however, not yet to be entirely freed from his worries about predestination, and once more he came very near dying.

A severe epidemic broke out in Padua in the summer of 1590. Forty-two of the French students, as de Sales wrote on July 26 in the second of his letters which have survived, contracted what seems to have been typhoid or paratyphoid. He caught it too, and was unable to shake it off. By January, everyone thought him a dying man. His tutor even asked him for instructions about his funeral. Always original, de Sales's answer contained a bequest that must have been rare in those days. "As for my body," he said, "let it be given after my death to the medical students. Seeing that it has been useless during my lifetime, I would like it to be of some use after my death. I am happy to think that I may be able in this way to prevent one at least of the fights and killings to which students resort when they are trying to get hold of the corpses of the executed for dissection." Stealing recently buried bodies from cemeteries, à la Burke and Hare, was then another common way of solving the problem. When we think of the pomp and ceremony with which nobles were interred at that time, de Sales's bequest is all the more remarkable. Spiritually, de Sales on his deathbed, as everyone took it to be, was content to put himself without any qualifications into the hands of God. But after receiving the Last Sacraments from Possevino, he slowly began to recover.

This complete trust in God expressed itself once more when his studies threw him again into the seemingly insoluble problem of predestination. By this time, the Jesuit or Molinist solution[25] had been put forward as an answer to the too often misunderstood teaching of St. Augustine and St. Thomas, and Francis found relief in it. But with his usual grace, he threw himself at the feet of the great Doctors of the Church to ask them pardon for his inability to take them at their word:

[25] Spanish theologian Luis de Molina (1535-1600) held the belief that God directs a person's free choice without coercing him. If God desires that a person make a particular choice, He will create the situation that will lead the person to make that choice.

Kneeling at the feet of St. Augustine and St. Thomas, I am ready to know nothing so that I may know Him who is the Word of the Father, Christ crucified. I stand by what I have written because I can see nothing that raises a serious doubt about it. Yet I do not understand everything, and I know this deep mystery to be such as to blind my human eyes, conditioned to darkness.

If, then, in the future I should find myself seeing things differently (I do not think this will ever happen) — still worse, if I were to see myself damned (which God avert) by that will which Thomas attributes to God so that God may manifest His justice, I would bow my head in my horror and, looking up at the Supreme Judge in astonishment, I would from my soul say with the prophet, "Shall not my soul be obedient to God? Amen, Father, since it seems good to You, may Your will be done."

And I shall go on saying this in the bitterness of my heart until the day when God will alter my life and change His verdict with the answer: "Take courage, my son; I do not wish the death of the sinner, but rather that he repent and live.[26] The dead will not praise me, nor those who go down into Hell.[27] I created you, as I created everything else, for myself. Even the sinners doomed, through their own fault, to the day of perdition I created for myself. My will is but for your sanctification,[28] and my heart has no hate for anything which it has brought into being. . . . You are not dead, but sleeping.[29] . . . Courage, little son, in my service — you may be worth little,

[26] Cf. Ezek. 18:23.
[27] Cf. Ps. 6:5.
[28] Cf. 1 Thess. 4:3.
[29] Cf. Matt. 9:24.

but you are faithful. Since you still hope in me, put your trust in my mercy."[30]

Later, as we shall see, Francis de Sales was to be called upon to play an important part in settling the great controversy between the Jesuits and the Dominicans over predestination and freedom in the *De Auxiliis* Congregation in Rome. But Maritain, the great Thomist writer of today, has said: "It is not, however, a course of theological science that we should ask of him, de Sales. The human-divine dynamism of the life of grace in us, of which St. Thomas Aquinas is the great doctor and which he has analyzed better than any theologian, is hardly touched upon by our Bishop of Geneva; there is little to warrant the claim that he even tried to penetrate the central intuitions of the Angelic Doctor in their profound exactitudes."[31]

Meanwhile, under cover of a normal student's life, Francis, apparently resurrected from the dead, would conceal his personal practice of spiritual perfection according to the precepts contained in a little book which greatly influenced him: Lorenzo Scupoli's *Spiritual Combat*. The book had only just been published anonymously. Scupoli was a member of the Theatine Order who, at about this time, was in Padua, living privately because of a grave accusation laid against him, but completely unjustly. It is likely that the two men met and that Scupoli himself gave de Sales the copy of the book.

---

[30] *The Works of St. Francis de Sales*, Vol. 22, 64, and also André Jean Marie Hamon, *Vie de Saint François de Sales*, Vol. 1, 56.

[31] See Jacques Maritain's foreword in C. F. Kelley, *The Spirit of Love* (New York: Harper and Brothers, 1951).

At a period when exceptional spirituality was usually measured by strict enclosure and the practice of great bodily mortifications, the *Spiritual Combat* made a great impression.

In the opening chapter, Scupoli points out that "fasts, vigils, genuflections, sleeping on the bare earth, and other similar austerities of the body" are in themselves by no means the perfection of Christian life. They may well be the instruments of the Devil. Where it is a case of people finding holiness in them, the Devil "gleefully refrains from interfering. . . . [E]xperiencing with this certain spiritual stirrings and consolations, such people begin to imagine that they have already reached the state of angels and feel that God Himself is present in them. . . . [H]owever, anyone can see clearly how sinfully such people behave and how far they are from true perfection, if he looks at their life and character. As a rule, they always wish to be preferred to others; they love to live according to their own will and are always stubborn in their decisions; they are blind in everything relating to themselves, but are very clear-sighted and officious in examining the words and actions of others. If another man is held by others in the same esteem, which in their opinion they enjoy, they cannot bear it and become manifestly hostile toward him; if anyone interferes with them in their pious occupations and works of asceticism, especially in the presence of others — God forbid! — they immediately become indignant, boil over with wrath and become quite unlike themselves."[32]

---

[32] Quotations from Scupoli are taken from the edition titled *Unseen Warfare*, translated by E. Kadloubovsky and G. E. H. Palmer (New York: Macmillan, 1952), 77-79.

One has met such people!

"I will tell you plainly," wrote Scupoli at the very beginning of his book, "the greatest and most perfect thing a man may desire to attain is to come near to God and dwell in union with Him."[33]

Here were a freedom, a common sense and an insight into human psychology which anticipated points which Francis de Sales would, in rather more kindly fashion perhaps, exploit in his own spiritual direction and in the most popular of his books, the *Introduction to the Devout Life*. Meanwhile, Scupoli, with Possevino's practical help, led de Sales to set down for himself a rule of life.

Much of this rule followed the post-Reformation ordering of the day with careful preparation by thought and prayer, daily attendance at Mass, weekly Communion, with spiritual considerations from time to time. De Sales had known it all from the Jesuits at Clermont. But certain unusual points stand out. He writes of a "forward examination" rather than of the more usual retrospective examination of conscience. He was more interested in arming himself against the dangers to come

---

[33] One day Francis was to write a letter of spiritual advice which echoes Scupoli's words. "When we see a person in ecstatic prayer, rising away from and above himself, yet far from ecstatic in his life — in other words, not leading a life raised to God and united with Him by turning away from worldliness and mortification of natural will and desires, by inner meekness, simplicity, humility, and, above all, love — then we may deduce that all these ecstasies are very doubtful and dangerous. . . . To be above self in prayer and sink below self in life and work; to be an angel in prayer and a beast in one's relations with men: that is to go lame on both legs."

than in inviting scruples through dwelling too much on what is over and done with. Then he makes much of what he calls a "sacred sleep." The phrase suggests something resembling the "prayer of quiet" of the contemplatives: a wordless and simple attending to God by a gentle act of the will. But this "sacred sleep," as he describes it, reads more like a meditation on the holy mysteries and considerations about the foolishness of living one's life in worldly dissipation — the term *sleep* being used to indicate spiritual rest for the mind during the working day by analogy with the body's need for sleep during the night. But the use of the word, so contemplative in its nature, is significant of the future when Jane Frances de Chantal would encourage him toward a truly contemplative "sacred sleep."

This rule is also marked by a spiritual optimism. Better to think of the attraction of virtue than to dwell on the evil of sin, which is "unworthy of a well-born person equipped to understand true values." And, anyway, sin is offensive to God — that is enough. But as for virtue, it is virtue "which makes the inner and outer man into something beautiful. It makes him wonderfully pleasing to God. It suits man extremely well, because it is man's proper state. How much consolation, delight, and true pleasure it always brings him. Christian virtue sanctifies him, turns him into an angel, makes him a little god, takes him into Heaven, even on earth."

For de Sales, the *honnête homme* of the humanist ideal inevitably becomes the man enlightened enough to pursue sanctity within the world. Appropriately, therefore, much of his rule of life concerns his relations with the world. There is charm in the simple gravity with which he lists his maxims for conduct:

I shall never despise anyone, nor altogether avoid him. The more so in that it would give the impression of being proud, haughty, severe, arrogant, critical, ambitious, dominating. . . .

I shall talk little, but well, so that others may enjoy meeting me again rather than think how boring this would be. . . .

I must always use judgment and prudence, for every rule has its occasional exception, save only the foundation of all rules: nothing against God. . . .

So in life's interchanges I shall always be modest without insolence, free in manner without austerity, gentle without affectation, flexible without contrariness, unless reason require otherwise; welcoming without dissimulation, for men like to get to know those with whom they have to do business. . . .

Since we must often have relations with persons of different qualities, I must be ready to put before some of them only what is exquisite, before others only what is good, before others still only what is indifferent; but never what is evil before any.

If I am obliged to be with the great, I shall remain carefully on my guard — they are like fire, approachable but not too close. A good deal of modesty is necessary in their presence, but it must be an open and sincere modesty. Great people generally like to be loved and respected, and love demands some freedom; respect, some modesty. A certain ease is therefore no bad thing in their company, so long as respect is not forgotten and yet does not destroy that ease. As between equals, ease and respect are just as necessary. With those of lower station, we may well be freer and show less respect, but with those of higher station and with our superiors, it is much more important to be respectful than to be too free.

In other words, if the *honnête homme* should, like any other man, be a saint, the saint should concentrate also on the virtues of the *honnête homme* in the worldly wisdom and etiquette of the society in which he is born. To do so would always be second nature to de Sales, but his love of God and his neighbor would never allow him to let convention, etiquette, and worldly wisdom stand between him and the human person, of whatever class, with whom he had to deal.

Francis de Sales spent just over three years in Padua, leaving it at about the same time as Possevino with a brilliant doctorate of law which led the celebrated professor, Pancirolo, to foresee for him a career which would make him the "luminary of his century." His old father was at last so delighted with his eldest boy that he had been quietly collecting a legal library with which to greet a son who confessed that in Padua he had only studied law to please his father and had given all the time he could to theology to please himself.

No young man of his class would have missed the opportunity of a grand tour in Italy before returning home to settle down to his life's career, and de Sales had devotional reasons for returning to Savoy by a very circuitous route. He wanted to visit the Holy House of Loretto on a pilgrimage of thanksgiving for his preservation from death, and he naturally wanted to see Rome.

When Déage asked him on the eve of leaving Padua whether he would wish to pay a visit to the lady who had nursed him in his illness and thank her, he answered with his usual delight in any play on words: "Quite right, I will go and thank the Lady who gave me the most help during that time." But we may be sure that he did not fail to say goodbye to the lady of Padua before setting off to thank the Lady of Loretto.

Francis, Gallois, and Déage sailed from Venice to Ancona, north of Loretto. But the disturbed state of the Papal States[34] after the death of Gregory XIV forced them to return to Padua for the winter of 1591.

Among the crop of stories of providential protection during journeys which in those days were indeed perilous, there is a very different story which at least brings out de Sales's sense of fun even at his own expense. On board a little vessel, he lost his hat in a high wind. Apparently, to be hatless in those days was as socially awkward as to lose one's trousers today. So poor Francis could do no better than wear his nightcap, to the enormous amusement of the sailors and passengers. When they landed at a small town, Déage, who certainly had no sense of humor and treated his charge like a small boy, refused to buy a new hat. So the party, with the gentleman in the nightcap, caused as much laughter among the townsfolk as among the visitors. In the end, the victim grew a little tired of the joke and begged Déage to procure him a new hat. Perhaps it was too late in the evening — perhaps (as the story has come down to us) the tutor implacably told him to make the best of the mortification and wait until they reached Venice. Related thus as an edifying tale by Charles-Auguste de Sales, Francis's nephew who wrote his uncle's life twelve years after his death, we need little imagination to see it also as an evening's lark which Francis enjoyed no less than the rest of the company.

What journeys on the stormy Adriatic could mean is vividly enough depicted in a letter de Sales wrote some years later

---

[34] The areas in central Italy that were under the authority of the Pope from 755-1870.

to a novice in a Paris convent who asked for his spiritual advice. "Imitate those who are suffering from distress and stomach troubles at sea," he wrote, doubtless recalling these days. "After they have lurched up and down the ship, their minds and bodies more than they can bear, they seek what alleviation they can get and finally put their arms around the mast, tightly clinging to it to overcome the giddiness they suffer. True, the relief is both short and uncertain. So you, if you grasp the foot of the Cross with humility, may not, it is true, find much remedy, but at least your patience will there feel sweeter and your troubles more bearable."[35]

The grand tour made a fresh start in January 1592, this time by road and on horseback, and one would dearly like to know what impression cities like Ferrara, Florence, Perugia, Assisi, and Rome itself made on the young man. But at no time in his life did Francis de Sales describe or record his views on art and architecture, and this suggests that they made little impression on him. Certainly, his real love, as illustrated so continuously in his writings, was for the wonders of nature and the hand of God always directly at work in it, providing men with endless lessons about Providence and human nature. In this respect, at least his native Savoy meant much more to him than the man-made wonders of Paris, Padua, Venice, and Rome itself.

The final family reunion took place at La Thuile, to the south of the Lake of Annecy, where the family had now settled because of the fighting taking place in the Chablais. Complete happiness in the reunion was marred by the tragedy that

---

[35] *The Works of St. Francis de Sales*, Vol. 12, 180-184.

Francis's mother, who was only just over forty, was beginning to lose her sight. As for his father, what delight for him in the certainty that his handsome and brilliant son and heir, now named Seigneur de Villaroget, would make a fine marriage and sweep upward to the highest positions in the magistrature and government of Savoy. When his time came, he would die happy in the knowledge that the greatest glories of his family were yet to come. He was quite right, but in a way of which he had not the faintest conception.

The time had now obviously arrived when Francis had to disclose the secret he had guarded so carefully and mysteriously since early childhood. Yet even now, at twenty-five — almost a late vocation — he seemed to wait on events rather than to confront them.

Imprudently, in view of his secular hopes for his son, M. de Boisy took the young man, already ruddily bearded, we may suppose, to pay a formal call on the Bishop of Geneva, the Benedictine Claude de Granier, whose episcopal residence was in Annecy.[36] Granier, a holy man, was much impressed by the young de Sales and jokingly said to him, as he pointed to some episcopal vestments on a chair, "If you want to become a priest, there's a miter ready for you." Later, his guest, because he had taken his Padua legal degree, was called in consultation on a point of canon law. His judgment seemed so learned and

---

[36] The bishop and chapter of Geneva had had to leave their cathedral city in 1534 in the face of the political and religious risings which were to establish Calvin's authority. Two years later, they settled in Annecy. The loss of the rightful episcopal city of the diocese would always be a sorrow and a challenge to de Sales.

helpful that Granier said to some bystanders, "What do you think of this young lord? I believe he will become great and a pillar of the Church, and succeed me in this See." Such stories get exaggerated in the telling, but Granier evidently discerned the priestly vocation and the inevitable preferments for so worthy a candidate.

M. de Boisy's plans were very different. He must get his son married as soon as possible. The lady of his choice (the father's, not the son's) was a neighboring heiress, Françoise Suchet de Mirebel, the fourteen-year-old daughter of a counselor of the Duke of Savoy. A first meeting was arranged with the company eagerly watching for the young suitor's smile, the change in tone of voice, that would indicate that all was going well. Francis was indeed prodigal of excellent manners, but he showed no deeper feelings. Mlle. de Mirebel understood, for before the next meeting was arranged, she had turned her attention to another suitor.

By no means best pleased, M. de Boisy had been pursuing his second and much easier plan — to have his son named to the Savoy Senate in the expectation that he would soon be made a senator. But the one solid fruit of de Sales's journey to the capital, Chambéry, was the first step in the life-long friendship with the ten-years-older senator Antoine Favre, one of the most distinguished lawyers of his day and the author of the internationally celebrated *Codex Fabrianus*.

Mysterious in different meanings of the word was the next event. Riding back from Chambéry with Déage, de Sales on three occasions was unseated from his horse, and, each time, his sword fell to the ground and, slipping from the scabbard, lay crossed by it. Once or even twice, this sign of the cross might be accident. But a third time? De Sales was so impressed that, for the first time in his life, he told the ever-present Déage the whole story of his vocation. Incredibly, Déage had never suspected. The mystery was not only a mystery of the three crosses, but a mystery as to why Francis de Sales would require a miracle to bring him to the disclosure even to Déage, now a canon, of what must have been the very basis of his life. Nor did he at once act on the sign from Heaven.

Even now, it seems, no one dared break the news to M. de Boisy, and one may reasonably suppose that by leaving it so late, de Sales had only made things harder for himself.

De Sales consulted his cousin Canon Louis de Sales, who promised to help. Unknown to Francis, Canon Louis talked to the bishop and, with his consent, put forward Francis de Sales's name to the Holy See for the provostship of the diocese, which happened to be vacant. While Francis, as Seigneur de Villaroget, continued to lead the life of a studious country gentleman, everyone but he waited for Clement VIII's answer. At last, in May 1593, the bull nominating Francis de Sales as provost of the chapter of the Geneva-Annecy See arrived. Since the provostship was next in rank to the bishop himself, it was felt that the old man would not object to this sort of ecclesiastical career for his eldest son.

When de Sales was told the extraordinary news that he was named provost, he was so stupefied that he could only take it as another and final providential sign that he must now act. At last, he showed his father the papal bull, explaining that Providence, entirely without his own knowledge, had thus arranged things to confirm his long-standing vocation for the priestly state. Even so, M. de Boisy was far from pleased, although it is much to his credit that he gave way because his son's future work would keep him near his parents and his family rather than because of the brilliant prospects which this appointment to a layman held out.

It is not altogether surprising that the episode of the projected marriage and the trick of the provostship were exploited by Protestant writers unable to forgive de Sales his future conversion of the Chablais. As late as 1878, an Anglican clergyman, the Rev. L. Woolsey Bacon, seeking to prove de Sales to be a dishonest person, argued in *Macmillan's Magazine* that he had first returned the affections of Françoise de Mirebel and then jilted her in order to take up the provostship which he had secretly procured.[37]

One would scarcely bother to mention this completely unfounded version, but for the fact that it picks out the one puzzling episode in a life so singularly above even *prima facie* reproach. De Sales, argued Woolsey Bacon, was clearly the sort of person who would later use dishonest methods to convert Calvinists. But the only puzzle is why de Sales kept his vocation so absolutely secret. In the absence of any surviving letters for the period, there is no satisfactory answer.

We know from his own testimony that from the age of twelve, he felt called to be a priest. We know, too, that he was never to hurry the great decisions of his life, whether for himself or for others. We are left therefore to suppose that, what with the great trial in Paris and the somewhat unnatural opposition of his father to any but a brilliant secular career, he came to the conclusion that he must wait for God to manifest His

[37] *Dublin Review*, January 1882.

will in His own time. The unexpected provostship, even more than the three crosses, would then be taken without further question as the signal from on high to act. Even so, this explanation seems overly simple and suggests that we know too little of what went on within him during these early years of his life.

However this may be, the course was now definitely set for what would be a rather late vocation, but which in those days was time enough, since no special theological training was then required in the Geneva diocese for the priesthood, least of all for a graduate of two great universities.

Chapter Three

Bringing the Faith
to Those in Darkness

1593-1594

The transformation of the country gentleman into the ecclesiastic was in the end rapid. On May 10, 1593 — three days after the receipt of the papal bull — Francis de Sales put on the soutane in the parish church of La Thuile: "the breastplate, the belt, of those enrolled in Christ's militia," as he described it.

Two days later he rode along the lakeside to Annecy to be sworn in at the curial office and to receive the provostship in the name of the Church of Geneva. Already he was second to the bishop.

A week later, the renewal of the tonsure, received in boyhood according to local custom, took place. Much later he admitted that he had felt a pang as his fine, fair locks were shorn. "For a couple of days," he told his confessor, "I have been suffering from a temptation against my vocation. The Devil has tempted me in all parts of my spirit, even to the tips of my hairs." Here is another hint that his vocation was not as simple and straightforward as appears on the surface. However, unlike Samson, strength came back to him as the golden curls were cut off.[38]

On June 9, just over a month since the arrival of the bull, he received the four minor orders and, three days later, the subdiaconate. Ordination to the priesthood was delayed until Advent. But he did not wait until then to start his active pastoral life. The minor orders and the subdiaconate, thus received without any specific preparation, save a retreat, were enough to convert the layman into a zealous and outstanding ecclesiastic.

The best proof of this is that Calvinists of the district were attracted to his first sermon preached in the bishop's presence. After all, the story of the young heir of the Saleses turning priest all of a sudden must have been more than a nine days' wonder — and all the greater wonder in that the new ecclesiastic preached so well as to impress the heretics. Two of them, destined to be distinguished converts, admitted that this first sermon of de Sales set their minds thinking that way.

Was this effect due to the matter and manner of the sermon or to the earnestness and sincerity of the man behind the words? To this first sermon, preached on the octave-day of Corpus Christi, he gave much time for preparation, writing it in the ornate oratorical style of the period. But it was not long before his apostolic zeal was moving him to preach to any audience and on any occasion in the simple words that first came into his head — so much so that his father, used to the old, dignified way, had a fresh grievance against his son. "My father, hearing the bell for the sermon, used to ask who the

[38] Judg. 16:19.

preacher was," Camus, Bishop of Belley, reported Francis's account. "They said to him, 'Who else but your son?' One day, he said to me, 'Provost, you preach too often. The sermon bell rings even on working days, and they keep on telling me, "It's the provost again." In my day, things were different. Sermons were rare events — but what events! They were learned and well thought out. We heard marvels. Why, there was more Latin and Greek in any one sermon than there is in a dozen of yours. . . . Now you are making preaching such a common thing that no one thinks anything of it — and no one looks up to you as they should.' "

The voice of old M. de Boisy goes on ringing down the ages, deploring any change, any innovation, however obviously it may be for the good of souls.

De Sales's comment was: "Believe me, we can never preach too much. We can never repeat too often what we cannot say enough — especially in this part of the country, so near to the seat of heresy, for heresy is only kept up by preaching and can only be defeated by preaching."

Meanwhile, having already startled everyone, even as a mere subdeacon, by using his apostolic imagination in visiting the sick and poor, lending a ready hand to anyone in distress, and even founding a confraternity of the "Penitents of the Holy Cross," which still exists, he came near the great day of Ordination, December 18, 1593.

We know for certain the state of his mind before this all-important event, for the letter which he wrote in Latin to his new-found friend, Antoine Favre, still exists, although in it we must allow something for his anxiety to turn a fine phrase and work out a rounded period rather than speak spontaneously from the heart. The "devout humanist" is very much present in these early letters.

> The awe-full day — to use St. Chrysostom's[39] words — is now close upon me: the day when by the will of my bishop, who is my interpreter in my search for the will of God, I shall, after having received other Holy Orders, be raised to the dignity of the priesthood. . . . I beg you to wish me well, for never before in my life has anxiety so deeply affected me. . . . Unless I am mistaken, nothing more difficult nor more dangerous can happen to a man than to hold in his hands and bring to be, through his words, Him whom the angels, so far beyond our conception and praise, cannot comprehend or sufficiently extol. I have indeed always known the terrible nature of the responsibility which this holy and August dignity brings with it, but distance veils the eyes, and it is a very different matter to be so close to it.
>
> I feel that you are the one person capable of understanding my sense of perturbation, for you observe, venerate, and understand the things of God so well that you can appreciate the danger and the awe of possessing responsibility for them, the ease with which one may slip into sin, even grave sin, and the difficulty with which one avoids treating them lightly. If you really understood how weak I am, I would ask no more of you than sympathy, which you would feel called upon to give me. But I am not without courage, a courage that so far has remained firm and strong.
>
> I have said enough, and said it, truth to tell, rather to excite your sympathy, for this is how one consoles oneself. . . . Sympathy is the infallible sign of friendship, that most perfect of relationships which, in friends, is so much more precious

---

[39] St. John Chrysostom (c. 347-407), Bishop of Constantinople.

when there is a community of feelings rather than a mere good will which does not share suffering.

But do not believe that the holy mysteries so much frighten me as to destroy my sense of hope and happiness which are well beyond my personal merits. I am so happy to think that I shall be able to make myself one with you in the best way of all — by my sacrifices, by the highest sacrifice. . . .[40]

After Ordination, he wrote to his old master, Possevino: "I have been made so much of an ecclesiastic that I celebrated Mass on St. Thomas's feast in our cathedral church of Saint-Pierre, where I am the unworthy provost — the highest dignity after the episcopal. By my bishop's command, I have preached the Word here and elsewhere in the diocese. Rashness would have been the explanation of this, had not obedience taken away my scruples. I have done this — and continue to do it as well as I can — by often thinking of you as I stand in the pulpit. Would to God I had but half of your assiduity in the service of God."[41]

Francis de Sales would always vividly remember his first priestly ministration. It was the baptizing of Jeanne, the thirteenth child born to the Saleses, the little sister he was so dearly to love — and to lose fourteen years later, when she died while staying with Jane Frances de Chantal and her daughters. "I engendered her to the Lord," he would then write to Jane Frances, "for it was I who baptized her with my own hands about fourteen years ago. She was the first creature on whom I exercised my priestly orders."

[40] *The Works of St. Francis de Sales*, Vol. 11, 37-40.
[41] Ibid., 104-106.

As priest and provost, de Sales seemed to sweep everything before him according to a predetermined plan. Those long years of preparation and meditation and hesitation seemed to convert automatically into a precise and carefully thought-out apostolate into the highways and byways of Annecy and the surrounding country — so much so, that people began to whisper in the bishop's ear that these Saleses were all alike, ambitious and ever seeking the main chance. If things went on like this, there might as well be no bishop. Msgr. Granier, who at Francis's Ordination had wept with pleasure at the thought that he was ordaining his successor, grew anxious and worried. Happily, he was soon reassured after a conversation in which, no doubt, the provost explained his apostolic plans. The first of these, clearly the fruit of his long preoccupation with the Calvinist challenge and how best to meet it, was openly declared during his speech of acceptance of the provostship.

"Love will shake the walls of Geneva," he told the chapter. "By love we must invade it; by love we must conquer it. . . . The smell of powder and steel, the taste of them, suggest the furnace of Hell, and I do not propose their use to you. I have no interest in organizing those camps, the soldiers in which are without piety or faith. Our camp must be God's camp, where the trumpets sound in harmonious melody: 'Holy, holy, holy is the Lord of Hosts.' My comrades in battle, it is in that sense that you should be thinking. Ardent prayer must break down the walls of Geneva and brotherly love charge them. . . . Everything gives way to love. Love is as strong as death,[42] and to him who loves nothing is hard. . . ."

[42] Song of Sol. 8:6.

Even more boldly, he imputed the present discontents to "the crimes of our times and our forbears." He took heart from the fact that Geneva had retained the names and monuments of the Catholic past. "Heresy, as it moves forward, overthrows and destroys churches and hacks the images of the saints. But Geneva has preserved its temples; the stalls of its canons are still there. These, my good friends, are good signs, a providential sparing which recalls to our foes their usurpation, but stirs us to recover what belongs to us and to choose our last rest in the same tomb as our ancestors. But the way to this is the propitiation of Almighty God by our penances."

Today, such an attitude might be commonplace, but then, when the inevitability of the heretic's damnation was generally assumed, delicacy as to the quality of the means by which they could be rescued from their fate was rare. It is remarkable that this newly ordained priest, brought up at home and in Paris to think of Calvinists and Huguenots as religious and political criminals, could invite his countrymen to overcome by spiritual arms alone their opponents' intolerant usurpation. Even more impressive was the confidence and sureness of this fresh voice, so lately hesitant even in accepting his own ecclesiastical vocation.

Another surprise: Francis, brought up to be so conscious of his rightful place in the world and the legitimacy of the honors which it could bestow on the deserving, now unhesitatingly refused his friend Favre's offer of a seat in the Savoy Senate — a seat which his own predecessor in the provostship had held. Nor did he this time mind offending his father in rejecting a position that could have been of great value to him in his ecclesiastical mission. "Go in peace, then," his father said bitterly to him when he heard the news. "I see I would be wasting my time trying to change your mind. I suppose your heart will never allow you two masters." It was the first step along the lowly way which would bring him to his end as the humble bishop of a country diocese-in-exile when, with only the slightest push on his part, he might have been cardinal and the holder of one of the Sees of France. Whereas, when he was a layman, his devout humanism had encouraged a life on two levels — the temporal upheld by the spiritual — now as a priest, he would grow ever more spiritual — the spiritual, however, always expressing itself in deep relations of love and courtesy with men and women of all ranks and stations in the world.

The Latin letters which he exchanged at this time with Favre were still the letters of the ex-classical student, but under the quaint expression, we can discern the deeply personal quality of his relations with those he loved.

"As for your last letter," he wrote to Favre in March 1594, "written on the same day as mine, so closely does it match mine in its sentiments that we might be brothers in friendship — not, alas, in our way of writing, for you are far ahead of me in elegance of style. It is fitting, then, that you should be for me and do for me what I am and have done for you, for with all my heart I want to be your most loving friend — mine in the fullest way — as I am yours almost to the point of feeling other than myself."

In another letter: "Since you allow me to look forward to being with you during the coming carnival, my heart is so filled with delight at the prospect that no one ever looked more eagerly forward to Easter after the unpleasant Lenten fasts than I do to this coming carnival. Then will be revived that ancient form of Christian courtesy according to which the days before Lenten fasting were celebrated together in a little holiday — thus preparing us for the silences of the season and the higher thoughts to which it should raise us. . . . If you come here [Annecy], I shall take good care not to be otherwise engaged. Even if you do not come, I shall not go [in reference to the marriage party of a friend's daughter]. How should I, having no wedding garment?[43] Besides, I dread that sort of convivial gathering."

It seems a far cry from this personal correspondence, this conscious delight in deep friendship, to the pastoral task which the provost undertook from the start. Then, as sometimes now, an insufficiently trained clergy, readily accepting old abuses, often class-conscious and exercising an authority that was not wholly pastoral in that peasant land, did not always regard its job as being "all things to all men."[44] Francis de Sales did.

In his ministry to the lowly folk, the devout humanist went so far as to make use of the local patois which he had picked up as a small boy. A provost and a Sales! How could he? The poor people themselves were surprised and shocked. Was he trying to make fools of them? But it was only a question of learning by experience the always delicate task of breaking through conventions without suggesting ulterior motives.

It soon became clear that he had only one motive in his tramping about the countryside, preaching on every occasion,

[43] Cf. Matt. 22:12.
[44] 1 Cor. 9:22.

taking the place of priests who were ill or away, giving his attention as fully to the poorest as to the well-to-do — it was to make known to them the love of God through his love of them. It might be strange for a provost and a Sales to do this, but, at any rate, he had no option but to share a good deal of their poverty.

Short of Geneva, the Annecy diocese was extremely poor, and he had no fortune of his own. But rather than accept stipends for his personal ministry, he looked to his family to meet the absolute necessities of his office. In his life, he would do a great deal of not very successful begging for the basic needs of the Church's ministry, but, brought up always to look to his tutor for necessary funds, he was always to make do on the very insufficient revenues that came his way. So ready to accept social conventions in other ways, he would never be ashamed of the outward marks of personal poverty in tattered and remended clothes, simple fare, and the plainest of lodging. If it was the aristocrat in him that made him unconscious of money, he knew how to convert his advantage into a conscious practice of the holy poverty that should mark priests and bishops as true followers of Christ.

The reports to Bishop Granier that the new Provost de Sales was above himself, like the rest of his family, as well as complaints from the poor, who feared he might be making a fool of them with his newfangled ways, make it clear that de Sales's ardent pastoral zeal, combined as it was with intelligence and fresh imagination, did not win through without opposition and criticism from those whose maxim in every century is: "What was good enough for our forefathers is good enough for us." It was not to be expected.

Nevertheless, the impression he quickly made was overwhelming, the best proof of the fact being that, within a few months of his Ordination, he was chosen, with his cousin Canon Louis, for a task considered utterly hopeless where any other of the clergy of Annecy were concerned. This was no less than the wresting of the Chablais from the Calvinists and the recovery of Catholic worship within it. It must have seemed almost as hopeless for the ardent young provost, aided by his cousin, to attempt it. But everyone agreed that if anyone could make headway, it was this born apostle.

To understand how the opportunity arose and what was involved in it, it is necessary to study the complex religious history of the district, that had from his earliest days filled the imagination of Francis de Sales.

The Chablais is the country, then part of the domains of the Duke of Savoy, to the south of the Lake of Geneva from east of Geneva to Saint-Gingolph and due north of Annecy and Thorens, where de Sales was born. It is cut in two by the river Dranse, east of Thonon. As the result of the highly complex political and religious situation, just before and just after the Reformation, in which the Swiss patriotism of the "Eiguenots," or confederates, was strengthened by adherence to the Reformers, Geneva and the districts of Savoy around it, including the Chablais west of the Dranse, were occupied by the Bernese Protestants, and Francis I of France[45] undertook the conquest of the Duchy of Savoy.

As de Sales was to describe it later when reporting to Clement VIII: "The people of Geneva shook off the sweet

---

[45] Francis I (1494-1547), King of France from 1515-1547.

yoke of Christ and the authority of their sovereign at one and the same time, thus most unhappily plunging into the seditious democracy which now oppresses them."[46] The people of the West Chablais were made subject to a violent persecution, all outward signs of the Catholic Faith being destroyed and the people heavily fined for worship in the old religion. The result was the virtual elimination of the Catholic Faith.

Twenty-eight years later, in 1564, a new Duke of Savoy, Emmanuel-Philibert, managed to recover his authority over the Chablais, but tacitly allowed the new religion to retain its hold — an astonishing tolerance for the times, due not to any broader views, but to the duke's unwillingness to add to his military commitments. De Sales was to call it "an iniquitous arrangement which was accepted in the hope of better days and the fact that, given the times and the place, there was no alternative."

In 1589, when de Sales was in his first year's study in Padua, Charles-Emmanuel of Savoy, called "the Great," took up arms once more against the insurgent Calvinists who were now seeking with French help to recover their political and religious rights over the Chablais — "sheer perfidy," reported de Sales to the Pope, "but, incredibly, it proved propitious and profitable to us, for the duke, in view of their broken word, restored the Catholic Faith to these people."

This was agreed to on paper by the Treaty of Noyon, the terms of which involved the Calvinists' undertaking the re-establishment of Catholic liberties, while they would retain for themselves only three churches in the Chablais. A mission

---

[46] *The Works of St. Francis de Sales*, Vol. 12, 229.

of some fifty priests was immediately sent by the Bishop of Geneva-Annecy to re-evangelize the unfortunate land. But when the duke decided to use his forces to support the Catholic League in France, the Calvinists in 1591, although still political subjects of the duke, once more imposed Protestantism and drove out the priests. The conversion of Henry IV of France in July 1593 led to a truce in the Chablais. The truce recognized Savoy's political authority, and agreed to the religious position defined by the Treaty of Noyon, namely, that Catholic worship should be free and Protestant worship severely restricted.

Thus, by a singular accident in those days of confused and cruel politico-religious warfare, the involved story of the fighting for the marginal land of the Chablais left the Catholic record unblemished so far as treaty rights went. Charles-Emmanuel would have been acting fully within his rights if he had enforced by military action the terms of the Treaty of Noyon so far as it affected religion. Luckily, he was too busy to do so, and a spiritually ideal situation was created. It was left to the spiritual arm of the Church alone to take an apostolic advantage of the religious rights of Savoy.

Had the diocese possessed the means, it would have organized a fully equipped mission to tackle a job which was bound to prove dangerous, since Savoy's political authority possessed little more than a token reality, the effective rulers remaining the Calvinists, supported by neighboring Geneva. But the diocese was so poor and the danger so great that it was left to Provost de Sales, with his cousin Louis, to win back to the Church the sixty thousand or so inhabitants of the Chablais. The missionary conditions of the first apostles had been granted to

these lone workers, traveling on foot as poor men with virtually no financial resources. It was only two years since Déage
had been making fun of the hatless Padua student during his
Italian tour. However drawn out his humanistic adolescence,
his maturing as priest and apostle was proving unbelievably
rapid.

De Sales, of course, knew the Chablais and had many
friends and relations in it. He was not unduly perturbed by
the mission. "We are not dealing with barbarians," he said.
"What would it be if they were sending us to the Indies or to
England — yet we would have to go." A degree of local physical safety would be ensured by the Savoy garrison established in the Allinges fortress on the high ground south of
the chief town, Thonon. De Sales could have made it a fairly
safe mission, and no doubt this was the general expectation.
If so, the zeal and character of the missioner had not yet been
understood.

Some of de Sales's sufferings in the Chablais apostolate
were due to his father, a man whose narrowness and stupidity,
while they may have been tolerated by Francis, who was a
saint and a loving son, soon began to wear down the good will
of the biographer. One would have thought that the old soldier
might have appreciated his son's lone apostolic battle against
heresy. But not a bit of it. He was furious. Perhaps he thought
that this was not the road to ecclesiastical preferment.

His anger was such that he refused to give the material aid
in the way of money, equipment, and service which he could
easily have afforded and which would have done so much to
ensure safety and some degree of comfort. For one of the greatest physical dangers would come from the bitterly cold winters

in a desolate snow-covered and frozen country in which de Sales would tramp by day and by night, ill-clad and ill-fed, hoping to make a friendly contact, or sleep in a hayloft — or, as on one occasion, tied to a branch of a tree, lest he fall off in his sleep, to be untied by peasants the next morning, too frozen to do anything for himself. It was left to his mother to give surreptitiously what little material help she could and at least arrange for messengers to keep him in contact with his family.

The greater danger came, of course, from physical attacks by rabid Calvinists or ruffians employed by their betters. Much of this danger he could have avoided, had he agreed to be escorted by soldiers from the garrison, but only once or twice did he permit this, when the actual danger had been foreseen and the governor was adamant. To preach the Gospel under the protection of soldiers was no part of his plan.

The provost's spiritual ideal was hinted at in a letter written a month before his departure:

Yes, I suppose it is very easy for a Christian to follow Christ curing the sick and bringing the dead back to life. We can all do that. It is another matter to follow Him suffering and dying. Only a few are capable of this. It is not so hard to embrace the Cross when it is standing up and when no one shakes it or tries to uproot it; but to hold it up in the face of those who would bring it down betokens a tried courage.

Blessed struggle when we are both dying and living for Christ. . . . Knowledge alone never raised to the heights the Martins, the Chrysostoms, the Hilarys, the Damascenes. It was the Christian magnanimity with which they declared war for Christ's sake against the emperors and the false brothers, showing themselves intrepid in fighting the wars of the Lord.[47]

Little did he think as he tried to work up a courage fitted to the task before him that he also one day would be numbered among the great apostles and Doctors of the Church.

So on September 14, 1594, the two cousins set out on foot, with their packs on their backs, to realize the impossible: to convert a population of sixty thousand (among whom were but a hundred or so remaining Catholics) sustained and supported by Calvinist leaders who had already often shown that they would stick at nothing to prevent the restoration of the old Faith. Some forty miles they must have tramped that first day to the Allinges fortress, setting from the start the sort of scale by which they would measure the vastness of the enterprise that lay ahead of them.

---

[47] *The Works of St. Francis de Sales*, Vol. 11, 85-86.

Chapter Four

Winning Souls
Back to the Faith

1594-1596

The story of the four-year Chablais apostolate in which, from start to finish, Francis de Sales played so much the leading role that success seems inconceivable but for his imaginative zeal, his winning character, and his indefatigable endurance, demands a book in itself. Here we must be content to treat it as a passing episode in his spiritual development and an indication of the kind of person he was. This is all the more important in that there is always the temptation to misunderstand his charm, his sensitivity, and his humanity, and to suppose that there was an element of softness in him hard to reconcile with great sanctity. The Chablais episode, when he was between the ages of twenty-seven and thirty-one, reveals for the first time the strength of character which was more and more to make itself felt as the real explanation of the balance and attraction of his personality. In this, the reader will doubtless feel, as the biographer must, how spontaneously and inevitably, as it seemed, Francis de Sales was to model himself on the pattern of perfection, the Christ we know from the Gospels.

Among Thonon's three to four thousand inhabitants, there were only some twenty Catholics. How to make contact with such a people? Foreign missionaries today may at least expect a certain initial curiosity on the part of those among whom they come. In the English mission of that time, Catholics were in sufficient number to shelter the priests from abroad and to make the necessary introductions. But de Sales's theoretical security under the legal Savoy sovereignty and the local protection of the Allinges garrison were in themselves another apostolic handicap. He was an intruding political as well as a religious enemy of the people.

The governor, who was a friend of his, at once put the position to him in idealistic and realistic terms. Pointing to the guns protecting the fortress, he said, "We shall not long need these, providing, please God, that the Huguenots down there are ready to listen to you." It was a formidable proviso. The missionaries could give fresh heart to the scattered handful of Catholics, but how to make contact with the Protestants? When de Sales invoked his legal right to preach in the bullet-pocked church of Saint-Hippolyte, only a few nervous Catholics were there to listen to him. The Protestants passed by, jeering at him and shouting, "Squint-eyed, squint-eyed" (*louche* in French, having the double meaning of the physical defect and a shady person). The preacher, in fact, was simply sent to Coventry.

Francis wrote to Favre after a fortnight: "The governor, together with a few other Catholics, has spared no pains and no persuasions to get the neighboring peasants and bourgeois of Evian to come to our sermons. He has done his best to promote the interests of religion with his enlightened zeal. But the Devil soon saw to it, and the leaders of Thonon assembled their council and swore perfidiously that neither they themselves nor the people would come to our sermons. . . . Their object is to make us lose hope of ever succeeding here and so force us to quit. It shall not be. So long as the truce lasts, we shall by the will of God and the state's authority continue absolutely resolved to carry on our task."

He gave a fuller explanation to his bishop: "The excuse the people give is that they may be maltreated by the Bernese and the Genevese as deserters to their Faith if they approach otherwise than with insults on their lips and stones in their hands. The truth is that our job here is not only to get rid of heresy, but most of all, of worldly self-interest."[48]

So it continued that first year in utter frustration, as autumn turned to an exceptionally cold winter. The task seemed hopeless even if de Sales could take courage from some signs of thawing in that one or two of the Calvinist leaders went out of their way to be personally polite and even friendly. That was where he would score, for his personal charm was irresistible.

When Louis returned home for a while, Francis, we are told, felt a special strength in his absolute loneliness as he trudged from door to door, seeking out the occasional Catholic home and hoping to obtain an introduction to a Protestant one. Physically strong and well built, de Sales suffered all his life from poor circulation, which in the end caused his early death. One can then imagine him, his hands covered with vicious chilblains and easily chilled through his whole body,

---

[48] *The Works of St. Francis de Sales*, Vol. 11, 90-95.

enduring day by day and often even at night exposure in that hard winter.

Physical attacks on his life occasionally occurred, sufficiently serious to terrify Georges Rolland, a servant from Thorens whom de Sales's father had at last consented to send. Rolland, an intelligent boy of eighteen, was not born brave. After an ambush in which two men threatened his master with swords, Rolland could stand it no longer and sent a message to tell the story to M. de Boisy. The latter immediately ordered his son to return to civilization. For once de Sales answered with a certain asperity: "If Rolland had been your son instead of only being your servant, he would not have been such a coward as to run away from the little trouble in which he was involved, exaggerating it into a great battle. No one need have any doubts about the bad will of our enemies, but at least spare us the wrong of doubting our courage. I earnestly ask you, therefore, not to see in our determination to stay here any sign of disobedience." It is strange that the old man could not see in his son the same spirit as he himself had once shown at the siege of Landrécies, many years before.

Still, M. de Boisy could say, "I told you so" as time passed and no appreciable progress was made. It was imperative to discover some way of breaking the deadlock.

De Sales wrote to Favre in January 1595: "My mind is turning over the idea of some meditations on the mutations of heretics in our times"; and a little later: "You wish to see the first pages of my work against the heretics. I want it very much too, and I would not like to carry my standards into the enemy lines with the spirit the cause deserves until I obtain your approval of the plan, the battle, and the tactics to be adopted.

But I realize the difficulties of the undertaking, and, moreover, I am short of the auxiliary troops I need: I mean the books necessary to a person who holds in his mind only a small number of ideas.[49]

His plan was simple — to reach by the written word those he could not reach by word of mouth. The idea seems simple enough to us. But apart from the physical difficulties of printing and distribution, the plan to write doctrinal tracts in much the same way as we should write pamphlets or magazine articles seemed hazardous. Writing in those days was, as he expressed it in his announcement of the project to the "Messieurs de Thonon," the prerogative of "the learned and most polished intelligences. When speaking, your action, voice, and appearance help on the word, but in order to write, you must 'know a great deal.' " It was a strange doubt on the part of a person who would always find it easier to express himself by the written word than the spoken. He would pour out his feelings in his letters, but he talked, we are told, slowly and hesitatingly. Anyhow, now there was no alternative if he was to carry on, despite the lack of books, which included only the Bible, Bellarmine's *Controversies*, and Canisius's catechism.[50]

The idea, as it worked out, was to write a series of doctrinal extracts from his sermons in the defense of the Catholic Faith — extracts short enough to be copied and slipped under the doors of the citizens' houses. But it became evident that if

---

[49] Ibid., 108-111.

[50] St. Robert Bellarmine (1542-1621), Archbishop of Capua; St. Peter Canisius (1521-1597), Jesuit theologian. The *Controversies*, by Bellarmine, is an apologetic work.

these tracts were to do their work, they would have to be printed. Soon, the doctrinal broadsheets were postered up in convenient places, as well as distributed by hand. In modern terms, it was a kind of Catholic journalism, published by a writer who had to work by candlelight after a day's tramping on arduous and disappointing apostolic missions. The writer could not have imagined that a day would come when these sheets — sets of which were to be discovered at Le Thuille, thirty-six years after his death — would find permanent publication under the name of *Controverses*. In his letters, he called them *Memorials* or *Meditations*. Their aim, in fact, was not so much controversial as expository. The straightforward journalistic style has a natural appeal today, and the *Controverses* often read more easily than his later and deeper writings. One can open the book at random and take a passage as illustration. Here is an example on infallibility.

> Surely it is not reasonable that any individual should call himself infallible when interpreting or explaining Scripture. See the result! Who would be willing to accept his authority? Why this person rather than the other? Let him talk as much as he likes about analogy, enthusiasm, the Lord, the Spirit — well, I for one would never thus restrict the freedom of my mind. If I have to take my chance, let it be my own judgment rather than someone else's, be he able to speak Greek, Hebrew, Latin, Tartar, Moorish, or any language you can think of. If we must risk being wrong, surely we should prefer to follow our own judgment than enslave it to a Calvin or a Luther! Everyone would certainly feel free to think as he wants to and follow up different points of view. Who knows — he might strike on the truth as readily as the next man!

Really it is an impiety to think that our Lord left us no supreme judge on earth — a judge to whom we could look for the solution of our difficulties; a judge so infallible in his judgments that we could not make a mistake when we followed Him. I maintain that that judge is none other than the Catholic Church. . . .

In another example, he refers to Theodore Beza, Calvin's successor, whom he was soon to meet at the Pope's request:

You will tell me that Beza says that the Roman Church errs today in necessary beliefs and this was why he left it, but that he does not hold that the true Church has ever been in error. He certainly cannot wriggle out by that path. Which Church existed in the world two, three, four, five hundred years ago, if not the Catholic Roman Church exactly as it is today? There was no other. It must therefore have been the true Church in error or else there was no true Church in the world.

If so, Beza must agree that this state of affairs arose from intolerable error even in things necessary to salvation, for I have already sufficiently shown the absurdity of his idea of a secret Church within which the faithful are dispersed.

Besides, when they admit that the visible Church may err, they are undermining the Church to which our Lord tells us to appeal in our difficulties — the Church which St. Paul calls "the pillar and foundation on which the truth rests,"[51] St. Paul's witnesses could only refer to the visible Church. If you do not believe that, you must admit, first, that our Lord wanted us to consult something invisible, imperceptible, and completely unknown or, second, that St. Paul was telling

[51] Cf. 1 Tim. 3:15.

Timothy to speak to a gathering of which he himself had no knowledge.

It was all straightforward, hard-hitting stuff coming into the hands of ordinary men and women who, for a couple of generations, had hardly heard a word against the teaching of their religious leaders.

The tracts were slowly to do their work, and de Sales decided early in 1595 to leave the security of Allinges as a headquarters and stay with friends in Thonon itself, where he could at least minister to the few Catholics. For Mass, however, he had to ride each morning across the Dranse into the Catholic part of the Chablais, an undertaking as perilous in winter as so much else, for the stone bridge had been washed away and a wooden plank, often covered with ice, substituted for it.

There was no optimism in a letter he wrote to Possevino at this time: "I need not underline for you what it means to me to make a resolution involving the abandonment of my interest in the affairs of the world and in my family. It is as much as we can do to keep the Catholics going here — such is the cost to them of keeping the faith. . . . However, I have some relations and friends who respect me for special reasons. These reasons I cannot entrust to others. That is what keeps me here. Only the hope I have of better times prevents me from being too depressed. . . . Anyway, it would be a waste to have someone else working here uselessly — someone likely to be of better service elsewhere than I could be. Besides, I am the sort of preacher who is only good enough to preach to walls, as I have to do in this town."[52]

[52] *The Works of St. Francis de Sales*, Vol. 11, 121.

However, he was soon a little more optimistic. To Favre he wrote, "Just now some ears are beginning to ripen in this great harvest, and if, in this unhappy time, I do not gather them, the danger is that the grains of the true Faith will be dispersed, especially if the wind blows from the north — as the prophet says, 'Every evil comes from a north wind.' Among the ears I refer to, I count Pierre Poncet, a learned jurist with his heart in the right place. Despite his gross errors in regard to nearly everything about our Faith, he has for a long time held correct views about the Real Presence of Jesus Christ's body in the Eucharist. So it was not hard to draw him away from Calvin's sect with its false views about this August sacrament, views which have deceived so many. But it was much more difficult to bring him back to the fold of the Church."

That hard and spiritually so disappointing winter was indeed ending as the sun of April shone across the lake again. Not only was Poncet converted, but so was the Baron d'Avully, a Calvinist who had first been moved by de Sales's first sermon in Annecy nearly two years earlier. D'Avully, one of the leading figures in the Chablais, professed himself converted, but deferred his public abjuration for political reasons.

The ice was breaking, despite de Sales's recent pessimism, and all the sufferings, dangers, and depressions of so unrewarding an apostolate for so young a priest were proving not to have been in vain. The example of such leading figures would slowly spread.

After seven months, de Sales had earned a rest, and for a few weeks, he returned to the spiritual peace of Annecy, whose arcaded ways alongside the waters seemed to him like a monastic cloister where he could pray again and peacefully greet so many friends among rich and poor. But the Chablais mission was not to everyone's taste in the episcopal town. Was not the young provost stirring up political trouble in the district? Was he certain that the highest political circles in Savoy approved of his mission? Such was the talk of the town he was overhearing.

In a letter to Favre on May 16, he turned from congratulating his friend on a volume of poems dedicated to himself ("Staying as I am with my relations amidst the birds singing in the springtime, I keep on admiring all the details of this flowing poem") to more practical matters: "I am getting ready to return to Thonon. You are about the only person who really approves of my determination. When, in another four months, my year's work will have been finished, only you will be able to persuade me to carry on. The general belief is that we are working in that province without the duke's consent, and many go so far as to say that our work is against his will. Seeing that a word from him would make all the difference, his silence is certainly an effective argument. But there is another: the sight of men at work within the domains of the Church and under a Catholic prince, living in so precarious a way and, one might say, just from day to day. But do not breathe a word of this to anyone, for you know how easily it could be misinterpreted."[53]

His nephew Charles-Auguste de Sales tells us that God sent Francis a special grace on the feast of Corpus Christi that summer. When in prayer, his sense of closeness to God was such that he could only mutter, "Hold back, O Lord, this flow

[53] Ibid., 138-140.

of grace. Come not so near me, for I am not strong enough to endure the greatness of Your consoling touch which forces me to the ground." This was the first, so far as we know, of similar spiritual experiences which indicate how close to God he was living his inner life — so close that it was as if the normal frame and space and time occasionally broke away to allow a sensible revelation of the reality which self-love, sin, and constant preoccupation with the things of earth shut off from normal human experience. The time would come when he would acquire a deeper spiritual perception too close to the divine for even this kind of sensible consolation. This first experience may well have been God's compensation for his patience and determination in his frustrating and criticized work.

After his return to the Chablais in June, he could still write in a mood of depression to Favre: "The Thonon harvest is beyond my own strength, although I am determined not to give up, save with your agreement and at your orders. Meanwhile I am doing all I can to prepare new workers for the task and to find means of arranging for their upkeep. [He was writing from Annecy.] I can see no end, no way out, given the infinite wiles of the enemy of the human race. I have been tormented, as I still am, by the thought that amid so many threatening catastrophes, we have hardly a moment to give to the spiritual preparation of which we are so much in need."[54]

This discouragement must have been largely due to fatigue, for in fact the tide was now slowly turning. His preaching — even apparently only to blank walls — his tracts, and, above all, his personality were causing many to think again.

[54] Ibid., 153-155.

We are told that children could not resist him, and that as he chatted and played with them, their parents realized what sort of man he was. He had the gift, too, of patiently gossiping with the simplest folk. We hear, for example, of the case of an old woman, worried about her faith, who loved to talk to him. One day she got onto the subject of the celibacy of the Catholic clergy, a matter that, she said, scandalized her. "But, my dear," he said to her, "you keep on coming to see me. Think of the time it takes to talk to you. How on earth could I manage to help you with all your difficulties if I had a wife and children!"

By September, he was writing much more cheerfully to Favre: "A wider and more beautiful door is opening out before us in the harvest of Christians. . . . They are now so keen on hearing my expositions of the Catholic Faith . . . that, not having been able to come publicly because the law forbids them, they listen at a spot where they cannot be seen. I only hope the weakness of my voice has not spoiled it all. . . . I am sure that now that they are ready to come to terms, they must soon, according to the proverb, capitulate."[55]

The best news of all at this time was the Pope's official acceptance of the abjuration of Protestantism by the King of France, Henry IV, for this would free the Duke of Savoy from his commitments to support the Catholics in France against the Protestant king, and enable him to give at least moral support and the necessary funds absolutely needed if the individual conversions were to lead to the re-establishment of normal Catholic parish life in the Chablais. No wonder de Sales, who, as a student, had not been able to stomach the idea of a

[55] Ibid., 158-159.

Protestant Henry IV in France, was now delighted to join with the Pope in welcoming the Catholic Henry IV. "If the news is true," he wrote to Favre, "may peace reign in the strength of the Lord — a peace all the happier in that the heretics will hardly relish it, I think. I am pressing forward now with these 'Messieurs de Thonon,' and I shall be pressing on even further when I have finished, as best I can, the little work I have so long been engaged on."[56]

By this second winter, the tally of converts was some two hundred — a tiny number, whose true significance, however, was to be measured by the wider signs of good will achieved through an apostolate resting only on love, fair argument, self-sacrifice, and prayer — an apostolate practically unique in those times because it was in no way supported by customary Catholic force. On the contrary, it was even denied the political sympathy and resources that could legitimately be expected of his own country by any missionary in any period of history.

In the circumstances, it is not surprising that he wrote at the end of the year to his sovereign, Charles-Emmanuel I of Savoy. "It is absolutely necessary," he said, "to have sure and reliable funds to support a goodly number of preachers. . . . Equally will it be to rebuild the churches and to provide for parish priests." He also wanted a commission of senators to enter the Chablais and invite the people in the name of the duke "to listen closely to the reasons given by the preachers to encourage a return to the Church from which the people had been torn, not through reason, but by sheer Bernese force."

[56] Ibid., 161-162.

The presence of some young soldiers would give heart to youth, "and would not be a useless means of stimulating courage in the religious question, provided the soldiers are organized in a religious spirit and linked to some Christian institutions." A Jesuit college would also be useful. "In obstinate cases, those persisting in their errors should be deprived of their judicial and public positions."

The Anglican clergyman, L. Woolsey Bacon, to whom we have already referred, tried to account for the success of the Chablais mission by de Sales's being "flush of money and resources of every kind, backed by the treasury and army of Savoy." He also maintained that conversions were politically dictated by the threat of the use of military force by the soldiers stationed in the country. Such charges are today no more than a curiosity of religious controversy, for few can have been less well-founded. Nevertheless, it is necessary to realize that Francis de Sales at the end of the sixteenth century by no means shared all the views Catholics would take today.

To understand this, we must distinguish between his attitude toward heresy as a political evil and his attitude toward the person of the heretic. "There can be no convention between Jesus Christ and Baal," he declared, and heresy, however many Catholic faults had contributed to its origin, was the work of Baal.[57] He could not therefore conceive of a Catholic state giving equal rights to heretics and Catholics. The Duke of Savoy would have been fully within his rights to use political and military force to drive heresy and obstinate heretics out of his country.

[57] Baal was the false god of storm and fertility; see Num. 25:3.

Had Woolsey Bacon's contention been true, de Sales would not have been intellectually scandalized. But since de Sales, as a person of deep spiritual insight, understood very well the difference between the method of love and Christian charity and the method of force, whether political or military, he himself was only personally interested in conversions by purely spiritual means. "I assure you that I have never used invectives and reproaches without being sorry for it," he confessed. "We must hold it an absolute fact that men do more through love and charity than through severity and harshness." So much was this the case that even among the different means of obtaining truly free conversions, only the best really appealed to him. Bossuet,[58] in the panegyric he preached after Francis de Sales's death, reported the charming words of Cardinal du Perron[59] on methods of conversion. "If you want heretics to be convinced," du Perron said, "I believe you could do worse than refer them to me; but if you are anxious to have them converted, you must take them to Francis de Sales, the Bishop of Geneva."

As we shall see, the conversion of the Chablais was completed with the help of the Duke of Savoy's political authority, whose rights de Sales did not deny, but for three years, de Sales prepared the way and brought about the conversion of thousands by purely spiritual means. It should also be remembered that the leaders of the Protestants who had used force to

---

[58] Jacques Bénigne Bossuet (1627-1704), French preacher and Bishop of Meaux.

[59] Jacques Davy du Perron (1556-1618), French cardinal, statesman, and convert from Calvinism to the Catholic Faith.

Protestantize the country saw no more virtue in toleration than the most rabid of Catholics. But for their fear of the duke's revenge, they would have driven de Sales out of the land or killed him. The unusual circumstances on both sides might have been designed to enable a saint to show the world how a true Christian apostolate should be carried out.

Chapter Five

The Fruits
of Perseverance

1596-1598

Francis De Sales, at the earliest possible moment, made it clear to the people of Thonon that his whole spiritual work was based on the central act of Catholic worship: the Mass. Despite the fact that he had to write to the nuncio in Turin that his mission was without any resources, he was determined to bring the Mass back publicly to the Chablais. "Besides, no church has been restored, no permanent altar set up," he wrote to Msgr. Riccardi. "We are even without chalices, missals, and other things indispensable. . . . In the church at Thonon, everything is topsy-turvy, without any furniture, except for a badly made, simple wooden altar we put together for Christmas."

But on that badly made, simple wooden altar, the Mass of Christmas 1596 had been celebrated publicly for the first time in Thonon for sixty years. "I am planning," de Sales had written to the duke, "to have an altar erected in the church of Saint-Hippolyte, where I have been normally preaching for these last two years so as to be able to celebrate Mass there during these good days of Christmas. The syndics of the town have tried to stop me, but they have given way. I cannot imagine on what grounds they dared to make their opposition, since the Treaty of Noyon is not violated."[60]

The fact that the Protestant leaders' opposition was not pressed home and that the first public Mass in Thonon could be held without disturbance of the peace is a striking indication of how much de Sales had accomplished behind the scenes in the course of two years by his prayers, his personality, and his preaching. From now on, Mass was to be celebrated publicly every Sunday in the chief town of the Chablais.

The spiritual effect of this first public restoration of Catholic worship was bound to be immense. The scattered, hidden Catholics were given new heart, and the many Protestants, shaken by the apostle's personality and arguments, began to feel that there was a definite religious option ahead of them. It was more than just talk. Before long, they might have to act.

This change, however, inevitably brought fresh dangers from the frightened extremists. When de Sales, at the beginning of Lent 1597, made up his mind to restore the old Catholic custom of placing the ashes on the heads of the faithful, the people, taught to regard such ceremonies as the grossest superstitions, were infuriated. They closed in angrily on him and called for his imprisonment, some of them openly threatening to kill him on the spot. The situation became so ugly that he had to give way and finally make his escape through an open door and up a staircase. "A la garde de Dieu," he shouted spiritedly as he disappeared, and this name is still given to the remains of the house where he found refuge.

[60] *The Works of St. Francis de Sales*, Vol. 11, 225-226.

Such incidents made the Duke of Savoy nervous. He was anxious to avoid trouble, and Favre again warned de Sales that Charles-Emmanuel, so far from wanting to support the apostolic task by political and military means, was determined to do everything possible to maintain peace and order. In the circumstances, the duke thought it best to send a regiment into the Chablais — a decision which some historians have seized on to prove the political nature of the apostolate. But neither the duke nor the missioner had any intention of using the "Martinengo" regiment as a threat. De Sales's only concern was to minister spiritually to the men, and to make sure that they behaved themselves properly and were of as little burden as possible to the people. As such they would be an encouragement and an example, not a menace. A little later he was to write to a military captain to beg him not to bring troops, since their presence would scandalize both Protestants and Catholics.[61]

How could anyone suggest that this apostolate, set in conditions of abject poverty within a legally Catholic land under a Catholic ruler where the lives of Catholics were still not safe, was a political undertaking carried out under threats of Catholic political violence? It is clear that the young Provost of Geneva had undertaken a humble spiritual work of personal apostolate that we more naturally associate with religious of a missionary order than with a scholar and priest of the world due for high promotion. It was inevitable that the zeal and brilliance with which he was carrying out his mission would bring him a fame that he might not so easily have earned in

[61] Ibid., 347-348.

Annecy itself. Although Bishop Granier had no immediate need of a coadjutor, rumors and more than rumors were already spread about that de Sales would shortly be appointed to the position that would give him one day the prince-bishopric of Geneva.

In a letter to Favre of February 1596, he refers to the fact that the duke was talking of "magnificent prospects for him" and added that he himself would much prefer to follow the example of a friend who had become a Capuchin. In another letter, he refers openly to the coadjutorship, and writes, "Every reason and my own experience prevent me from wanting it. Besides, the duty, honor, and zeal I feel toward the bishop would stop me from ever thinking of it so long as God keeps us our prelate, while my own incapacity would hold me back once God has deprived us of him."[62]

A more unexpected recognition of his work in the Chablais came from the Pope, Clement VIII, himself. He received a papal brief telling him that Father Esprit, a missionary who had come to help in the work, had a special message for the provost. The message was that the Pope wanted de Sales to go to Geneva and see no less a person than Theodore Beza (or de Beze), who had played a leading part in the growth of French Protestantism and succeeded Calvin as the leader of the Reform. Now, Beza was approaching his eightieth year, and it is astonishing that the Pope should have entrusted to a priest of only twenty-nine the task of seeing what could be done to bring the Calvinist chief back to the Catholic Faith he had professed until that same age.

[62] Ibid., 182-183.

In a letter of April 1597 to the Pope, de Sales briefly described his first attempt. "My first duty," de Sales wrote, "was to make use as prudently and carefully as possible of the first chance of learning from Beza himself what his real feelings were and to talk to him about them. With this in mind, I very often entered Geneva on the excuse of having business there. But I was unable to find any way of getting into close and secret contact with the man I was seeking until Easter Tuesday. I then met Beza alone and found him fairly easy to approach. When at length I left, after having tried every means of penetrating into his mind, not leaving any stone unturned, I had to see in him a heart of stone that was not to be moved — or at least sufficiently moved. In a word, he was a hardened old man full of evil days. So far as I can judge from what he said to me, I would say this about him. If one could see him more often and in less hazardous circumstances, one just might bring him back to the fold of the Lord, but for an octogenarian, all delay is dangerous."[63]

A little later, de Sales paid a second visit, taking with him this time his friend Favre, whose learning and official position in Savoy might help to impress the veteran Calvinist. Naturally, on these visits, the provost had to wear secular clothes, for Geneva would not have tolerated a Catholic priest freely walking through its streets.

This time Beza seemed pleased to see his visitor and to welcome Favre. But the small talk was leading to nothing when de Sales pointed to a number of dusty tomes lying in the corner of the room. Although he had recognized them, he asked

[63] Ibid., 269-270.

his host what they were. The old man said that they were volumes of the Fathers of the Church and he did not think much of them. De Sales saw the opening and said that he took a very different view of them. Over a volume of Augustine, the three men discussed together de Sales's old problem of grace, justification, and predestination. Beza seemed to enjoy the conversation and to appreciate the charm and learning of his visitors, as well he might.

This introduction enabled de Sales to ask Beza the direct question — to which Church should a man trust himself if he wishes to be certain of his final supernatural destiny? Beza had to admit that the Roman Catholic Church was a true Church, but maintained that the Reformed Church was also true and an easier Church within which to be saved. After this, it was a question arguing whether Christ had founded an easy Church in which a man depended on faith alone or a hard one in which salvation depended on living up to the good works that proved a real faith.

Charles-Auguste de Sales, to whom we owe the details of this meeting, tells us that Francis's servant, Georges Rolland, overheard Beza saying as the visitors were leaving: "If I am not on the right road, I do pray God every day that His mercy will guide me to it." Eight years later, Beza died, a Calvinist, it seems, but no one can know what effect Francis de Sales may have had on him in his inmost self.

But if the interviews with Beza seemed barren, de Sales did not leave Geneva without a consolation which was to mean very much to him. On a previous visit when he was disputing with the Calvinist minister de la Faye, he had met a simple, but most courageous Catholic servant in the Ecu de France where he stayed. This girl, Jacqueline Coste, used to help the occasional Catholic priest entering the town. Each time de Sales saw her, he confirmed her in her religion and he brought her Holy Communion. A few years later, Jacqueline was to convert on her deathbed the wife of the owner of the inn, but rather than stay and marry the widower, she left Geneva to settle in Annecy near its new bishop, Msgr. de Sales. Later, this brave woman would find a niche in history as the first *tourière*[64] of the Visitation Order, a truly beloved figure in the golden legend of the beginnings of the contemplative nuns established by the inspiration of two saints, Francis de Sales and Jane Frances de Chantal.

From now on, the Chablais apostolate was to be for the provost, who was beginning to be thought of as Coadjutor and future Bishop of Geneva, a long administrative headache. The increase in the number of converts set the problem of establishing parishes and finding clergy to run them — and this with hardly any financial resources. Letters to the duke and the nuncio followed one another. In one letter, it is a question of organizing personnel. Second to de Sales himself was the young Capuchin preacher Father Chérubin, ardent, impetuous, but without de Sales's tact. Jesuits also were needed, and would it be better to have a certain Jesuit from Turin or a Frenchman from Milan, and what about Fr. Alexander Hume, the Scotsman? In another letter, how many parishes? M. d'Avully thought twenty-two were necessary, but "I have always thought eighteen would suffice." As for money, de Sales was for years to try to induce the Knights of SS. Maurice and

---

[64] A lay sister who looks after the community's material needs.

Lazarus, to whom had been temporarily given what was left of the old Chablais church revenues, to disburse what was now needed — and with very little success.

The good work in the Chablais made him keenly interested in the Calvinist oppression in those parts of the diocese which lay within the jurisdiction of the King of France, such as the Pays de Gex on the other side of the Lake of Geneva. This, too, would be a vexatious problem that would haunt him through life. In a letter at this time to the Pope, he wrote, "I know of many places which daily complain that being Catholics, they are prevented by the tyranny of Geneva from fulfilling their Catholic duties, even though that republic oppresses these people, not in its own name, but in that of the very Christian King of France. Is the king aware of this tyranny weighing on Catholic consciences? . . . I believe that if the king were informed of the situation by the Apostolic See, things would work out differently."[65] But although Henry IV was to become his friend, that monarch was too wily to bring trouble on himself by interfering too much in this difficult problem.

It was providential that the lone apostle of the Chablais, destined to succeed to the bishopric, should gain all this experience in his own difficult mission-field. It seemed that he would not have long to wait before facing the greater problems of the diocese, since in the summer of 1597, Bishop Granier had a very serious illness. Everyone was awaiting the official nomination of de Sales as coadjutor. The appointment was in the hands of the duke, subject to papal approval, and the nuncio

[65] *The Works of St. Francis de Sales*, Vol. 11, 270-271.

in a letter had already hinted to the provost of "the greater position" for which His Highness destined him. Everyone was already calling him "Monseigneur."

De Sales's letter to the duke, when he understood what was happening, is a model of humble realism: "Knowing that your favor in this high business springs from Your Highness's goodness, persuaded perhaps that there is something in me that corresponds with your favor, I must blush with shame at my own unworthiness, but I must also praise God, who has enabled Your Highness to wish to appoint good pastors for your people. Although I am the least worthy of those whom Your Highness could have thought of, the good intention is nonetheless very commendable."

And the writer could not resist the opportunity of reminding the duke of other matters that seemed much more pressing to him: "I have lately written about the needs of the Chablais, and although I do not doubt that the zeal with which the Lord has warmed your heart has kept the memory of these matters fresh in your mind, I have nevertheless asked the Baron de Chevron to bring them again to your attention."[66] Writing to princes was something which Francis de Sales understood very well.

Bishop Granier, however, recovered. Even so, he asked de Sales for his consent to the appointment so that papal approval might be obtained. De Sales, who did not know that the duke had already signed the letters patent, felt he could speak his mind more openly to his bishop and he begged to be spared the honor. He was not, he said, made to command, but

---

rather to have charge of a simple parish. No one could have been less ambitious than he, and his natural, as well as supernatural, inclination was to defer important decisions until he could no longer doubt the will of God. To make quite sure of this, he went to the church of Thorens, where he had been baptized just thirty years earlier, to say a votive Mass of the Holy Spirit. Asked what his mind was after saying this Mass, he answered, "You will tell the bishop that I have never wanted this for the reasons I have already given you. But since it is his wish and, as you say, his command, I am ready to obey. If I do any good, the merit will be his."

The prospect of the succession to the See of Geneva, although highly honorable, must have seemed to him a great burden and responsibility. For a man like him, it could only mean a lifetime of dedication and service to others without thought of himself and of the many interests of family, friendship, social graces, scholarship, and writing, which were so very much part of the *honnête homme* that had marked his character and tastes since the beginning. The appointment — although not the honorary title of coadjutor — was, in fact, never to be officially taken up, partly through inevitable delays, but also because of his own complete disinterest in the matter.

One of the causes of the delay was another grave illness. The labors and vexations of the Chablais mission had worn him down, aggravating his poor circulation and causing him to suffer from varicose veins, an unfortunate affliction for a man who was always on his feet ministering to the needs of others. In this weak state, he seems to have caught a contagious disease which was going about in Savoy in that winter of

1597. For the second time in his life, he was considered to be a dying man. By January 1598, he seemed to have turned the corner, and he could write to the Nuncio Riccardi: "After the Lord in His goodness visited me with a continuous fever and recently allowed me to have so serious a relapse that for seven days my death was expected, now, through the same divine goodness, I am getting better. But I am left so weak, especially in the legs, that I doubt whether I can make the journey to Rome before Easter, despite my great desire to be there for Holy Week. I shall do my best to manage it."[67]

The visit to Rome was to obtain the Pope's personal approval of the ducal appointment to the coadjutorship. But the illness dragged on, and, in the end, he was cured, we are told, by the supreme remedy of the time — drinking a medicine containing gold. He would not be able to get to Rome until the autumn.

During that long illness, he again suffered something of the spiritual anxiety about his eternal fate as in his student days in Paris and Padua. Another temptation that assailed him was some undisclosed difficulty about the Real Presence in the Eucharist. So terrible was it that he would never confide to anyone its nature nor the answer to it. Such weaknesses under stress of illness make it clear that his habitual and characteristic spiritual serenity was not just a happy natural disposition, but the result of a strong willpower deliberately turned to God and brushing away the temptations which arose within him when illness enfeebled him. He struggled like the rest of us — only much more successfully.

[67] Ibid., 313-314.

By the time he had completely recovered, he was able to begin to reap the fruits of those first hard years in the Chablais. Thonon was by now one-fifth Catholic, and the mission had become a question of organization and development, although in conditions of poverty which broke the missioners' hearts. Father Chérubin, who could never have started the work with any hope of success, was just the man to carry it through with his more forceful and rougher ways. The provost was always in the background to stand by him in trouble and smooth out any difficulties which he made.

De Sales's relinquishing of direct control came between two great public demonstrations of faith which underlined his own constant insistence on the primacy of the spiritual in the work of conversion. These demonstrations were the *Quarant' Ore*, or Forty Hours, of Annemasse and of Thonon.

The *Quarant' Ore* was a recently established popular devotion in Rome and Italy, unknown as yet in France and Savoy. It consisted of the solemn exposition of the Blessed Sacrament for forty hours with constant popular prayers and general rejoicings. It appealed to de Sales as a spectacular answer to the Calvinist denial of the Real Presence of Christ in the consecrated bread and wine — one of the chief points of controversy about which he had for so long to instruct and to preach.

To hold Catholic celebrations in Thonon itself on the large scale called for by this public devotion of the whole people was thought to be too provocative for the time being, so the town of Annemasse, two or three miles east of Geneva itself, was chosen. Annemasse had remained in large part Catholic, so there could be less objection from the Calvinists. The choice, moreover, gave the excuse for a great Catholic procession from Thonon to Annemasse — a distance of eighteen miles.

On the morning of Saturday, September 6, 1597, about five hundred Catholics set off from Thonon, headed by poor Georges Rolland, bidden by his master to carry the cross at the head of the procession. He was terrified, for he expected to be attacked by the Calvinists and sacrificed for the general good. But his master insisted, and the young man's fears at least remind us that a demonstration of this kind still had to be carried out at some real danger to those taking part. Another procession came up from Annecy with the bishop. As these processions wended their way through the sun-drenched countryside, more and more people joined in, so that a great mass of Catholics at length entered the little town for the High Masses and the mystery play. So confident had the Catholics become that de Sales felt able to lead the pilgrims along the road to Geneva in order to set up again a wayside cross which had been destroyed. Under it was affixed a notice explaining that it was not the stone or wood which Catholics worshiped, but only God Himself, who died on the Cross. De Sales never missed an opportunity of preaching in deeds as well as from the pulpit. Some thirty thousand people, including some curious Calvinists, are said to have been present at this Annemasse Forty Hours.

A year separated this first mass spiritual demonstration from the Forty Hours of Thonon, and the contrast between the two occasions is another measure of the missionary progress constantly being made. Annemasse was a public and solemn act of devotion of a still slightly nervous minority. Thonon was virtually the celebration of a work successfully accomplished over four long and weary years.

Church and state at last appeared in all their glory, the Pope sending his legate in the person of Cardinal Alexander de' Medici and Charles-Emmanuel himself coming as sovereign of his Catholic people. Francis de Sales had done the work by purely spiritual means and without their help. It was for others to reap the glory. Even so, the great princes were so delayed that the Forty Hours had to be held twice — the first time for the impatient people; the second for Church and state.

The celebrations, even on the first occasion, September 20, 1598, were on a far greater scale than in Annemasse. From many parts of Savoy, the people poured into Thonon, but the real sign of the times was the number of Protestants who now declared themselves convinced and asked to be baptized and confirmed — two hundred from one parish, we are told, sixty from another, some from the nobility, many from other classes. As the ceremonies were taking place and the people enjoying the theatrical representations and tableaux in the town, priests were all the time hard at work, and even Bishop Granier had to be dragged out late to confirm some converts whose jobs forced them to leave at once.

Excitement was caused by the rumor of a miracle effected by the apostle of the Chablais, as de Sales was freely called. A newborn baby, the child of a Protestant mother, had died without Baptism. De Sales had gone to explain Catholic doctrine to the mother, praying that the infant might recover for the time necessary for Baptism. His prayer was answered, and the whole family became Catholic. Perhaps the chief interest of this miracle lies in the fact that it is the only one recounted in the story of the apostolate of the Chablais, a fact well in tune with the sense that this remarkable apostolate has been recorded and has come down to us in terms of sober historical fact, not of wonders and legends exaggerated in the telling. It was a sufficient miracle in itself.

A fortnight later, the duke and the legate arrived for the second Forty Hours. Charles-Emmanuel, who had done so little to help de Sales, sent a message to the bishop to say that he was coming as a judge to punish the Calvinist leaders who in 1591 had driven the priests out and imposed Protestantism. Only the entreaties of Bishop Granier, supported by de Sales, persuaded him to change his mind. When later the duke presented Francis de Sales to the legate, he found the right words with which to describe him: "My lord," he said, "here is the true apostle of the Chablais, a man of God whom God has sent us. It was he who dared to enter this country alone and in danger of his life. . . . I have come with my sword to further this holy enterprise, but no one can deny that all the glory belongs to this zealous missionary."

That glory was indeed made public when in the great church of Saint Augustine, its walls draped with cloth of gold and silver, the legate, with the duke at his side, received the abjurations of the notabilities of the land. So many were they that secretaries could not keep pace with them, and they had to be content with listing the heads of families only. A list of 2,300 is to be found in the Vatican Archives. No doubt, the changed circumstances and fear of the consequences of refusal were now strong motives in some of these abjurations, but Francis de Sales, who had made it all possible, is not to be blamed for the inevitable consequences of the links between Church and state in those times. Moreover, even these abjurations were to leave a third of the people Protestant. The purely political pressure cannot have been very heavy.

Invoking in their own favor the religious clauses of the Treaty of Noyon, the Protestant leaders now begged the duke to allow them to retain the three Protestant ministers legally permitted to them. Charles-Emmanuel's answer was, one must in honesty confess, subtler than that of de Sales. The latter feared a recurrence of Protestant proselytism and was against the petition. The duke neatly clinched the matter by asking whether the Protestants would allow him to send in return three Catholic priests into Geneva and Berne. Merely to ask this question made it absurd for the Calvinists to press their petition. But afterward, when the duke insisted on expelling Protestant leaders who refused to abjure, de Sales had the courage to step forward and explain that it was not a question of expulsion or abjuration, but only of a readiness at least to study with an impartial mind the Catholic teaching and the reasons for it.

From these political events, one may easily derive a very false picture of the true state of affairs in the Chablais after four years of apostolate. The reality behind the political show-piece of Thonon is described in a letter to the nuncio by de Sales himself, and it explains his own nervousness about the future. "The happy harvest of many thousands of souls which has been gathered in during these last days in Thonon," he wrote, "has given us an unbelievable consolation, but . . ." And he goes on to explain. "Our affairs are in such a state that more than ever we need a protector and promoter like Your

Lordship. From His Highness we have the right to expect and desire no more than the mere maintenance of the very Christian works he has accomplished. There is nothing for us to do but to beg for an active, prompt, and generous cooperation from the Holy Apostolic See. . . . We could wish that His Holiness, in accordance with the views of His Highness, should insist on the restitution of the benefices held by the Knights. . . . In this business, caution is out of place and all delay dangerous. . . .

"It is true that the Holy Faith has been re-established in most parts, but the churches are ruined and we are still without sacred ornaments, chalices, and crosses. Where shall we get them? The parish priests cannot be fifty-ducat men; each needs an assistant. Woe to the man who is all alone, especially in the neighborhood of leopards, bears, and wolves. If necessary, chalices and precious objects that other churches do not need should be sold so as to raise funds to nourish hungry souls."[68]

The truth was that he had had extremely little assistance from first to last from state or Church. Alone at first and then with the help of other priests modeling themselves upon his pioneering zeal, two-thirds of the Chablaisiens returned to the Faith of their forefathers. The work, in fact, ran far ahead of the resources of a poor and disorganized diocese, and ahead, too, of the practical interest and assistance of the Church as a whole and of the political responsibilities of the state.

Nervous as de Sales might be of the future, all this only brings out the more forcibly the quality of his own realistic

[68] Ibid., 356-360.

driving force which alone could have accomplished this unique apostolate. One hardly recalls that all through he was still a young man and a young priest, scarcely emancipated from his long student days and still humbly deferential to parental, legal, and ecclesiastical authorities, a young man who could still so greatly value the charm of a happy turn of phrase in letters to his dearest friend.

The attraction of his personality, the untiring zeal, and the freshness of his missionary endeavors, the saintly dedication of every moment of his life to God's work: all these are rightly insisted on by his biographers. They should not, however, be divorced from a business capacity and a determined will which would have made him a leader of men in any walk of life. There was always hidden strength behind the sympathy which made him already so well loved, so fully appreciated as a man even by his opponents.

Yet this apostolate, outstanding in the long history of the Church's missionary work, was only a prelude to the great responsibilities of a prelate whose personality, genius, and sanctity raise his fame far above the circumstances — however heroic — of a small diocese in a small principality.

Chapter Six

Meeting Saints and
Winning Souls Abroad

1598-1602

Francis de Sales was at length able to set off on his long-
planned visit to the Eternal City in November 1598. By this
time, the nervous Rolland had blossomed under his master's
tutelage into a cleric and secretary whose value would continuously increase. Favre, called to Rome on diplomatic business,
and Louis de Sales (favorite brother, to be distinguished from
the Canon Louis de Sales) were of the party. The main reasons
for the visit were, first, to deputize for Bishop Granier in one of
the periodic so-called *ad limina* visits to the Pope — which
bishops are called upon to make to report on the state of their
dioceses — and, second, to obtain Clement VIII's agreement
to the coadjutorship with succession to the Geneva diocese.
In fact, however, de Sales's three months' stay in Rome was to
be a matchless experience for a future bishop and diplomat. In
Rome he would learn to do as Romans do and make friends
with outstanding ecclesiastical personalities of the day.

As Dom Mackey has written: "He mixes with Roman society, meets influential personalities, visits cardinals and holy

religious, makes friends here and protectors there. Above all, the movement, the style, the ways, the customs of the pontifical court keenly interest him. He watches, he observes, he listens, he learns. . . .

"Francis de Sales was then thirty-three years old. At that happy age, perspicacious minds interest themselves above all in the serious side of real life. Their vision is just, their ability to learn rapid, their memory good. The Roman court and the religious houses numbered among their members, at the time when the envoy of Msgr. Granier came to Rome, many men of singular merit, most of whom have lived in history. It is not difficult to guess the value of meeting them for a person of such unusual and subtle sagacity with the experience behind him of a long and varied ministry and rich already in moral observations and memories. It is impossible not to believe that this contact, however short, with a court always viewed as the best school of diplomacy in the world was in the case of our saint the best apprenticeship in the handling of business."[69]

Among the friends he made were the cardinals Bellarmine (made cardinal in this year, 1599), Baronius,[70] and Borghese.[71] Borghese (the future Paul V, whose condemnation of the terms of the English oath of allegiance under Elizabeth was to perplex English Catholics and cause the execution of some of them) and Bellarmine were to live the rest of their lives as contemporaries of de Sales and to die a year before him in 1621. Baronius, himself twice nearly elected Pope, succeeded

---

[69] *The Works of St. Francis de Sales*, Vol. 12, 6.

[70] Cesare Baronius (1538-1607), ecclesiastical historian.

[71] Camillo Borghese (1552-1621), Pope from 1605.

St. Philip Neri[72] as superior of the Oratory and in the charity and honesty of his mind in controversy shared the de Sales outlook. De Sales would always feel himself much inferior to such great people, but had he possessed even a touch of worldly ambition, such friends at court could have raised him to ecclesiastical heights.

As regards his immediate business, de Sales found Rome very tough, and one is surprised to note how close in those days of difficult travel and continuing laxity in many parts of the Church was the vigilance of Rome over diocesan affairs. A long letter written to Bishop Granier in mid-January 1599, lists the first of the applications to Clement for various helps needed by the diocese: "We proposed to His Holiness ten articles on your behalf. Some of them have been accepted; others he has referred to the nuncio; and the rest he has practically refused." The refusals included the application to transfer the diocesan capital from Annecy to Thonon.

It was not before March that it proved possible to ask the Pope's approval, with the necessary accompanying bulls, of the coadjutorship given by "the good pleasure of His Most Serene Highness the Duke of Savoy." The Pope's reply was a shock. Clement insisted on a formal examination of the candidate in full consistory of cardinals. De Sales feared the anger of the duke, since such examinations were not normal where Savoisien bishops were concerned, but the Pope admitted the Savoy rights and insisted that the examination was only for his own edification. The great Bellarmine was among

---

[72] St. Philip Neri (1515-1595), founder of the community of priests known as the Oratory.

the examiners, and the Pope afterward said that no previous
episcopal candidate had given him so much satisfaction. De
Sales was appointed to the See *in partibus infidelium* ("in the
district of the unbelievers") of Nicopolis. Only the consecration would, of course, actually make him a bishop, and this, as
we shall see, was never to take place until his succession to
Geneva.

To his cousin, Canon Louis, he wrote that more than ever
after these signs of papal favor, he must be "a good boy and a
good servant of the Holy Roman Church — and whatever our
friends may say to you in their letters, remember that friends
exaggerate merits as often as enemies exaggerate faults. In the
end, we are only what we are in the sight of God."[73]

In Rome, then as now, there were, of course, *longueurs*, and
there was surely a touch of humor in de Sales's remark that
Providence had permitted Roman delays so that "visitors may
quietly visit the holy places and again and again recommend
their business to God and His saints." Slow himself, however,
he sincerely appreciated "the so great weight of this court,"
where everything was pondered and pondered again.

Among the friends that de Sales made in Rome was the
Oratorian Juvenal Ancina, who was beatified in 1889. Saints
recognize saints, and this spiritual friendship meant much to
both of them. A letter to Ancina, written by de Sales on his
way home from Rome to Turin, conveniently affords us an account of the journey:

> Although I have not yet finished my return journey, being
> miserably stuck at this court for a whole month, I feel I must

---

[73] *The Works of St. Francis de Sales*, Vol. 12, 6.

send to Your Reverend Paternity an account of the favors I have received through your help. At Loretto, the most reverend Bishop and M. le Primicier [the third dignitary of the chapter] were as kind and welcoming to me as you foresaw, but in "good measure and pressed down."[74] They invited us to say Mass in the Holy House, touch the holy image, and view all the precious objects. [De Sales was, in fact, rather scandalized by the value of the treasury at Loretto and thought it might well be sold to fight the Turks and for good works. No doubt, he had the pressing needs of the Chablais in mind also.] The bishop would have liked to give me a copy of his writings, but he had no other copy than the one he uses himself. He asked me to remind him to send them when a carrier was available.

In Bologna, the most illustrious archbishop embraced me with much love and showered me with favors even though I was only able to meet him just as I was leaving. On the previous morning, he was suffering so much from catarrh that I could not ask for an audience without showing a lack of discretion. Enough to say that I have made myself known and been lovingly treated by these two distinguished prelates whose memory can do nothing but stimulate in me the desire to lead a good life.

Here in Turin, I have made it my business to greet the archbishop in the name of Your Paternity, and he told me how highly he thought of you. I have also paid my respects to His Highness and given him a succinct account of my business in Rome. He said he was well pleased, except for the examination which seemed to him at first sight out of order. In our conversation, His Highness came to talk about Your Paternity and in the polite terms to be expected of a prince of

[74] Cf. Luke 6:38.

his type — still he expressed sorrow in affectionate terms about the refused bishopric. . . .[75]

On his return home, much of the work accomplished in the Chablais seemed to be threatened by political events. Because of the 1598 Treaty of Vervins, the war between Henry IV of France and Philip II of Spain had been brought to an end, and a religious settlement of the Chablais had been made possible. But by the terms of the treaty, Charles-Emmanuel (who had looked to Catholic Spain for support) had been obliged to give to France the provinces of Bresse and Bugey on the left bank of the Rhone in exchange for his right to keep the marquisate of Salluzzo in Piedmont. Furious at this, he readily entered into a conspiracy with the French Duke of Biron, who was promising himself Burgundy as a private possession. By this means, Charles-Emmanuel hoped to retain his lands beyond the Rhone.

Henry IV, the victor of so many battles, was not the man to submit to such arrogance, and by the second half of 1599, the Calvinists in Geneva were licking their lips at the thought that war and the humiliation of Catholic Savoy would restore their power in the Chablais. They expected that the ex-Calvinist author of the Edict of Nantes would give them

[75] Ancina had refused the bishopric of Salluzzo, the place which Charles-Emmanuel was so reluctant to yield to Henry IV of France, according to the terms of the Treaty of Vervins. In the end, the Pope forced him to accept it. When Francis later visited Ancina as Bishop of Salluzzo, he was greeted with the Latin pun "Sal es," i.e., "You are the salt of the earth" (Matt. 5:13). This de Sales capped with "But you are 'sal et lux' " ("salt and light").

complete freedom in places they held to be Protestant.[76] De Sales was warning the nuncio that "the Genevans and the other enemies in the neighborhood were opposing the holy negotiations [with the Knights] through spreading rumors of war and making threats. They also distribute books and writings and secretly spread spies and corrupters of souls."

In the late autumn of 1599, Henry IV, always a brilliant soldier, had moved through Savoy as far as Annecy. The duty of religious leaders, faced with a situation like this, when one's own country is occupied by a hostile potentate, is always delicate; Annecy, spiritual and temporal, received the French king with marked coolness. Bishop Granier and his coadjutor had one responsibility uppermost in their minds — to seek Henry's protection from the Calvinists, many of whom, as high officers and men, served in the French army. One cannot help wondering what these holy men really thought of Henry IV, a rough libertine in his private life and a convert whose tolerant attitude to people of his former Faith seemed to Francis to mean grave danger in those parts of the diocese so long religiously controlled by the Calvinists.

In those days, a favorite time for discussion was High Mass, and it was during High Mass that the king and Granier conferred. Henry solemnly promised that he would tolerate no change in the Chablais — "truly royal words," as Charles-Auguste de Sales commented in his life of his uncle. But kings cannot control their followers, and de Sales would have to

---

[76] Signed by Henry IV on April 13, 1598, the Edict of Nantes ended the French wars of religion and allowed the Huguenots to exercise their religion freely except in certain towns.

report to the nuncio that "both in Thonon and Ternier there has been much suffering under the government of the Huguenot M. de Montglat, through various Genevan insidious acts (in Ternier they behave particularly badly, committing unspeakable acts against sacred things). Nevertheless, despite all this, only four from among the immense number of converts have fallen away, and these low-born types."[77]

Although greatly consoled by such evidence of the toughness of his catechumens, de Sales had reason to be anxious about other consequences of the peace between France and Savoy which was signed in January 1601, after the complete defeat of Charles-Emmanuel. The bailiwick of Gaillard to the south of Geneva was to be returned to Savoy, but the much larger Pays de Gex, west and north of the Calvinist capital, was to be handed over to the over-tolerant Henry IV.

Gaillard, like the Chablais, had been under Calvinist control, but Catholics had resisted with more effect, and it was soon reconverted — one hopes without too much help from the sinister-sounding Corsican Captain de Basterga, who drove out the Protestant ministers. Its people, de Sales wrote to the nuncio, came over "without any force or artifice, but simply by preaching."[78]

Very different was the case of the Pays de Gex, under French rule. The problem of this district of the Annecy diocese, outside Savoy's jurisdiction, was to haunt Francis de Sales all through his life. Within it the Edict of Nantes operated, and this in practice meant that the rich Calvinists could

[77] *The Works of St. Francis de Sales*, Vol. 12, 58.
[78] Ibid., 65.

prevent or greatly hinder all attempts to bring the people back to Catholicism. De Sales could not accept a nominal tolerance which protected the avowedly political authority of Protestant ministers. The latter had even appealed to Elizabeth of England and had sent a delegation to Paris to induce Henry to stand firm against any Catholic intrusion into Gex. De Sales, on his side, was appealing to the Pope and traveling post-haste to Lyons, where his friend Baron de Lux, the French governor, was to be found. But the wily Henry IV was more interested in playing the two sides against each other than in following de Sales's idea of what was right — namely, to allow the old religion full apostolic scope in Gex and to have the old Catholic parishes and property restored to his diocese. Undeterred, de Sales would soon be traveling to Paris to bring the matter to the king personally.

These years, immediately following the Chablais triumph, seem indecisive and even full of frustration, as though the very success of the Chablais had caused the coadjutor in his early thirties to run ahead of himself and not quite know where he stood. The war had threatened what he had accomplished, and lack of material means made the realization of de Sales's vision of a truly Catholic country impossible. He himself was only coadjutor in name because he was too busy to attend to the formalities of getting the bulls from Rome and being consecrated.

Typical of his vision and the difficulty of making that vision real was his plan of founding in Thonon a great center of Catholic training, spiritual and temporal, for the mass of new converts. One rubs one's eyes as one reads of this plan and remembers that even the reforms of the Council of Trent had hardly as yet touched this poor rural diocese lost in the sub-Alps. Most of its monasteries and convents were still in a state of scandalous laxity. The establishment even of a seminary for the training of priests was only a dream. Most of the clergy had to live lonely lives in little peasant communities completely isolated, the one from the other, and where superstition still abounded. Yet, against that background, this young priest in his early thirties was planning the "Holy House of Thonon" or "Hostel for all the Sciences and Arts."

This "Holy House" — the name doubtless reflected de Sales's devotion to the Holy House of Loretto — was to be a kind of super-mission center under the direction of a group of secular priests, living together in a manner that resembled Ancina's Oratory. Apart from offering various spiritual services to the converts, it would organize apprenticeship courses for technical training in various trades to give them employment. Among these de Sales naturally had a special place for the printing press he had already started. The apostolate of the printed word was always a priority for him. Such home industries, he fondly believed, would successfully compete with the too successful Calvinist-inspired trade of Geneva.

It seems strange that a man so naturally cautious, so realistic, should have dreamed this dream. It was, in a way, a young man's fancy, yet much of the pastoral work of the future Bishop of Geneva was to be a slow and patient carrying out through the years of the purposes he was now envisaging as springing from this missionary center on the Lake of Geneva.

Nothing was to go well with this Thonon project. Promises of money were not fulfilled. The secular priests did not relish a community life for which they had no vocation. Some Jesuits who had been sent to help did not like not being able to live in community. An Oratorian seminary, a Jesuit university — none of these further projects could be realized. In the end, under Barnabite priests from Milan, the Holy House survived its founder, but it was never to be the grandiose spiritual communal and technical center which its young enthusiastic planner was conceiving.

One solid reason for failure was the simple one that when de Sales became Bishop of Geneva, he was far too much engaged in episcopal duties, as he conceived these to be, to be able to attend personally to the Holy House. The project was in the hands of the equally optimistic, but far less realistic and capable, Father Chérubin and others. De Sales had as much as he could do getting these out of trouble and difficulties. When we remember that this early-seventeenth-century plan for a diocesan center was far ahead of the times and that the aims behind it remain often still unrealized today, it is hardly surprising that they were then doomed to failure.

But the imaginative vision remains and the fact that Francis de Sales could even entertain such a vision throws light on the paradox that one of the most realistic and dedicated bishops of the Church was to rule his obscure diocese and yet speak to the whole world in a manner that seemed to transcend both time and space. The devout humanism of his early years was to be raised to a quality of behavior, understanding of human nature, zeal, and love that (one may think) has come closest among the saints to the universal charity and understanding of the Incarnate God.

Somehow or other, during these busy and difficult years of overwork and worry, de Sales managed to publish his first full-scale book, *The Defense of the Standard of the True Cross of Our Savior, Jesus Christ.*

Despite the printer's trick of calling the first edition the second in order to suggest that the book had already been in great demand, this book, which in effect is a lengthy refutation of the charge that Catholics pay to the Cross the worship due to God alone, did not make a great stir at the time and is the least known of de Sales's books. Yet it contains clear argument, still valuable (and sometimes necessary) today, to distinguish between the prayer that is due to God alone and the honor and veneration due to exterior signs closely associated with God and honored by Him with miracles and graces.

"Our affections are not fixed on the Cross or other relics; they are fixed on the kingdom of Heaven. In seeking the latter, we make use of everything which can help us to raise our heart toward Him whom they recall. We must climb toward Heaven. That is our aim and our final resting place. Holy things here below are no more than steps useful for reaching it.

"The sign of the Cross has in itself no virtue; but done for God's honor and to symbolize His Cross, it becomes a very holy ceremony of which God often makes use to bring about great consequences."

Just as the war between France and Savoy was ending, Francis de Sales, writing to the bishop on a business matter, went on: "Seeing that the business was not a pressing one, I am forwarding the two letters and remaining here [at Sales] because of the duty I owe to my father. Day by day, he is hastening to the other life and growing so weak in this one that unless God intervenes miraculously, I foresee myself losing in a very few days the consolation which I, as with everyone else at home, have always derived from so good a father. May God, the Lord of our lives, ever be praised in all His decrees."[79]

M. de Boisy lingered on a few weeks, and de Sales was obliged to leave his family to preach the Lenten sermons of 1601 in Annecy. On April 6, a messenger reached him as he was ready to enter the pulpit. His father had died the previous evening. At the end of the sermon, the preacher said, "I have to tell you that François de Boisy, your friend and my father, is dead. As you loved him, please pray for his soul and allow me two or three days' holiday that I may pay him the last rites."

It does not seem that the old man, who died at seventy-nine, had ever become fully reconciled to his eldest son's ecclesiastical career, nor had he any inkling of the fact that the name of de Sales would become immortalized through a vocation so much below the proper aspirations of the head of the Saleses. On the other hand, the love and reverence which Francis had always felt for his family fully included the father who had so little understood him and had done so much to thwart his bent and his call. But his father's death, no doubt, brought him even closer to his beloved and still young mother, to Louis (now returning from his studies in Rome) and his other brothers, and to little Jeanne, his sister, strengthening even further a rare gift for personal relationship which would express itself later in the deep spiritual friendships he would make as he guided men and women along mystical paths.

Much later, his friend Camus, the Bishop of Belley, was to say to him, "You have no reason to be dissatisfied with life. Everything smiles for you; everything succeeds. Your enemies

[79] Ibid., 53-54.

respect you, and even the enemies of religion pay you honor. You delight all who know you." And de Sales answered, "All this amounts to very little and is not to be relied upon. Those who shouted, 'Hosanna to the Son of David!' cried out three days later, 'Crucify Him! Crucify Him!'[80] Besides, nothing really counts except the soul. If I could live as long again as I have already lived with the certainty of all the happiness and prosperity which life can offer, what would it all amount to in the light of eternity?"

Perhaps the successful, admired, and beloved Bishop of Geneva was then thinking back to these days of difficulty, frustration, unsuccessful plans and negotiations in a kind of overbusy half-world, a bishop and yet not a bishop, the maid of all work to whom everyone looked to solve a problem or get them out of a difficulty. Humble as he was, de Sales, one feels, was not a good second. His constructive imagination, bubbling with ideas, his spirit, filled with the love of God and man in selfless service, needed the genius's personal responsibility and freedom. Yet for a young man with such a future, how valuable the discipline of the Chablais and the practical knowledge of men and affairs which these harsher years were affording him.

∞

All this training was to be added to by an experience even more valuable than the visit to Rome. He felt he had to see the King of France in connection with the ecclesiastical position in the Pays de Gex. This meant a journey to Paris — Paris, for him now, not so much the capital of culture as a center of fresh

---

[80] Matt. 21:9; Mark 15:13.

spiritual endeavor after the cruel days of the Wars of Religion. Just as Paris in his student days had raised him above the cultural limitations of provincial Savoy, so now it could bring him into contact with men and women who shared and could define the spiritual forces within him that were reaching out for a deeper and more vital religion suited to ordinary men and women growing out of the old ecclesiasticism and the bitternesses of Reformation controversies and quarrels.

With Antoine Favre and Déage, he set out for Paris at the beginning of 1602, and a January 3 letter makes clear the nature of his immediate business:

> In a few words much to say, for I am in a hurry. Here I am in Meximiaux with the president [Favre], staying in his property, and just about to start together for Dijon. His business concerns a lawsuit of importance to him; mine is to see the Maréchal de Biron and the Baron de Lux. From both I hope to obtain a powerful recommendation to the monarch. From Dijon I shall go to him to deal with our business of Gex, the state of whose affairs is as follows. The Baron de Lux took our bishop last month to the bailiwick of Gex and handed over to him three parishes where the religion would be Catholic — the town of Gex itself, Farges, and Asserens — and gave him possession of their revenues. But we are not satisfied with this. We ask for everything, both so far as the exercise of religion is concerned — and this first — and as far as property. Our purpose is not only our own convenience, but the distress of the Huguenot religion, which will very quickly and certainly fail if it is to depend on the money of the people. With all this in mind, Baron de Lux is sending us to the king and his council, and I am going backed by so much good reason that if only we are supported, victory will be ours. . . .

As for the coadjutorship, I am deeply grateful for your interest. We shall see what happens. Whichever coast the ship makes for, the harbor will suit me.[81]

The anticipated few weeks of business were to turn into months. Not until Easter could an audience with the king be arranged, and the first appointment was deferred. "I was never so frustrated," he complained in a letter, and "I am terribly afraid that I shall be returning without anything better than a mere hope, but my conscience tells me that I have done all I can."[82] Nicolas de Villerio, the secretary of state, made empty promises, but the truth was that the Calvinists were pressing their claims equally hard and with more political backing.

At last, his luck seemed to turn, for he ran into Antoine des Hayes, a gentleman-in-waiting on the monarch, whose private secretary he was. Des Hayes was a former comrade of Paris student days. Des Hayes had no difficulty in securing his friend an invitation to preach before the court on Low Sunday.[83] "If I had not already been converted, Monsieur de Genève [as he was always called in Paris[84]] would have done it," commented Henry IV, and the next day, de Sales and the king were walking together in the gardens of Fontainebleau. They took to each other at once, but on business matters, Henry was too experienced to allow personal relations to

---

[81] *The Works of St. Francis de Sales*, Vol. 12, 98-100.

[82] Ibid., 108.

[83] The first Sunday after Easter, so called in contrast to the high feast of Easter.

[84] "Here I am treated as a bishop. . . . [T]his spurious honor is very useful to me, even though I do not like to be so called before my time; but *manco male!* It is the lesser evil."

affect policy. "I fear," wrote de Sales to Claude-Nicolas de Quoex, "that the negotiations will not prove very useful, despite the high favor in which I find myself with the great people here, and even with the king."[85]

Henry neatly assessed de Sales's qualities: "A rare bird indeed; devout, learned and a gentleman into the bargain. . . . He does not know the art of flattery; his mind is too sincere for that. . . . He is the person most capable of restoring the ecclesiastical order to its first splendor. He is gentle, good, and humble — deeply pious but without useless scruples." The affable and libertine monarch's pen-portrait of de Sales is as neat as any that has been made.

And the king, seeing the nature of the renewed friendship between de Sales and des Hayes, asked to be allowed to be the third party in it.

This success with the king might have gained him something, but unfortunately "M. de Genève" suddenly found himself involved in considerable personal danger. The Duke of Biron, whose treasonable plot to carve himself out a personal kingdom in southeast France had been discovered, was arrested. De Sales's friend Baron de Lux was also arrested, and suspicion fell on de Sales himself as likely to have been involved in the conspiracy against France.

Just as de Sales was about to preach on Corpus Christi, he was warned that he had been reported to the monarch for having come to Paris as the political agent of Charles-Emmanuel to further the machinations of the king's enemies. The charge sounded plausible enough in those times, and few men would

[85] *The Works of St. Francis de Sales*, Vol. 12, 115.

be able to hear such news without some sign of shock or fear. But de Sales remained completely undisturbed and preached his sermon as though nothing had happened. He then went straight to the Louvre to see Henry himself.

Once suspected of being involved in a political conspiracy, it is never easy — nowadays as much as in the past — to clear oneself. But de Sales had made so strong and so good an impression on the king that it was enough for him to be himself. "I cannot help reports reaching me," the king said to him, "but I could never have suspected you." And de Sales could answer with a smile that if he, ignorant as he was of affairs of state, were ever to engage in them, he would certainly not be so foolish as to start in that way — especially after the king's kindness to him.

Instead of sending M. de Genève to prison, Henry IV begged him to stay permanently in France, offered him a pension, and hinted at a fine See soon likely to become vacant. "Sire," answered de Sales in the famous words, "I have married a poor wife, and I cannot desert her for a richer one." His *mot* became the talk of the town.

Far more than such honors, de Sales wanted fair play in Gex. But the political atmosphere was less propitious than ever. Biron was soon to be executed, because he would not confess; de Lux and others were in the end pardoned. De Sales had to report to Clement VIII the royal answer. "More than anyone else," Henry had said to him, "I should personally like to see the entire re-establishment of the Catholic religion, but my wishes do not go hand in hand with my powers." And de Sales, in his letter to the Pope, sighed, "After nine months, I must return having accomplished virtually nothing."

But, looking back, we can see that these months in Paris bore far more important spiritual fruit than any ecclesiastico-political victory could bring. They completed Francis de Sales's training — the training which would make him a bishop of international fame and a saint.

He had arrived in Paris with a quickly growing reputation as an exceptional man, and, possessing as he did the *entrée* to the families on the steps of the throne, he soon had the opportunity of becoming widely known as priest and preacher. It happened that the pious Duchess of Longueville, to whom the Mercoeurs were kin, had been asked by the queen, Marie de' Medici, to find at short notice a substitute preacher for the Queen's Chapel in the Louvre. De Sales, intent only on his business, accepted with some reluctance and only out of politeness.

Inevitably, however, he proved to be a startling success with his fresh, simple manner of speaking quietly and thoughtfully from the heart to the hearts and consciences of congregations more accustomed to hear fine words and subtle arguments. Yet this was no half-educated simpleton. He was a great gentleman and a learned person. We know, from some brief surviving notes, that he preached of "pure love by which God is loved for Himself with a complete dedication of the heart." Perhaps he was recalling those days of temptation in Paris which he overcame by his generous and instinctive élan of pure love. Certainly he was anticipating the spiritual approach which from now on was to win him immortal fame.

Calvinists, as well as Catholics, were moved by this personal religion of love rather than fear and the letter of the law. De Sales was to explain later how this experience drove home the lesson that "he who preaches with love is preaching well enough against heretics, even though he does not utter a word against them." Soon he was everywhere in demand as preacher and personal adviser in matters of the spirit. There were other great spiritual men in Paris at that date, but the people were captivated by this combination of spiritual fresh-ness addressed to the hearts of all, united as it was with gentle-ness, graciousness, affability, geniality, and a *douceur* which was neither soft nor sentimental and that seemed connatural to this young and impressive figure. His personality made its immediate mark.

Even so, his mind, as we have seen, was not on the pastoral opportunities of the capital, but on his unsuccessful business, and it was an accident that so many men and women in Paris, among them Madame Acarie, the famous mystic, had the chance of appreciating the spiritual value of what he himself as yet hardly suspected — namely, the all-importance of his own instinct for getting at the heart of true religion and being its own best exemplar. De Sales was now to enter into the company of those whose lives were being consciously — al-most scientifically — dedicated to the *unum necessarium*, the one necessary and truly meaningful aim in human life — namely, the seeking of God within oneself rather than the seeking of oneself within God, as Fénelon[86] was so neatly to put it.

From Mme. Acarie, one of the most interesting and aston-ishing contemplative women in the annals of the saints, de Sales was to learn to formulate what he already instinctively lived — namely, the science of detachment from creatures

---

[86] François Fénelon (1651-1715), Archbishop of Cambrai.

and attachment to the divine through the love of Him who alone is pure love. In the annals of the saints she is known as Blessed Mary of the Incarnation, but almost alone among the saints and the *beati*, she lives for posterity by her married name, Mme. Acarie.

Born Barbe Avrillot, her lifespan (1566-1618) was nearly parallel to that of Francis de Sales. Married to Pierre Acarie at the age of sixteen, she had by this time borne him six children. Few women can have led a busier and more normal life as wife, mother, and Parisian hostess. Her husband, whom she loved deeply, got himself into trouble through his activities on behalf of the Catholic League, and after the triumph of Henry IV, he had been exiled from Paris and disgraced. He was away from home for about fifteen years, and during that long period, Barbe had to make herself entirely responsible for her children and the running of her house. Into the bargain, she had to deal with the impaired finances of the family and satisfactorily settle them.

There could be no doubt that she was a strong and capable person with all her wits about her — the last kind of woman who would be likely to fall for spiritual illusions. Amazingly, Barbe Acarie succeeded somehow in combining her domestic and business duties with a rare contemplative life in the closest union with God. In a 1606 letter to Mme. Brûlart, de Sales was to refer to "a lady, one of the greatest souls I ever met," almost certainly Mme. Acarie. "She was long subject to the moods of her husband, who insisted that even in her most ardent devotions, she should be décolleté and covered with vanities. She had also to go to Communion secretly, except for Easter. Had she disobeyed, she would have raised many storms in her house. Yet by this road she rose very high as I know, having heard her confession many times."[87]

It all began, oddly enough, because her husband thought she was wasting her time reading light novels. Pierre Acarie gave her what he thought more suitable reading, if read she must. Thus she came across a sentence from St. Augustine: *"Trop est avare à qui Dieu ne suffit"* ("A person must indeed be a miser to need more than God"). This sentence was a revelation to her. Not long after, Barbe was found in church, immobile, hardly breathing, rapt. On emerging from this consoling but frightening experience, she first worried that she had been neglecting her household duties. And was it, she asked herself, the effect of a diseased mind? Was it a visitation of the Devil? Was it truly from God?

Barbe Acarie had to wait some time before she met a priest who was experienced enough in such matters to judge of what it all meant, the more so in that there were many false mystics about in Paris. It was the English Capuchin Benet of Canfield, who, as we have seen, must have met de Sales in his university days. This experienced mystical theologian had no doubt that this immensely active woman, full of common sense, had been chosen by God from the first for this rare intimacy with Him. Barbe Acarie, indeed, was the sort of mystic who, when she felt the movement of the divine presence within her, began desperately to play the spinet to ward off the intensity of the experience, and if she started reciting the Rosary with her

---

[87] *The Works of St. Francis de Sales,* Vol. 13, 228; see also St. Francis de Sales, *Thy Will Be Done* (Manchester, New Hampshire: Sophia Institute Press, 1995), 61.

daughter, she went off into an ecstasy at once, leaving the daughter, not at all surprised, to continue on her own.

There is something almost comical about the setup in the Acarie home which resulted. The place buzzed with distinguished clerics and lay people. Theological experts, spiritual directors, pious men and women seeking edification, ladies organizing the charities and good works that spread from this spiritual center: these were always coming and going, while Barbe, insofar as her ecstasies allowed, carried on her wifely, maternal, and domestic life. Poor Pierre, deprived of normal married life, not (as one might have thought) because of his wife's exalted vocation, but because she could not have more children without grave physical danger, could no longer call his home his own. Barbe, now wisely directed, seems to have reached a state of almost habitual union with God so perfectly controlled and so detached that she could carry on her normal, overfull life. Nor did she write a word about her experiences, nor found any spiritual school of her own.

Barbe was evidently impressed by this new preacher from Savoy, for she recommended a well-known Calvinist lady to come with her and hear him. The personal introduction was, however, made by Pierre de Bérulle, the future cardinal, diplomat, and mystical writer, but then a young cleric and member of a family with close personal relations with the Acaries.

De Sales, somewhat awed by it all, must nevertheless have been happy indeed to find in the Acarie home a whole world of learning and holiness — the highest-level focus, it seemed, of the spiritual renovation which was so marked a feature of the capital. Regular visitors included Dom Beaucousin of the Carthusians (the order that needed no reform); André Duval, of the Sorbonne, and Barbe's future biographer; the Jesuit Coton, who brilliantly handled the spiritual direction of the wayward monarch; the fascinating de Brétigny, who was a kind of Don Quixote in dedicating himself to bringing the Carmelites from Spain to France; François du Tremblay, or Father Joseph, the future Grey Eminence of Richelieu; Ange de Joyeuse; and Benet of Canfield himself. Such men, and many others, were the general staff of Bremond's "mystical invasion" of the seventeenth century.

Soon de Sales was a regular visitor to the Acarie home, crossing Paris on foot "in any weather, sun or rain, and through the mud, of which there was plenty in Paris," as Charles-Auguste reports. Some were already looking on him as a saint, and Barbe herself chose him as her confessor — a puzzling commission, since, as he later recorded, she never seemed to commit the smallest venial sin and was guilty at worst of mere imperfections.

Even so, it was clear that de Sales was very much the disciple, and the mistress of the house, the teacher. After her death, he wrote, "She was a great servant of God. What a mistake I made in not profiting enough from her conversation, for she was very willing to speak to me of all that went on in her soul, but the infinite respect which I had for her prevented me from asking any questions." The fact was that de Sales's humility and slight fear of the spiritual "experts" then and later, while never preventing him from carrying out his spiritual duties toward them, made him move very cautiously with them. Anyway, Acarie was not destined to be his teacher, partner, or disciple in the mystical way. This was reserved for another saint whom he would soon meet and with whom he would link himself with unique bonds of holy friendship. Nevertheless, the importance of Mme. Acarie and her circle in his development should not be underestimated. The experience had all the force of a first encounter with a world of which he knew little, yet which he knew was his world also.

"Simplicity," sums up Bremond. "Forgive me repeating so often that all-important word. None is more in tune with the spiritual movement which we have undertaken to describe. Francis de Sales was to be the great Doctor of the mystical life reduced to its essential and beneficent simplicity; Mme. Acarie was its great inspirer and its perfect model. Both of them, equally definite, equally liberating, equally wise, followed different ways in their teachings, for their gifts and their rank in the Church were different. But what they taught was the same. The *Treatise on the Love of God* formulates, establishes, defends and spreads, with the authority of a theologian and a bishop, something which, long before that work appeared, everyone could have read, and many had read, in the living book which was Mme. Acarie."

Where for the moment Monsieur de Genève, friend of the Pope, friend of the king, and well-versed in diplomatic ways, could do useful work was in giving his aid and authority to the great project to bring to France St. Teresa's reformed Carmel.[88] The plan was not new, and Bremond recounts in one of his most delightful chapters the adventures of the Seigneur de Brétigny who had been engaged in trying to carry out this plan. The times, however, had not been propitious, for France

---

[88] The Carmelite Order had been reformed by Spanish Carmelite nun St. Teresa of Avila (1515-1582).

and Spain had been enemies and the Carmelites were themselves terrified of the French heretics. Barbe Acarie herself had not been very impressed by what she had read of St. Teresa, for she was deeply distrustful of visions and marvels. St. Teresa herself undertook to answer that criticism by personally appearing to Barbe in Barbe's first vision, and she asked that the Carmel should be brought to France. From then on, the project was taken seriously, and de Sales strongly supported it. It fell to de Sales to write to the Pope about it.

"During my stay in Paris," he wrote, "where I was occupied with the business whose outcome I have reported to Your Holiness, I had to accept invitations to preach many times to the people and in the presence of the king himself and the princes. It was on such an occasion that Madame Catherine d'Orléans, Princess of Longueville, a most illustrious lady not only because of the nobility of the princes of her house, but far more because of her love of Christ, asked me to join with other theologians of eminent piety and deep learning in studying together a plan of the duchess to found in Paris a monastery of the Order of Reformed Carmelites. We worked together on this plan for some days, and, having fully examined it, we agreed that it was inspired by God and would contribute to His greater glory and the salvation of many souls." The letter went on to acquaint the Pope with the difficulty that it did not seem possible also to introduce Carmelite friars to govern the convent, but three men, suitable for this purpose, had been chosen instead. "It remains for me to express the wish that the Holy Apostolic See should approve this undertaking and entrust its carrying out to the will of the king, who has given it his consent, a consent which, against expectation, he gave at once. Thus it is that the bearer of this letter throws himself at Your Holiness's feet, praying for the grant of the apostolic bulls necessary for the establishment and carrying through of this work."

By the autumn of 1604, six Spanish Carmelites under Anne of Jesus, accompanied by Bérulle and Brétigny, had entered France, expecting daily to be martyred by the French and heroically waving crucifixes and rosaries from the coach window in order to bring this fate upon them. Very soon they had changed their views to the extent of believing that the fervor of French Catholicism recalled the glories of the primitive Church. From Anne of Jesus and the first Paris Carmel, which de Sales helped prepare, all the reformed Carmels of England and, one supposes, America today are derived.

Barbe Acarie herself, after the death of her husband, entered Carmel as Mary of the Incarnation. She was to die in Pontoise, and the Bishop of Geneva, then in touch with Angélique Arnauld in nearby Maubuisson, was to make more than one pilgrimage to her grave.

De Sales's planned six weeks' visit to Paris had extended to months. Although it was time wasted so far as the business which had taken him there was concerned, one might adopt the word *tertianship* to describe its value to him. Just as the Jesuits, after their Ordination, spend a third year of novitiate, called the tertianship, to prepare them for their ministry, so Francis de Sales obtained in Paris the spiritual and social preparation for his life's great work as bishop, spiritual director, and writer of the love of God.

It seemed to have been providentially planned, for on his way home, he was given the news of the unexpected death of

Msgr. Granier and his own consequent automatic succession to the See of Geneva-Annecy. He had never got around to taking up the bulls appointing him coadjutor bishop of Nicopolis, although he had got as far as writing from Paris to his mother to arrange about the payment, "for after having received all this promotion and all these favors, I cannot in decency hold back from it."[89]

Of his predecessor he wrote in a letter to the Pope: "By his own efforts, together with those of his collaborators, he brought back to the fold of the Lord twenty-five thousand lost sheep. A man of ancient faith, of ancient ways, of ancient piety, and ancient constancy, he is surely worthy of immortality, and his memory calls for universal blessings."

The apostle of the Chablais, who was now giving the chief credit to his predecessor, seemed already to belong to the past. He was getting ready to be married to his "poor wife" of a diocese, of which he was to be the saint with a fame even in his own lifetime that spread far beyond the boundaries of Savoy.

Deeply filial, he chose to be married to it from his home in Thorens. In the large village church, rather than in the pro-cathedral of Annecy, he would be consecrated and on the feast of the Immaculate Conception, December 8, 1602.

During the ceremony, as he himself later explained to Jane Frances de Chantal, he experienced a vivid inner sense of the Holy Trinity directly operating on his person that which the consecrating prelates were externally operating with their symbolic actions and words — and the awareness of this divine action within him remained with him for six weeks.

---

[89] *The Works of St. Francis de Sales*, Vol. 12, 104.

"God," he was to say to St. Chantal, "deprived me of myself to make me His and to give me to my people. In other words, He changed me from what I had been for myself into what I would become for them." The dedication, as will be seen, was complete and until death through increasing suffering.

Six days later, he took possession of his diocese and was solemnly enthroned. All Annecy, magistrates, clergy, regular and secular, and the whole people joined in the enthusiastic welcome to the new Prince-Bishop of Geneva who, if still not well known to people generally in the great world of Europe, was certainly already a hero in his own country.

Chapter Seven

Father to His Flock

1602-1603

At the time when Francis de Sales became its bishop, the diocese of Annecy — that is, the diocese of Geneva without its episcopal city — had about 450 parishes, many of them in very difficult mountain country and almost inaccessible in winter. It was still very much a diocese of the past with unreformed monasteries, three rival chapters in Annecy itself (two of which were in angry and disedifying conflict), and no seminary or other organization for the education of the clergy. We have to remember the ease with which the Chablais, one of the more cultured parts of the diocese, accepted Calvinism, and we have no reason to suppose the state of religion and education in the rest of the diocese would have assured any tougher resistance there.

The cathedral of St. Francis in Annecy was also the Franciscan conventual church, so the bishop was not even undisputed master in it. There was no fixed episcopal residence, although the rented "Maison Lambert" had the advantage of being only a few steps from the cathedral. Annecy itself was a small town of some four thousand people huddled together within the waterways from the lake below the famous castle of the dukes of Savoy-Nemours.

In other words, despite the piety and zeal of his Benedictine (unreformed) predecessor and the established faith and piety of the people generally, the apostle of the Chablais was faced with an immense task of change and reform if the diocese was to correspond with his own high conceptions of a diocese in tune with post-Tridentine times and his own belief in living, personal religion. In fact, there was only one way in which the task could be tackled: to give a shining example of a father-in-God and to do all the work oneself. De Sales, now as in the days of the Chablais, had no thought-out paper plans. He simply filled the yawning gaps and did admirably what others had done indifferently or by rote.

He knew, for example, that the Council of Trent had laid it down that "the first and principal duty of the bishop is to preach." So he preached and preached. "Never allow any excuse to turn you away from this order of Trent," he wrote to a friend about to be raised to the episcopate. "Do not preach in order to become a great preacher, but simply because it is your duty and God wills it. A fatherly sermon of a bishop is worth more than all the artifice of any elaborated sermon of other preachers. A bishop needs little to preach well, for his sermons should deal with necessary and useful subjects, not far-fetched ones. His words should be simple and not affected, his mode fatherly and natural without art or over-care. However short his sermon may be and whatever the subject, it always means much that he preaches."[90] All this was de Sales's method, even

---

[90] *The Works of St. Francis de Sales*, Vol. 12, 193.

before he was a bishop. He preached slowly, deliberately, instructionally, and usually spontaneously, the choice of words, quotations, and images assisting and not impeding the sense. He spoke, as we have seen, from his heart to hearts.

Two years later, at a time when he was so overcome with work that his fatigue showed in his handwriting, de Sales was to sit down one day and, for the benefit of Jane de Chantal's brother, newly consecrated Archbishop of Bourges, write a letter of nine thousand words on the art of preaching. Little known, it remains today a document which every preacher, or indeed public speaker, may profitably study. Here one can only quote a sentence or two: "A preacher should have sufficient learning, but it is not necessary that it should be first-class. St. Francis was not learned, but he was a great and good preacher; and, in our times, the blessed Cardinal Borromeo was only moderately learned, but he did marvels. . . . By preaching, one becomes a preacher: the preacher will always know enough, if he does not try to give the impression that he knows more than he does."

De Sales distinguishes between the relish which comes from good preaching and the relish which a preacher seeks to give and, by doing so, ruins his sermon. He meant "a certain tickling of the ears[91] which results from a worldly elegance, from seeking curiosities, from mannerisms, ways, words which depend on mere artifice." Of stories in sermons, he writes, "They are useful, but they should be served sparingly, like mushrooms, to whet the appetite." Sermons should not be so short as to miss their point, nor so long as to be boring. "I think

[91] Cf. 2 Tim. 4:3.

the structure of a sermon should be clear and obvious, not hidden, as among those who think it very clever to be able to hide the structure. Of what use, I ask, is the structure if the congregation neither sees nor knows it?"

"Let us avoid the *quamquams* and the long periods of pedants, their gestures, their attitudes, their movements. All this is the curse of preaching. Rather, an action that is free, noble, generous, simple, strong, holy, serious, and rather slow . . . The sovereign artifice is not to have any artifice. Our words should be burning words, but because of what we are truly feeling, not because of our cries and our extravagant actions. They must come from the heart, not the mouth. Say what you will, the heart speaks to the heart; the tongue only speaks to the ears."[92]

Speaking one day to a nobleman, soon after becoming a bishop, he said in comment on congratulations being offered him: "If only those of my calling, my lord, love God, they will always be ready to speak of His love, and this does not require much preparation."

What he could do to many at a time from the pulpit, he endeavored so far as he could to complete individually through the confessional. His own advice to his priests was certainly based on his own practice.

"Above all," he said, "take care not to be rough with penitents. . . . Within the kingdom of grace, gentleness alone is in place. Our Lord's anger is like the summer rains that only touch the earth. The Son of God is the stuff of mercy, and He purposely became man to exercise a merciful temperament.

[92] *The Works of St. Francis de Sales*, Vol. 12, 299-325.

His divine soul is united with His humanity in order to bear with patience, and it is attached to His body in order to sympathize gently with His creatures and to become like unto His brethren. I do not understand sympathy which provides a pillow for vice and a cushion to ease sin; no, but I do understand that we must accommodate ourselves to the reach of each person, yielding something, not to the malice, but to the weakness. Souls do not wish to be bullied, but gently brought back: such is the nature of man."

One of the bishop's first acts has always been recorded, and it cannot be omitted here because it bears on a custom which survives today in English-speaking countries. In the second month of his episcopate, in February 1603, de Sales publicly condemned and forbade the strongly entrenched local custom of sending Valentines. It appears that the custom had led to a good deal of impropriety and sin, because not only did the young have their Valentines, but the married also. This was certainly not good for maintaining harmony among married couples, since the duties of escorting one's Valentine to dances and entertainments were taken seriously. The bishop's edict caused a good deal of anger which, doubtless, was not assuaged by Francis's idea of picking out a saint in the calendar as one's spiritual Valentine for the rest of the year.

The need to stop the Valentine custom points to looseness of morals in the town, and it was because of this that the new bishop felt the need to give himself over personally to the formidable task of catechizing the children and setting them on the right path from the start. Here we see for the first time in action one of the most charming characteristics and tastes of Francis de Sales. Just as toward the end of his life, he would love chatting away to the Visitation nuns in the orchard of their convent, so now he was at his best, seated on a little platform of the church of Notre Dame de Liesse, surrounded by the delighted little boys and girls of Annecy, explaining the Faith almost in their own language.

An early biographer has described the scene: "There was an atmosphere of absolute happiness as he told them in simple language of the first principles of the Faith. For every subject, he could think of fruitful images which he would describe as he looked at his little world and the little world looked at him. He became a child with them in order to form in them that inner man, that perfect man according to Jesus Christ."

"When we are born, how are we born?" he would ask the children. "We are born blind like the puppies whose mothers lick their eyes to open them. It is the same with us: our Mother the Church, when we are born, makes us see by Baptism and by the Christian teaching She gives us." Often, we are told, the episcopal catechist and the children around him were to be heard laughing heartily at the stories which the bishop told them or at the strange answers which came from the children's benches.

It was the beginning of the catechetical age, and de Sales in the Chablais had written to Peter Canisius to tell him how valuable he had found his catechism in instructing distinguished converts there. But we imagine that this, perhaps first, of episcopal catechetical instructions to children saw the question-and-answer method used more intelligently and humanly than the practice when the catechism was reduced to a textbook to be learned by heart whether spiritually understood or not.

The first enthusiasm of the new bishop, expressing itself in this personal giving over of himself to immediate needs could not, of course, last. The manifold business of the diocese, the growing personal contacts over which he was never to spare himself, the crying need for the reform of manifold abuses: such matters took more and more of his time. But he knew what he was about, for the setting of the personal example as to how things should be done easily led to the setting up of organizations which could carry on his lead.

Soon a Confraternity of Christian Doctrine was established for lay catechists to assist him and the clergy in a pastoral work which de Sales considered vital. For more than ten years, the bishop would himself continue, whenever he could, to take his turn in the catechetical instruction, and he always enjoyed making an unexpected personal visit to see how the work of others was progressing. Not all good men are gifted with the power of becoming children again with children, but of those who in fact are able to do so with the success of a Francis de Sales one may safely say that they are indeed good men.

After the children, the clergy. The Council of Trent, while insisting on the establishment of seminaries for proper clerical education, did not make such education a condition of Ordination to the priesthood. Hence a poor diocese like this one had continued as of old, relying on university courses, private study in religious houses and presbyteries, and other means of satisfying the not very exigent demands of bishops. Even the new bishop was never to be able to establish a seminary, whether in Thonon or Annecy. The best he could do was to take the greatest care to examine each candidate with the assistance of a panel of priests and satisfy himself that no one was ordained without a sufficient standard of learning, morals, and spiritual qualifications. But once again it would be his own example and his own ordinances which would see to it that the clergy lived according to the calls of their vocation.

He ordered a diocesan synod for the second Sunday after Easter, commanding "all parish priests and others involved to come personally to hear the constitutions and ordinances necessary for their office and the care of their flocks." Meanwhile "we order residence for all who hold benefices which by right and custom require this. Within two months of the publication of these presents, they must return to their duties and personally exercise their charges and offices, or else give reason why they claim exemption. Failing this, they will be proceeded against according to the rigor of the law and canons." Incredibly, given all the work he was doing, the new bishop undertook for a time to give courses of theology in his episcopal residence to priests who could attend.

But in the end the raising of clerical standards had to depend on Francis de Sales's first apostolic weapon: his pen. His own writings could be printed and distributed all over the diocese, and so we get the succession of works whose purpose was to teach and help his clergy in the carrying out of their offices and pastoral duties: the *Synodal Constitutions of the Diocese;* the *Method for Teaching the Catechism;* the *Exhortation to Ecclesiastics for Application to Study;* and the *Instructions to Confessors.*

Among the synodal injunctions, one may mention the following. All priests were commanded to live in their residences, to wear decent, black clothes with the soutane and square bonnet, and to be tonsured and bearded. They were forbidden public games, hunting, and fairs. They were not to use the pulpit for secular announcements for "in the pulpit, one must only speak of what furthers the glory of God and the salvation of souls."

Most striking among his *Exhortations to Ecclesiastics* is his insistence on true learning in a priest:

> I tell you — and with truth — that there is no great difference between ignorance and malice, seeing that ignorance is not only a personal lack, but one which causes the priestly state to be despised. That is why I implore you to spend time in serious study. Knowledge for a priest is the Eighth Sacrament of the Church's Hierarchy. The latter's greatest misfortune has been that the Ark has passed into other hands than those of the Levites.[93] That was why we were taken off our guard by our miserable Geneva. Seeing our laziness and that we were not on our guard — that it was enough for us to recite our breviary and not trouble ourselves to become wiser — they deceived our fathers and predecessors in their simplicity and persuaded them that up until then, no one had understood Holy Writ. While we slept, the enemy sowed tares in the garden of the Church[94] and the falsity which he slipped in divided us and set the country on fire. That fire would have consumed us and many others had it not been for the goodness of God, who mercifully raised those powerful minds, I mean the fathers of the Jesuit Order who countered the heretics. . . .
>
> My dear brothers, since Divine Providence, disregarding my unworthiness, has made me your bishop, I beseech you to

---

[93] This is a reference to the holy Ark of the Covenant, which contained the tablets of the Mosaic Law and which was carried by the Levites (Deut. 10:8). — ED.

[94] Cf. Matt. 13:25.

study with all your hearts so that, being wise and of sound heart, you may be beyond reproach and ready to answer all who question you about the Faith."

As one considers this immediate effort to renovate a country diocese off the beaten track and not so many years after the disruption of the Reformation, one is astonished to find that the actions and the words of Francis de Sales seem only to date in the details of application. What he did and what he had to say always has a contemporary quality, and one may still imagine a bishop following with profit the methods and exhortations of this astonishing prelate 350 years ago. But there was another aspect of de Sales's work as bishop which, happily, is not needed today, although it is interesting to know about it, since it helps us to understand the conditions of Catholic life in which he had to labor. It was the reform of the monasteries and religious houses of the diocese. He himself has left us the best account of the situation in a letter he wrote to the new nuncio, Paul Tolosa, at the end of 1603:

> It is certain that the relaxation of all the monasteries of Savoy, with the sole exception of the Carthusians, is so deep-rooted that any ordinary remedy would be useless. To succeed, we need a reformer of great authority and prudence with ample powers, of which he would have to make use when necessary. I say not only ample, but absolute and without appeal, for the monks are very experienced and clever in chicanery. . . .
>
> I think it would be right in the case of certain monasteries to introduce religious of a different congregation, such as the Feuillants [reformed Cistercians] or the Carthusians, while, in others, the monks would be replaced by secular priests or

canons. Here is my reason. Since some of the monasteries are subject to unreformed superiors, the reform, even if accepted by the community, would not last.

Take the example of the Priory of Talloires, a very illustrious foundation, and near Geneva, the Priory of Contamine and the Abbey of Entremont. The first depends on the Abbot of Savigny in France, the second on the Abbot of Cluny, and the third on the Abbot of Saint-Ruph of Valence. How, then, could these superiors and their monasteries maintain discipline and reform in these dependencies, since they do not observe such reforms themselves and do not even know what such reform is?

That is why my view is that one of two measures will be necessary to avoid scandal: either to place in the monasteries other reformed monks or turn them into secular colleges. A third way would be to put them under a reformed congregation of the order to which they belong — a fourth, to make them subject to the bishops, as used to be the case with many excellent monasteries before the present exceptions came into force.

As for others, such as the monasteries of Sixt, Peillonnex, the Sepulcher in this town, and the like, these will have to be secularized, since the monks are Canons Regular of Saint Augustine, but belonging to a congregation which has no general, no provincial, no chapter, no visitor, no express form of vow, no rule, no constitutions. It is true that Sixt and Peillonnex are visited by the bishop. I have done so myself, but I was unable to make them observe the rule, for they have not got a rule. All I could do was to make them observe the ordinary constitutions, as though they were secular canons, pending the regularization of their situation.[95]

[95] *The Works of St. Francis de Sales*, Vol. 12, 239-243.

Thus de Sales did not possess the requisite power to succeed on his own in carrying out the vow he had made years earlier in connection with the Chablais monasteries: "Never will I cease to press for, to cry for, to obtain, through the bowels of Christ, the measures necessary for the reformation and change of the abbeys of Aulps and Abondance and others which are seminaries of scandal in this land."[96] But his own efforts, where he had the power, and his determination, where he needed higher authority, were to effect a great change in his own lifetime. The long-standing system of commendatory superiors — ecclesiastics or laymen who were given the nominal appointment and revenues, while a deputy of no consequence held the actual office — had caused these increasing scandals. On his own, he restored some sort of canonical order in Sixt and Peillonnex, insisting at least on enclosure and stability for the religious — a first change which was to bear good fruit even in his lifetime. In the case of the ancient and most celebrated of the abbeys of Savoy, Abondance in the Chablais, the six surviving canons of St. Augustine were replaced, with the authority of the Pope, by a community of Feuillants.

But his greatest worry and consolation in this work of monastic reform would be at the Talloires abbey, magnificently situated on the east bank of the Lake of Annecy under the Massif des Aravis, whose northern slopes enclosed his own native Thorens. Bishop Granier had been a prior of Talloires, and in the community were his own friends. In the monastery, the rule of St. Benedict had been relaxed, although some of the community observed it. With the consent of the commendatory

[96] Ibid., Vol. 11, 266.

abbot, the bishop ordered the return to the ancient rule and the election of a claustral prior, Claude-Nicolas de Quoex, whom de Sales had ordained and with whom he had long been closely bound. The community split in two and drove out the new prior. Frightened at their own boldness, the rebels asked the bishop's pardon, but, in the end, the authority of the Holy See was needed to effect the reformation.

One day, the bishop, exhausted by his labors, was to plan the luxury of retiring to Talloires, but in vain.

But perhaps the strangest relic of the old order which was to vex the bishop, so far ahead of his own times, was the curious quarrel between the chapter of Saint-Pierre, exiled from Geneva since 1535, and the chapter of Notre Dame de Liesse. The former was, of course, the diocesan chapter; the latter a chapter created in the fourteenth century by Benedict XIII. Historic and well endowed, this latter chapter, which also had parish rights in Annecy, looked down on the recent exiles from Geneva, even if they were the diocesan chapter. In particular, the canons of Notre Dame de Liesse had claimed and, in effect obtained, the right to be the only attendants on the bishop during the great outdoor feast of the year, the Corpus Christi procession of the Blessed Sacrament.

In his first year as bishop, the "gentle" Francis de Sales, who always turns out to be anything but weak when any matter of principle is involved, proclaimed from the pulpit on Trinity Sunday that he would carry the Blessed Sacrament in the procession, accompanied by the canons of the cathedral. The Notre Dame de Liesse canons replied by appealing to the magistrates and demanded back their older rights to carry the Blessed Sacrament themselves.

Furious — with that fury which, we are told, was sometimes shown by the little boy of Thorens — de Sales replied, "Neither I nor my canons should be taken for strangers, and I would never have expected such words from you. My predecessors in this pastoral charge may have been feeble, old, and infirm, but I, by the grace of God, am healthy and strong. Why, then, should I not carry the body of my Lord and Master as much as another?" And he made it clear that he intended to do so. The Notre Dame de Liesse chapter at once appealed to the Duke of Nemours, suzerain of Annecy under the Duke of Savoy, and so did the bishop. But meanwhile he insisted that his orders be obeyed. He even threatened with excommunication the dean of the chapter when, instead of obeying de Sales's orders that members of his chapter should assist in a lesser position at the procession, he nominated for this service ordinary priests. In the end, at the first procession, the bishop carried the Blessed Sacrament accompanied only by his own diocesan chapter.

Meanwhile the young Nemours sought the easiest way out by suggesting that the two chapters should in future processions walk in parallel columns, as was the custom with two chapters in Paris. But de Sales had no intention of compromising. Not only that, but in order to prevent the Notre Dame canons from absenting themselves out of pique once again, he ordered that in future all the clergy should be present for the procession under excommunication, and he set out the order of precedence, the Notre Dame canons taking second place, while the diocesan canons directly assisted the bishop. In 1604, the Notre Dame canons just did not turn up, but by 1605 peace was re-established on de Sales's terms.

This long-standing quarrel had indeed been a scandal, for de Sales himself, happy at the outcome, noted that his success would "increase piety among the laity." This odd story conveniently reminds us that behind the ways of harmony and peace which we associate with Francis de Sales, there was always a hard core of ruthless principle which was a necessary ingredient if charity was not to soften into sentimentality.

One asks oneself whether this new broom with a handle of iron, however soft the bristles, caused murmurs and encountered much opposition among his clergy and people. We know that his attack against the custom of Valentines was not popular, and one gets, from time to time in his episcopate, evidence of annoyance and dissatisfaction from different sections of the people. As we shall see, the political authorities and the Duke of Savoy himself were not best pleased by the independence of his attitude. But he certainly caused no opposition of a character sufficiently marked as to force his biographers to refer to it, nor do his own letters hint at any difficulties except from the unreformed religious houses.

This is a remarkable fact, for even sanctity and the highest principles do not normally prevent human nature from objecting to the man who shakes people out of their set ways. The attraction of his personality must have been immense to carry him through day after day, filled, from morning until night, with reformist pastoral work. How he ever got through these early days of preaching, catechizing, hearing confessions, and putting himself at the disposal of all who came to seek his advice or had business with him, is a mystery. For, apart from work, he left himself plenty of time for prayer and especially attendance in the cathedral at the Divine Office, which was one of his favorite devotions. Into the bargain we have the irrefutable evidence of his writings and especially his letters, laboriously and neatly written in longhand, not only to important clerical and political figures, but to the ordinary men and women who sought his personal spiritual guidance. This latter work was, of course, to grow enormously with the spread of his fame as the greatest director of souls of his time.

Even so, in these early days, he found time to write immensely long letters of personal advice and direction to a simple novice nun in a Paris convent, Jeanne de Soulfour, just because she was the daughter of a friend. The three letters written to her which we possess run to between five and six thousand words. Long quotations are impossible, but how admirable and finely expressed is the following spiritual advice from this activist bishop of only thirty-five years of age:

> Simplify your judgment; do not make so many reflections and replies, but go forward simply and with confidence. For you there is only God and you in this world; what remains should not touch you save only insofar as it is God's will and in the way it is God's will. I implore you, do not look around you so much; keep your looking focused on God and yourself. Never will you see God save as goodness, nor yourself save as misery; and you will see His goodness a blessing for your misery and your misery the object of His goodness and mercy. Dwell on nothing else but this — I mean, of course, fixed, concentrated, conscious dwelling; the rest consider only in passing.
>
> Further, do not look closely at the deeds of others, nor what they are going to do, but look at them with a simple, good, kindly, and loving eye. Do not demand of them more perfection than you have, and do not be astonished at the

variety of imperfections, for imperfection is no less imperfection because it is extravagant and strange. . . .

Let us practice the little virtues suited to our littleness. For a small dealer, a small basket. Such virtues are practiced running downward rather than climbing, but they may be best for our legs. Patience, helping our neighbors, service, humility, gentle courage, affability, tolerance of our own imperfections: such are the little virtues. I do not mean that we should not climb by prayer, but step by step.[97]

One learns with disappointment that this seemingly overanxious novice who had the privilege of such an adviser did not persevere with her vocation.

To a bishop-elect, de Sales writes another very long letter in which he offers a long list of spiritual reading, with Grenada[98] "*tout entier*" ("entirely"), to be used as a second breviary. Among the recommendations, the spiritual letters of "Jan Avila"[99] are to be found, but there is no mention of Teresa of Avila, nor of his beloved Scupoli.

His advice as to how to read a spiritual book is interesting because it once again reminds us that Francis de Sales, despite his endless activity, was a man by temperament slow and deliberate in action, in the pulpit and, as here shown, in reading:

To read with profit, avoid reading greedily. One must weigh and appraise, and, chapter by chapter, ruminate and apply

---

[97] Ibid., Vol. 12, 163-170, 180-186, 202-206.

[98] Probably Luis of Granada (1504-1588), Spanish author of the *Book on Prayer and Meditation* and the *Guide for Sinners*, two books of spiritual guidance. — ED.

[99] Probably St. John of Avila (1500-1569), Spanish mystic. — ED.

with much thought and many prayers to God. You should read the book with reverence and devotion, as a book which contains the most useful inspirations that the soul can receive from on high. Thus you will be remolding the powers of your soul, cleansing them as you grow to detest their evil inclinations and directing them to their true end by firm and strong resolutions.[100]

Sometimes in the way in which de Sales teases and worries at his subject matter, there is an unexpected affinity with the letters of the Baron von Hügel.[101] He liked simplicity, but was never superficial.

On November 13, 1603, he sent the long Latin report to the Pope about the whole history of the Chablais from which we have already quoted. Its ending conveniently sums up the position as it was when he succeeded to the See:

To sum up the history of this great work in a few words: twelve years ago, in sixty-four parishes near Geneva and almost under its walls, heresy was in occupation. It had invaded everything. Catholicism held not even an inch of territory. Today the Catholic Church in those places spreads Her branches everywhere and with such vigor that heresy can find no room. Before, it was hard to find a hundred Catholics within all those parishes taken together; today it would be just as hard to find a hundred heretics.

Everywhere the mysteries of the Catholic Faith are celebrated and frequented. Every parish has its parish priest. Finally, the three bailiwicks which, by treaty, were returned

---

[100] *The Works of St. Francis de Sales,* Vol. 12, 189-190.

[101] Baron Friedrich von Hügel (1852-1925), Catholic theologian and philosopher.

to the duke, are completely restored to the Church and, what matters most, their people, after faith and religion had been recovered, have persevered unshaken by the persecutions of the recent wars or the threats of the heretics. And this, most certainly, has been the one and only good thing which the wars have brought to the diocese.[102]

The new bishop was indeed happy, after three years of absence, to return in September 1603 to his beloved Thonon, where he had a special appointment in the church and pilgrimage center of Our Lady of Compassion of Thonon.

Shortly before, de Sales had had to go to the Pays de Gex, where the state of religious affairs, despite all the negotiations in Paris, was in unhappy contrast with those of the Chablais. While there with the Governor of Burgundy, the Duke of Bellegarde, his success in bringing back to the fold a number of distinguished Calvinists tempted some enemies to try to poison him. Happily, he was warned in time to take an antidote, and he suffered no more than bad sickness. In gratitude for his escape, he vowed to render thanks to Our Lady of Thonon.

So full of spirits was he at the prospect of seeing Thonon again that when he was reminded of the Ember-Day ordinations (to ordinations he always gave priority), he said that he would not return to Annecy for them — let the ordinands come to Thonon for the ceremony.

On foot, then, with Rolland, now the treasurer of the diocese, and his personal servant, François Favre, he trod the familiar miles from Annecy to Thonon, to be received in the

---

[102] *The Works of St. Francis de Sales*, Vol. 12, 237-238.

town, "in two respects his daughter," as Charles-Auguste puts it, by the whole happy people. In Thonon, he could not resist further discussion with Calvinists, and he was especially happy to be able to convince one of the obdurate on the famous day in 1598 when the duke demanded conversion or exile. The man in question admitted that he was a good deal better at wielding the sword than theology.

Consecrating the cemetery that had been Protestant, de Sales, accompanied by some curious Calvinists, was drenched by a sudden autumn storm. "You see how the Lord punishes the Papists," the Calvinists pointed out. "Not at all," replied the bishop. "It is the fury of the Devil whom we are chasing away from his unjust hold by the virtue of the Holy Spirit."

Reminding ourselves that the bishop, whether in Annecy or Thonon or even Gex, was never far from Thorens, just as the thought of his family can never have been far from his mind — he had recently ordained Jean-François and accompanied his especially loved brother Louis on his honeymoon, which was also a pilgrimage — we may fitly end this chapter with a letter he wrote at this date to his mother in which he underlines the better times:

> I write these lines, my most dear and good mother, as I get into the saddle to ride to Chambéry. This note is not sealed, and I am not worried by that. By God's grace, we are no longer living in those troubled times when even a letter of friendship or one merely carrying but a word of consolation had to be sealed.
>
> O my God, O my good mother, I must, it is true, confess that the memory of those days still has a touch of holy sweetness about it in my mind.

Remain joyful in our Lord, my good mother, and remember that your poor old son is, by God's mercy, well and expecting to see you as soon as he can and for as long as he possibly can, for I am all yours — as indeed I ought to be. You know I am

Your son,
Francis, Bishop[103]

---

[103] Ibid., 244-245.

Chapter Eight

Growing in Holiness
Through Friendship

1604

Until the year 1604, Francis de Sales, the Chablais apostolate apart, was just another bishop, even though one about whom many people were talking because of his growing reputation as an admirable, intelligent, and saintly prelate of quite exceptional personal charm. But those who knew him best through ties of friendship or because they had taken his spiritual advice realized that in a quite special way, this man seemed instinctively to go to the heart of the matter where real religion, the personal link between man and God, was concerned.

He ardently loved a loving God, and in this relationship between God, who is all love — i.e., infinitely wishing well to man — with man, called upon to do no more than return that love in ever greater knowledge and service of God, he saw — or rather he lived — the key to the purpose and meaning of human life. This new hammer of the heretics of his native land really loved the man within the heresy because God also loved him; this bishop, uncompromising in the cleansing of the part of the Church entrusted to him, was all love and gentle reason in his personal government; this preacher and teacher, who never dreamed of minimizing doctrine and standards, was also the compassionate, even indulgent (it seemed to some) priest who coaxed and gently drew men, women, and children along God's loving, seemingly easy, way.

Yet this spiritual flair, this taste, for the personal religion of love, of simplicity, of urbanity was as yet more potentiality than a thought-out, driving actuality, whether in himself or for others. To turn this taste and practice of his into a consciously realized, objective thing, the key of true spiritual progress itself, not only for himself or for special people, but for all men and women of any genuine spiritual good will, he needed help. He needed, as it were, to be able to see himself in another, to objectify in that way his own inner feelings.

Nor is it surprising that this was so. From the start, friendship and love had meant so much to him. His own family, Antoine Favre, Bishop Granier, Barbe Acarie and her circle, des Hayes: they all in some way mirrored back to him his own spiritual instinct which otherwise might be no more than the personal complement to his immensely activist nature. One can reason to this conclusion, not only by observation of his character with its natural diffidence, compensated for by his love of action and apostolic zeal, but also through the obviously providential nature of the immensely fruitful contact with Jane Frances Frémyot de Chantal — the contact that grew into a spiritual intimacy that places him apart and makes him unique in the ranks of the saints. She would teach him truly to know himself, as he would teach her how best to apply her spiritual vocation and genius. Between them, they would map out the way of spiritual perfection in its application to men and women of every kind according to the nature of their spiritual call.

As bishop, a matter of Church business made it desirable for him to go to Dijon, the chief town of Burgundy, on which the affairs of Gex depended. He was also unexpectedly invited to preach the Lenten sermons of 1604 in that city. Yet he was strongly advised not to make the journey because of immediately pressing diocesan affairs at home. He even wrote to the Pope, almost excusing himself for undertaking it. "I can never believe that Your Holiness would disapprove of this short absence which the need of the diocese imposes on me. I leave it well provided in spiritual matters, and I hope to return in two months."[104]

Much later, he confessed to Jane de Chantal, "God, whose will I looked to directly, so drew my soul toward that blessed journey that nothing could have stopped me."[105] One morning, indeed, while he was making his thanksgiving after Mass, he became somehow vividly and intimately aware of the fact that he would found a new religious order, and he saw before him the phantasm of a woman, dressed as a widow, with two other young women similarly dressed. Two years earlier, the widowed Jane de Chantal, praying for guidance in her own spiritual life, saw in the distance the figure of an unknown bishop and heard a voice saying, "Here is the guide, beloved of God and men, in whose hands you must put your conscience." These strange phenomena, of which there can be no doubt, may have been miraculous, or they may have been some

---

[104] *The Works of St. Francis de Sales*, Vol. 12, 259.
[105] Ibid., Vol. 13, 142.

mysterious psychological insight reflecting the need on both sides for help along the way of perfection and God's call.

The family with which Francis de Sales had business in Dijon was the Frémyots, old, rich, and distinguished in their service to king and country. Bénigne Frémyot had been presented by Henry IV with the archbishopric of Bourges and the abbey of Saint-Etienne in Dijon for his fidelity to Henry during the wars of religion. His son, André, had been captured during the fighting and threatened with death. Bénigne had declared, "Better for my son to die innocent than for his father to live ignobly." Twice married himself, Bénigne had passed on the archbishopric of Bourges to André, while retaining Saint-Etienne as his own private residence.

Preaching one day in the Sainte-Chapelle of Dijon, Francis de Sales noticed near his pulpit a lady with light brown hair and dressed as a widow, listening apparently with the closest attention to his words. Her figure seemed to him to recall the vision he had had before leaving Annecy.

After the service, he asked André Frémyot, the Archbishop-designate of Bourges, who she was.

"But it is my sister, Jane Frances," he answered. And de Sales said, "How very glad I am to know that she is your sister," and he proceeded to find out all he could about her.

Who was she?

Jane Frances Frémyot, the daughter, as we have seen, of Bénigne Frémyot (generally called President Frémyot because of parliamentary office), was born on January 23, 1572, and so was four and a half years younger than Francis de Sales. On the side of both father and mother, she was of noble blood. We know little of her childhood except, by inference, that she was extremely educated, developing a natural gift for writing beautiful French, a generation ahead of de Sales in style. She was to be grandmother of Mme. de Sévigné.[106]

Bremond sees in her childhood an upbringing which prevented her from ever being a "*dévote*" in manners and ways of speaking. "A beautiful, cheerful girl, liking to play, restless, soon to be much sought after in marriage." She called herself "*fille à toute folie*" and described how the starlings she used to feed with sugar followed her about wherever she went. "Saint Chantal," observes Bremond, "before leading her novices in Annecy wherever she wanted, had once charmed little birds in some garden of Burgundy."

Having lived for five years in her teens with a sister in Poitou, Calvinist country, she reacted like Francis to the destruction of churches and religious houses, often weeping at the desolation. The story is told of how on one occasion, as a child, she was offered some sweets by a Calvinist. She threw them into the fire and pointed out to the benefactor that that was how heretics would burn in Hell. One can imagine Francis doing the same, although at a rather earlier age. It was part of the religious climate of the times.

At the age of twenty-one, she married Christophe de Rabutin de Chantal, son of a veteran of the League who had lost a good deal of the family fortune in the wars. The marriage to a Frémyot was, no doubt, calculated to improve the Rabutin fortunes. Many years later, Jane confided to her friend and secretary, Mother Marie-Madeleine de Chaugy, most of what we

---

[106] Marie de Rabutin-Chantal de Sévigné (1626-1696), French writer.

know about her early years, and the latter, on what precise grounds we know not, gave this portrait of Jane at the time of her wedding: "Very tall, of full and noble figure, of gracious, charming, natural, and strong beauty, lively and gay in manner, with a clear, quick, and decisive mind and solid judgment." Her hair was fair, gradually turning chestnut brown — another resemblance to the young Francis.

Her husband was an observant Catholic, but one who had been strongly addicted to dueling in his youth, loving soldiering and action of every kind. He was a softened reflection of his father, who had been called "Guy the Terrible" in his family pride, his bellicosity, and his debts.

Although the marriage was a pre-arranged family affair, there is not the smallest doubt that it turned out to be a love match between two complementary characters. Christophe appreciated better than the young Jane herself her outstanding qualities, and to her he entrusted the task of managing the impaired family business affairs of the great castle of Bourbilly, and its lands, near Sémur-en-Auxois, some forty miles northwest of Dijon. To her daughter, Jane would one day write, "Take pains to concentrate on the running of your house. Had I not had the courage to do so after my marriage, we should not have had enough to live on."

Heavy responsibilities were thus thrown onto the young wife, responsibilities which she at first feared, but which she admirably carried through, not in any niggardly spirit, but with generosity and humor, if we are to believe the story of how she winked an eye during the year of famine when some of the poor, having been given help by her, walked around the castle and came again. She had been thinking how little she would have liked it had God refused to answer her prayers the second and third time of asking. Another delightful habit of hers was to rescue prisoners in the castle cell, give them a bed, and send them back to the cell before her husband returned. This combination of efficiency with charity and a sense of humor about it all parallels both Francis's strength and gentleness.

This happy Christian marriage was to last eight years, during which six children were born, of whom four survived: Celse-Bénigne, to be the third Baron de Chantal; Marie-Aimée, who was to marry Francis's brother Bernard de Sales; Françoise; and Charlotte. The marriage ended in tragedy. Three weeks after Jane's last child was born, Christophe went out shooting with a friend. Mistaking him, as he was taking cover behind some brushwood, for a deer, the friend shot at him and broke his thigh. He was carried home dying, messengers being sent at once to four neighboring churches to make sure of a priest before he died. Jane, after hearing the terrible news, insisted on leaving her bed and going to him.

By a strange inversion in the face of disaster, it was Jane, future saint, who was unresigned to the will of God; the young husband was resigned to die with the thought uppermost in his mind that no one must blame his friend who had shot him. For nine days he lingered, Jane never succeeding in becoming resigned and, after his death, she endangered her own life with the weight of her sorrow. The depths of her feelings were such that she could not bring herself to forgive the unwitting cause of tragedy. It is frightening to think of a reaction so intense that even five years later, Francis de Sales was writing to her about the young man in the following terms: "If he comes to see you, I want you to greet him with a heart gentle, gracious, and sympathizing. Of course I know that your heart within you will rise up, that your very blood will boil — but that does not matter. . . . Such emotions are God's way of reminding us how we are made of flesh, bone, and feeling. I have said enough. Again I say I do not want you to seek to meet that poor man — only that you should be kind to those who want you to see him again."[107]

It was Jane herself who was later to confess that when her husband was away from home, her mind turned eagerly to God with an *arrière-pensée*, growing stronger as she prayed that her husband might soon return; and when he was home again, her devotions considerably weakened. Even so, she had not failed to keep him up to his religious duties, for it had been her habit as a wife to rouse him out of bed in time for Mass. When he grunted and turned over to fall asleep again, she would take her lighted candle and wave it near his eyes so that in despair he had to get out of bed. The little scene is as human as any in the long annals of the saints and was recounted by the saint herself to her Visitation community. "Is it not delightful," writes Bremond, "to hear a great saint telling such a story to young religious?"

So far as ordinary life was concerned, she was saved from despair by her love for her little children and her duties to them. But on the spiritual plane, something more complicated was happening. Alas, we know little about it, because she could never bring herself to open her heart to anyone on the subject. Her old consoling, simple religious life had faded away to be replaced by a period of undescribed violent temptations

---

[107] *The Works of St. Francis de Sales*, Vol. 13, 67-68.

which nevertheless went with a new-found religious austerity of vowing perpetual widowhood, wearing only wool, turning her fine dresses into ornaments for the church, fasting, hair shirts, and vague dreams of total self-dedication in some unknown part of the world. It was a "dark night" of which she herself had no understanding whatever. "The happy clear light of faith which no sophism had yet troubled, the sweet ease of praying, the simple and straight appreciation of the line of duty, peace of conscience — of all these which were once her joy and her strength the soul is implacably stripped," so Bremond speculates about this period.

It was during this time of desolation that the widow had her vision of the "unknown bishop," now that, even more strangely, she heard a voice saying, "You must go beyond and further; never will you enter into the sacred repose of the sons of God save through the gate of Sainte-Claude." What could all this mean?

She returned for a time to Dijon, and there she found herself with some pious ladies on a pilgrimage. With them was a priest, whose name has never been disclosed. He was the religious director of these women, and when Jane spoke of her perplexities to these ladies, she was advised to put herself in his hands. Unwillingly she did so. Mme. de Chaugy tells us: "She let herself be bound by this shepherd who obliged her to four vows: the first, obedience; the second, never to change; the third, to remain secret about their relations; and fourth, to speak to him alone about her soul."

Under this strange priest, Jane was simply guided to more and more of her own recipe of mechanical prayer and penance to ward off the temptations of the Devil. Deep within her, she knew it was all wrong and that her director had no understanding of her needs, but she obeyed.

Hardly worse was the misfortune which recalled her to live in 1601 with her old father-in-law, Guy, now seventy-five years old. Always, it seems, slightly eccentric, the old man threatened to remarry and disinherit her and the children unless she came to live with him at his home of Monthélon, near Autun. There, the daughter-in-law and her children were to suffer from that most mortifying of trials, subjection to a servant, whose relations with the master of the house were questionable, and determined for obvious reasons to make bad blood between father-in-law and daughter-in-law. Although expected to keep house, Jane in practice could do nothing against the will of the old man's companion.

For seven and a half years, Jane de Chantal, once mistress of Bourbilly, with its gaiety, its social life, its successfully mastered problems of money and land, and, above all, the tender love at its heart, had to endure this horror, relieved only by the pathos of the fact that the old man had really called Jane to his house in order to help him escape from the pit which he had dug for himself. Bremond evokes the picture of how the old soldier of Henry IV would try to rise from his chair and hold out a shaking hand to his daughter-in-law. "Under the white moustache, his lips would move in a tender and ashamed smile. From the room next door came the noise of children playing and the spelling of alphabets. Somewhere in the distance, the phantom with her ring of keys was prowling — unseen, unheard."

It was while Jane de Chantal was living at Monthélon and making a Lenten visit to her father in his Dijon Abbey of St.

Stephen that she first saw from her chair in the church her "unknown bishop," preaching from the pulpit.

They met from time to time in the Frémyot house, where the bishop was always welcome. How strange these first meetings of the two saints who were to be spiritually bound together for twenty years! Francis, on his side, always cautious, always slow to move; Jane, still bound by her vows to her spiritual director who, when away from her, went so far as to have her watched lest he lose the guidance of so remarkable a woman. Surely both, deeply aware within them that God had called them to one another, were wondering with some nervousness how God's will was to manifest itself and how they must be careful to tread the way God wanted. It is hard enough for one soul alone to follow that way without mistake; but for two together, how much more difficult!

We know from her own account that she "was dying to talk" to this so "good-natured, charming," holy bishop. He was content to pray and closely observe this ardent chosen woman, with the perfect manners of the world hiding her personal sorrows and struggles.

Francis chose his time for a little probe, almost a hint about the future, perhaps only a hint that he already understood a great deal about her. He asked her one evening as they were at table whether she had intentions of remarriage. She answered, as he expected, that she had no such intentions. "Well, then," he said, "why not lower your colors?" He meant — as she well understood — the frills and ornaments which she still wore. By the next evening, she came down without them. The bishop surely smiled at her when he pointed and teased: "Madame, if there was no lace there, would you be improperly dressed?" And that night Jane herself cut the lace off her dress.

Bremond, in his earlier life of St. Chantal, but not in the later *History of Religious Sentiment in France*, showed less than his usual insight in suggesting that Francis misunderstood the significance of these last signs of worldly elegance, thinking them marks of continuing vanity. Rather, one would think, a little comedy was being played between the two future saints, almost a gentle leg-pull on the bishop's part and a gesture on hers to show that she had taken his point.

Meeting often at the Frémyot table, they must have had further opportunities of conversation. We know, at least, that Jane, despite her obligations to her director, plucked up courage to speak to the bishop of the temptations of discouragement from which she was suffering once again. Her behavior itself must have been affected by these temptations because her scruples were such that she only dared express to him "a part" of what was going on in her mind. Whatever he said to her, she took it as the voice of "an angel." It was a voice which pressingly recalled the voice that many months earlier had mysteriously told her that she must pass through the gate of Sainte-Claude.

Sainte-Claude is a charming and busy little town in the Jura mountains and had long been a place of pilgrimage to the seventh-century saint whose name it bore. More relevant perhaps at the moment was the fact that it was situated on the much-frequented road between Dijon and Annecy.

At dinner on Maundy Thursday, Jane mentioned that she greatly wished to go in pilgrimage to Sainte-Claude. Francis overheard the remark and said that his own mother had also long wanted to make that same pilgrimage. "Madame," he went on, "if I knew when you were going to Sainte-Claude, I could arrange to find myself there with my mother accomplishing her vow."

Francis, who described himself as "bound hand and foot" by the cares of his diocese, had, we recall, felt urged, against advice, to accept the invitation to preach in Dijon. Now, he, most uncharacteristically, engaged himself to leave his diocese at some unknown moment in the future in order to meet Jane at Sainte-Claude. The drawing of these two souls together must have been under a most powerful impulse.

After Easter, the bishop went so far as to hear Jane's confession, but he insisted that she must for the time being remain under the spiritual direction of the priest to whom she had made promises. De Sales was not yet ready to take the priest's place, for he could not see God's will for her. But he promised to write as often as possible. Thus ended the first encounter between Francis de Sales and Jane Frances de Chantal.

That he was leaving Dijon with her very much in his mind, despite the triumphant goodbye which the town was giving him, is shown by the fact that on the day he left, he wrote her a note: "God, I am feeling, has given me to you. That is all I can say. Pray for me to your guardian angel."[108]

Hardly was he home again when he wrote her a long letter. So slow to talk, so much at ease was he with a pen in his hand, telling her that the further away he was from her, the closer he felt to her within himself. He told her to build her spiritual life on a desire for Christian perfection and her holy state of

[108] Ibid., Vol. 12, 262.

widowhood. But as always, he warned her not to take advice too literally.

"In everything and by everything, my wish is that you should feel a holy freedom of spirit as to the ways of seeking perfection. . . . Beware of scruples, and rest entirely in what I have said to you by word of mouth. . . . Beware of overeagerness and anxieties, for nothing stands more in our way as we journey toward perfection."[109]

He had told her to keep her spiritual director, but what he wrote to her seemed to be advice exactly contrary to what that priest had for so many years recommended. The ambiguous position caused her to have fresh scruples, and in mid-June Francis had to write another long letter trying to explain to her that his advice was not incompatible with her duty to her director.

Frankly, it was not a very successful attempt, unless history has exaggerated the obtuseness of that priest. Jane had given his name to the bishop, and the latter in this letter reminds her that he would not object to her communication with him "so much do I see him as a friend of mine." But his real mind comes out again when he writes, "Respect for him must certainly hold you to the holy ways to which you have conformed with him, but it must not stamp out the just liberty which the Spirit of God gives to those He holds."

And in his next letter, written ten days later, he confesses that his last letter, "although written with all truth and sincerity," was written for her director to see and allay his suspicions. Now he could write in greater freedom and from heart to

[109] Ibid., 264-266.

heart. He had been reading Ribera's life of "the good Mother Teresa,"[110] who had vowed obedience to Father Gracian, but who confessed to have greatly profited from others whose advice she took, so long as it was not contrary to her vowed obedience.

"What importance has it for you to know whether you can take me as your spiritual director or not, so long as you realize how my soul feels in your regard and I know how yours feels for mine. I know you have a perfect and complete confidence in my feeling for you. Of that I have no doubt, and it much consoles me. Please be assured of my keen and extraordinary will to serve your soul with all my strength. I could not explain to you either the quality or the greatness of that affection for your spiritual service; but I can tell you that I think it is from God. . . . God has given me to you; believe me to be yours in Him, and call me what you will — it does not matter."

A dozen times, he tells her, he had to take up his pen again writing this letter. It seemed that "the enemy was heaping on [me] distraction and business to prevent [me] from writing it. . . . Interpret its length therefore in the light of my need to forestall, if possible, the replies and scruples which so easily rise in the minds of your sex. Beware of them, I beg you, and be of good courage."[111]

Francis in the above letter commented with pleasure on Jane's news that they would meet again in September, but in fact the rendezvous under the gate of Sainte-Claude was to be earlier.

[110] That is, Francis de Ribera's biography of St. Teresa of Avila.
[111] *The Works of St. Francis de Sales*, Vol. 12, 282-288.

In the third week of August, just before the feast of Saint Louis, a cavalcade of three women, with their servants, set out from Dijon: Jane herself with two close friends from near Monthélon, equally dedicated to the service of God and already correspondents of the bishop: Marie Brûlart and her sister Rose Bourgeoise de Crépy, abbess of the royal Abbey of Puits-d'Orbe, a relaxed Benedictine house whose abbess could do very much as she pleased. Traveling through plain and hilly country and over steep spurs of the Jura, they reached Sainte-Claude on the evening of August 24, and passed under the town's gateway. From the other and much harsher side, across the Faucille pass, a carriage had already brought the Bishop of Geneva, his mother, and his doomed youngest sister, Jeanne.

Both parties stayed at the same house, and that very evening Mme. de Chantal, for the first time, opened her heart to Francis. She told him the whole story of her life and the story of her soul. He allowed her to speak on as long as she would. And the fluent correspondent, not having uttered a single word, left her.

Next morning, before Mass, they met again. "Let us sit," the bishop invited her. "I am tired and have not slept. All night I have been pondering about you. It is true enough that God wills me to take charge of your spiritual conduct and that you should follow my advice." One can almost hear him slowly picking his words as, after a night's prayer, he had realized God's will clearly and strongly in regard to this woman with whom his life was to be so closely linked. He seemed all the time rapt, as Jane was to say. "Madame, how shall I speak? But I must speak because it is the will of God. Those four vows which you took — they can be good for nothing except to destroy your peace of conscience. Please do not wonder at the time it has taken me to give you a firm decision. I had to know fully what God Himself wanted; I had to be sure that nothing in this business should be done save as though His hand had done it." Gone were the hesitations and excuses of the letters. Now there was only plain, stark truth and decision.

At Mass after their meeting, Jane vowed perpetual chastity and obedience to her new spiritual director. But of future plans, of Francis's own vision of the religious order he would one day found with Jane, no word was said.

It was enough for Francis there and then to write out a series of points outlining the spiritual road he wished Jane to follow in future. This paper is now lost, but a few weeks after his return to Annecy, he wrote it all out in a letter of some seven thousand words.

"One word summarizes the spiritual direction which Saint Francis de Sales was to give to Saint Chantal," Bremond writes. "That word, in fact, may be said to be the direction itself. He freed both her soul and the grace to which she had not dared completely to yield herself, thus leading her along the mystical way far more successfully than any personal intervention could have done."

That was what she herself was to say: "How happy for me was that day. I felt my spirit changing and escaping from the inner hold where the advice of my first director had held me until then."

In that lengthy letter, whose advice was set out in nine points, one sentence stands out in Francis's own capital letters: "Everything must be done through love, nothing through force. Obedience must be loved rather than disobedience feared." And he went on in his normal handwriting: "I leave you the spirit of liberty — not the liberty that excludes obedience, for that is the liberty of the flesh, but the liberty which excludes coercion, scruple, or nervous eagerness. If you truly love obedience and submission, I want you to consider it a kind of obedience to give up your spiritual exercises for a good reason or through charity, and making up for this by love."[112]

Near the end of the letter, Francis wrote, "In one part of your letter, you write as though you were taking it for granted that we should meet again. May God will it, my most dear sister, but as for me, I see nothing at present which can give me hope that I shall be free to leave this place. In confidence I told you why in Sainte-Claude. Here I am bound hand and foot; and you, good sister, are you not worried by the difficulty of the journey? But between now and Easter we shall know what God wants of us. May His holy will always be ours! I ask you to thank God with me for the graces which have come since the journey to Sainte-Claude. I cannot tell you of them, but they are great."

In those last words, it would seem, Francis de Sales was hinting at the spiritual benefits which he himself had received from that meeting and that decision. He would, it is true, always be the director of Jane de Chantal, but Jane de Chantal in her sweep forward to ever higher states of mystical union with God would carry Francis himself with her.

Bremond wrote, "If they do not as yet see one another from the same point of view, nor penetrate together to the same point, the sole reality, it is that sole reality which equally fills

---

[112] Ibid., 359.

their minds, namely, the love of God, the supreme object of the devout life as it is the object of the mystical life. And since this supreme object is to be reached, whichever the goal, by the same discipline — by detachment and self-denudation — there is no reason to fear that the sternly mortifying spiritual direction of Saint Francis should hinder the progress of Saint Chantal. He may not understand these things yet — the presence of God in the fine point of the soul; that completeness of denudation which is both the condition and the consequence of that grace; even perhaps what Saint Chantal has to tell him about these perplexing matters.

"Even so, his spiritual direction, even of itself, goes straight to the point and infallibly so in helping toward both ends. His is a spiritual direction which both calms and denudes, which allows God to act upon us because we do not resist nor remain anxious. . . . He guides her from below, and in guiding her, he rises toward her without realizing it, while she, for her part, thinks she is following him and from a long way away. Thus between them there is — what shall I call it? — a charming misunderstanding."

Chapter Nine

Finding God's Will
Amid Life's Busyness

1605-1607

The effect of de Sales's extraordinary activity at this time betrays itself in the pages-long letters of his which have survived. He had promised, for example, to write an annual letter of spiritual advice to Bénigne Frémyot, Jane's father. In the letter of October 7, 1604, in which he fulfills his promise, he writes toward the end, "This, Monsieur, is surely enough, if not more than enough for this year, which is passing and running away before our eyes, and in two months we shall see how fleeting and vain it is, just as we realize the vanity of the past years that are now gone."[113] A tired sentiment for a man of thirty-seven, even though a saint.

And two days later, he begins a letter to the Abbess of Puits-d'Orbe with words that explain the reason: "I have kept your servant, Philibert, a long time, but the reason is that I have not had a single day to myself, even though I am in the country. The burden that I carry brings its martyrdom with it

---

[113] *The Works of St. Francis de Sales*, Vol. 12, 331.

in everything. I cannot say that I can call a single hour my own, except when I am saying my Office. So you see how earnestly I must ask your prayers for me." At the end of the letter, he asks pardon for his tired handwriting.[114]

Despite a holiday with his mother at Thorens, overwork was leading to an illness at the turn of the year which he himself took lightly, but which the doctors could only account for by some form of poisoning, although this time there were no heretics to blame.

In the middle of January, he wrote to Mme. de Chantal: "Brother John [from Dijon] has found me emerging from a continuous fever, the effects of which prevent me from writing save by another person's hand."[115] By the middle of February, he still needed someone to write for him, although he could add some words of his own. Despite this, he later brushed away his illness with the words: "My illness was nothing at all, I think. But the doctors who thought I was poisoned frightened those who loved me so much that they thought that I was going to slip away from them altogether."

The winter's illness, it need hardly be said, was not allowed to stop him from fulfilling his next important engagement: preaching the Lenten sermons in the little town of La Roche, where he had been at school for a short time. All the grandeur of Dijon and its famous Sainte-Chapelle one year; the humble Savoy townlet the next. It was all the same to him so long as he was helping others. Still, we may perhaps discern in a letter to Jane de Chantal the need he felt to strengthen his

---

[114] Ibid., 341.
[115] Ibid., Vol. 13, 2-3.

resolution for an undertaking to which his health was hardly equal.

He was explaining that the will of God is to be discerned in two ways: necessity and charity. "I want to preach in a little spot in my diocese. If, however, I fall ill or break my leg, I need have no regrets or worry at not preaching, for then it is certain that God wills me to serve Him by suffering, not preaching. But if I am ill, yet I have the chance of going somewhere else where the people may well become Huguenots unless I go, here, too, the will of God shows itself and makes me gently change my plans."[116]

But his illness was over and there were no Huguenots calling, so to La Roche he gave himself. And for him, preaching the Lenten sermons meant visiting all the people — most of all the poor — catechizing the children, spending hours in the confessional, and administering the sacraments of Confirmation and Ordination. What we today call a "mission," lasting a few days, when the mission priests seek to bring all the people of the parish to church, was Francis de Sales's idea of preaching in a little town, swollen by people from all the neighborhood. Incredibly, he found time to instruct a deaf-mute whom no one had thought worth consideration and to take the instruction far enough to enable him to make his First Communion. In doing so, he gained a personal servant, for Martin, the deaf-mute, joined the staff of his residence in Annecy.

The Lent at La Roche turned out to be a prelude to an episcopal labor which he had not been able to carry out since his consecration: the visitation of the diocese.

[116] Ibid., Vol. 12, 365.

By the Council of Trent, a bishop was obliged to make a formal pastoral visit to all the parishes of his diocese every two years. Even today this is a heavy burden in large dioceses, despite the facility of means of communication. In those days, traveling on horseback or jolting carriage or even on foot, bishops must have dreaded the fatigue involved. But Francis de Sales's diocese was no ordinary diocese. Its parishes were often far distant from one another, separated by mountains through which communication depended on primitive paths. Pastoral journeying from week to week would involve climbing and descending at all heights up to four thousand feet and more.

Such was the prospect that faced him after a summer in the middle of which he could write to Jane de Chantal: "Don't be jealous, I tell you again. You are not the only one to have a cross to carry. Yes, since you desire it, I must start speaking to you of myself from this aspect. After all, it is the truth: yesterday, all day and all night, I had to carry a cross like yours, not in my head but in my heart. . . . It is true that yesterday I felt my will to be so feeble that a mite would have been strong enough to crush it."[117]

In August 1605, he had a moment of consolation to set against the fatigues and depressions of the year. Ecclesiastical business took him once again to his beloved Chablais and Thonon. "I have just come back," he wrote to Mme. de Chantal, "from the Swiss end of my diocese. I have finished the establishment of thirty-three parishes where, eleven years ago, only Protestant ministers were to be found, while I had

[117] Ibid., Vol. 13, 82.

been for three years preaching alone the Catholic Faith. God enabled me to feel in this journey a sense of complete consolation, as I reflected on the fact that where once I found only a hundred Catholics, now I cannot find a hundred Huguenots. Yet it was a troublesome journey and very awkward, as I found much obstruction in regard to temporal matters and provision for the churches. But God's grace made everything turn out for the best, and some spiritual fruit resulted. I tell you all this because my heart cannot hide anything from yours. It cannot be different or other than yours — but just one with yours."[118]

And so he came to October, when the formal visitation of the diocese was to start. Actually, it took four years to complete, a number of months each year being devoted to it. "Delayed up until now by a number of difficult matters," he wrote on October 13 to Jane, "I am off on this blessed visitation, although I foresee crosses of all kinds at every corner. I tremble at the thought of it, but in my heart, I love it all."[119]

Different though the work might be, it is the apostle of the Chablais whom one meets again on these visitations, as he trudges along on horseback, with Rolland and his servant Favre, through every sort of weather, putting up at night with such rough accommodation as could be found, preaching — often in patois — confirming, hearing confessions, sometimes having to deal severely with negligent and tepid priests, sometimes delighted to find immense fervor and young men desirous of instruction for the priesthood so that he sighed at the lack of any diocesan seminary.

[118] Ibid., 88.
[119] Ibid., 113.

The enthusiasm of the mountain folk could be as embarrassing and fatiguing as the lack of proper accommodation, for they would demand souvenirs of his visit and even tear pieces off his clothes to keep as relics. Strange superstitions held sway in remote villages, and on occasion the bishop, so widely venerated as a saint, was criticized as being anything but a good man, since he put a stop to keeping wolves away with blessed bread or protecting houses from fire by throwing paper with one's name on it into Christmas bonfires.

"All things to all men"[120] — it is strange to think of the elegant and learned de Sales, sought after as prize preacher in Paris and Dijon, as spiritual director to men and women of sanctity and rank, as diplomat and writer, spending week after week among the simplest folk of the world, talking their language, sharing their living, solving their problems, and warming their hearts with the message of that same love of God as, in very different terms, he would explain in lengthy letter after lengthy letter to souls who could share in this high mystical vision. To him, the universal apostle, it was always the same work, the same will of God, adapted to an infinity of different circumstances and people.

The best story of his visitations is the one Rolland relates. On a visitation journey when the weather was very hot, the little cavalcade was quietly making its way from one village to another. Rolland and Favre were ahead. Looking back after a time, they could see no bishop. They halted their horses and waited. After a time, the silhouette of bishop and horse could be seen in the distance against the sunset. When he had

---

[120] 1 Cor. 9:22.

caught up with them, they exclaimed, "How slowly you are riding, Monseigneur!" The bishop smiled and answered, "My dear Monsieur Rolland, old friend, one jogs along as one can!" That was how de Sales always saw it: to shirk nothing, to accept everything as it came, and to do it at his own pace and in his own way.

Describing this first 1605 visitation, while en route, de Sales wrote in a letter to Jane de Chantal: "What more shall I say? I reached this place on Saturday evening, after scouring the country for six weeks, without stopping in any one place more than half a day. I have usually preached every day, and sometimes twice a day. How good God is to me. I never felt stronger. All the crosses I foresaw at the start have turned into palm trees and olive trees. I had expected vinegar, and it has proved to be honey — or nearly so. But I can truthfully say that except on horseback or during waking periods at night, I have never had a moment to think of myself and worry about my feelings, so busy have I been with one important matter after another. I have confirmed a numberless quantity of people. And you have shared in all the good done among these simple folk, just as you have shared in everything else that has been done and will be done in this diocese so long as it is in my hands. Why do I tell you this? Because with you I speak as I do with my own heart."[121]

De Sales was to refer to other visitations in his letters to Jane de Chantal, which greatly help us to see him at work and to understand his feelings. In the middle of 1606, he would write, "You know how ready I am to go to Burgundy, my dear

[121] *The Works of St. Francis de Sales*, Vol. 13, 125.

daughter, for visitations are necessary and a principal part of my duties. I go with great courage, and this morning I felt a special sense of consolation in undertaking it, although for some days past, I have been feeling a thousand vain apprehensions and sadness — but they only touched the skin of my heart, not the heart itself. It was like the shivering one gets just before a cold."[122]

Two months later he was writing, "During these last few days, I have seen some formidable mountains covered with thick ice, and the people of the neighboring valleys told me that a shepherd, trying to follow his cow, fell into a crevasse in which he died of cold. O God, I said to myself, was the zeal of this shepherd so keen in the quest of his cow that the thought of the ice did not deter him? Why, then, should I be so cowardly in seeking out my sheep? The thought moved my heart and, tepid as it was, it melted within me. I saw marvels in those places. The valleys with their many habitations and the mountains all covered with the simple people, like the valleys, so fertile, but the bishops, raised so high in God's Church, so frozen! Will no sun prove strong enough to melt the cold that runs through me!"[123]

And a little later: "It is one of God's little miracles, for every day I am so tired that I cannot move body or spirit; but in the morning I am brighter than ever. What a wonderful people I have found among these high mountains. What honor, what welcome, what veneration for their bishop! The day before yesterday, I came to a little town late at night, but the people

[122] Ibid., 192.
[123] Ibid., 199.

had so many lights and festivities that it was like day. How much better a bishop they deserve."[124]

After the evidence of what these visitations meant to a bishop like Francis de Sales, one can read — with a certain amusement — the way he distinguished between episcopal and lay life in the letter he wrote to Archbishop Frémyot on the art of preaching. A bishop, he wrote in that letter, must not be "vicious with mortal sin and must avoid certain venial sins, as well as some actions which are not sinful at all. . . ."

A layman may hunt, or go out at night for social chatting, and there is nothing wrong in this, nor as a means of recreation is there any sin in it. But in the case of a bishop, if such actions are not seasoned by thousands of circumstances not easily realized, they are scandalous and gravely so. People say, "They are having a good time; their hearts are given over to it." Preach mortification after that, and everyone will make fun of the preacher. I do not say that a bishop may not play at some decent game once or twice a month by way of recreation; but he must do this with great circumspection. Hunting is absolutely forbidden. And the same for unnecessary expenses in festivities, clothes, and books. Such things are superfluities for lay people, but for bishops they are great sins. . . .

Hospitality does not consist in giving feasts, but in willingly asking people to meals such as are suited to bishops and in keeping with the instructions of the Council of Trent: *Oportet mensam Episcoporum esse frugalem* ["It is fitting for the table of bishops to be frugal"]. I except certain occasions which prudence and charity will easily pick out."[125]

[124] Ibid., 221.
[125] Ibid., Vol. 12, 302.

It seems a long cry from the bishop in his Savoy mountains or even from the bishop writing his endless letters to the Baroness de Chantal and other women correspondents to the affairs of the great world outside. But it was in this private pastoral year of 1605 that Francis de Sales only just escaped the high ecclesiastical honors which would probably have forced him to separate himself from his poor wife of a diocese.

In 1605 the Pope, Clement VIII, who had supported him in the Chablais apostolate and had instituted the devotion of the Forty Hours, which the Provost de Sales had put to such good use in that mission, died. His successor could hardly fail to be one of the great cardinals with whom de Sales had made friends in Rome. In fact, the conclave unanimously elected the Cardinal Alexander de' Medici, who had been Clement's legate for the triumphal Forty Hours of Thonon. He took the name of Leo XI.

Soon de Sales had news that the new Pope intended to create a number of new cardinals, and his own name was on the list. His nomination, it seems, was largely due to the efforts of Henry IV, who was extremely anxious to press his view that Francis de Sales was lost to the world in his mountain diocese and should shine before the world from one of the great Sees of France.

"From two sides I have news that they want to raise me higher before the world," de Sales wrote to Jane. "My answer before God is 'No.' Be certain, my daughter, that I shall not blink an eyelid for all the world, which I heartily despise. Unless it be for the greater glory of God, there will be no movement that way from me. All this between the father and the daughter — it must not go further, please. And by the way, in regard to that word 'daughter': I do not want you to use in your letters any other title than that of 'father'; it is stronger, more pleasing, more holy, more glorious for me."[126]

When the chaplain at his home was at this time asking for instructions about any messages to his mother, the bishop answered, "Tell my mother to pray to God and to implore Him not to raise me to a higher position. The present one is already too heavy for me."

Francis de Sales was saved — if this is the right word — from the Sacred College (of Cardinals) by the untimely death of the new Pope, three weeks from his coronation. Leo XI was succeeded by Cardinal Borghese, Pope Paul V, whom Francis knew much better than he knew Leo. We seem to have no explanation of why Paul V, who was to live until a few months before de Sales's death, never raised the question again. But the last person to worry about this apparent neglect was de Sales himself, dedicated, as he felt himself to be, to what he called his *"cher Nessy"* (Annecy).

After his first visitation at the end of 1605, he once again fell ill. "You were ill after the Conception [December 8], and I was also for seven or eight days running," he wrote to Jane in January 1606. "I thought it was going to be much longer, but that was not God's will. I cannot write as lengthily as I would, for this is a day of farewells, as I have to start tomorrow for Chambéry, where the Jesuit rector awaits me for the five or six Lenten days that I am keeping apart to refresh my poor spirit, storm-tossed by so much business."[127]

[126] Ibid., Vol. 13, 85.
[127] Ibid., 139.

He had been asked by the Senate of Savoy to preach the 1606 Lenten sermons, and, in preparation, he was putting himself into retreat under the Jesuit Father Fourier, whom he made his spiritual director. The Bishop of Grenoble, in whose diocese, Chambéry, the capital of Savoy lay, had given him permission to act in his name during the Lenten preaching. At first, he seemed to make little impression on the people, and he confessed to Jane, "As for myself, I am here where I can see little happening, save a slight rousing to devotion on the part of souls. God will increase it, if He wills, for His greater glory."[128]

By Holy Week, the de Sales spiritual magic had taken full effect, and his days and nights (despite medical objection) were given up to the heavy apostolic round of preaching, confessions, confirmations, and personal visits to all whom he could help. Apart from this, there were the heavy Holy Week ceremonies. So busy was he that a critic grumbled that he must be thinking himself to be the Bishop of Grenoble — to which he answered in words that warn against episcopal jealousies: "It is rather a pleasant thought, but anyway, the bishopric of Grenoble is just like mine: one tiny portion of the heritage of Jesus Christ, our only and sovereign *Père de famille*" ("Father of the family").

It was on Good Friday in Chambéry that people saw the great crucifix above the preacher give out rays of light surrounding him. The figure of this crucifix, after a checkered history, rests today in the Visitation cloister in Chambéry.[129]

---

[128] Ibid., 144-145.

[129] This seven-foot crucifix was taken to the Chambéry Visitation convent in 1672, although apparently its story had been

But the year 1606 does not stand out in Francis de Sales's life for the Chambéry Lent, but for one of the other facets of his many-sided personality. In telling the story of his life, we have almost forgotten his close friend, Antoine Favre. But their intimacy had never been broken. Letters took the place of personal contact when they were separated. From 1597, however, they had been close to one another, for Favre, appointed to the presidency of the Council of Genevois, had left Chambéry to live in Annecy.

Delighted at the change, he had hoped to be able to spend half the day with Francis, discussing together literary matters and reading to one another examples of fine poetry and prose. It was, of course, a vain hope, but Francis, apostle, missioner, spiritual director, priest, and bishop, had never lost his taste for fine writing and the turning of a classical phrase, nor for the ideal of devout humanism: beauty and style in the service of the good, in the service of God.

Favre convinced de Sales that the time was ripe for founding in Annecy a literary academy in which the best minds of Annecy and Savoy could devote themselves together to the study of science and the arts in the service of the Church.

It was one of the ideals of the Sainte Maison of Thonon, but doomed there to remain dormant. Called the Académie Florimontane — interestingly a purely secular name, commemorating the beauty of Savoy — it was established in the autumn of 1606, with a severe and almost stoical ideal.

forgotten, for it was sold and then rebought. It was hacked about during the French Revolution and finally returned in 1830 to the Chambéry Visitation, where the figure was repaired, repainted, and affixed to a new cross.

"None of the academicians will show any sign of frivolity of mind, however small — or else they will be reprimanded by the Censors" one of the constitutions reads. "The style of speaking or reading will be grave, exquisite, rounded, and it must not in any way smack of pedantry. The lessons will comprise theology, politics, philosophy, rhetoric, cosmology, geometry, and arithmetic. The style of languages, especially of the French language, will be treated." Public sessions would be held to which could come "the worthy masters of honest arts, such as painters, sculptors, carpenters, architects, and the like."

Annecy, it was hoped, would blossom into a Christian Athens. But the high hopes were never realized, no doubt because the bishop, however delighted with the idea, was no longer in a position to give his full mind to such a project, nor had he the time to spare to ensure its standards and its success. Certainly, when one reads his letters and remembers the constant burden of work falling on his tiring shoulders, it is difficult to see him concentrating on a project, very much in tune with his ideals, but outside the present range of the spiritual interests which more and more absorbed him.

No reference to the founding of the academy is to be found in de Sales's surviving letters, and he would surely have described it to Jane de Chantal, herself a woman of literary interests, had he considered it of great importance. It was he who opened it, however, in the absence of the Duke of Nemours, but no records of its meetings were apparently kept. When, after a few years, Favre had to leave Annecy for good, the academy fizzled out. Its chief interest lies in the fact that it was a precursor of the French Academy, founded thirty years later by

Richelieu.[130] One of the first of the French academicians was a son of Antoine Favre who would have attended the open meetings of the Académie Florimontane, which held its sessions in Favre's house in Annecy.

De Sales was now coming to the end of his first four years as bishop — Bishop of Geneva, not of Annecy, as he never forgot. The thought that he remained exiled from his rightful episcopal city was never far from his mind, not because he had the smallest interest in the worldly glory attached to the title "Bishop and Prince of Geneva," but because even the spiritual cure of the Chablais was but the cure of the body, while the head remained mortally injured so long as Geneva remained, as he put it in a letter to a cardinal, "the throne of Satan."

"I plead today the cause of this diocese," he wrote in this letter, "which, more than all the other dioceses of the Christian world, merits the support of the apostolic good will, the favor of prelates, and the sympathy of men of good will. . . . My adversaries are men who hold the doctrine of the Devil."[131] It was now time for him to journey to Rome and make his canonical visit to the new Pope, Paul V, and the thought of what his old friend, then Cardinal Borghese, could do to recover Geneva and settle the problems of the French part of his diocese was uppermost in his mind. Yet, despite this great urge, he felt unable to make the journey to Rome himself.

"At the approach of the fifth year of my episcopate," he wrote to the Pope, "I have a duty, according to the constitution

---

[130] Armand Jean du Plessis Richelieu (1585-1642), French cardinal and politician.

[131] *The Works of St. Francis de Sales*, Vol. 13, 240.

of the Apostolic See, to visit the tombs of the holy Apostles. But this journey is so lengthy that I cannot undertake it, owing to my lack of means, the difficulty of travel, and the care of the diocese itself. So I am sending my brother [Jean-François], canon of my Church, in my place. He will bring as clear and precise a report of this diocese as possible.

Here it is in summary. Large is its extent, but equally large is its devastation. Yet its restoration demands reforms which cannot be carried out, save in virtue of the authority of the Holy See. . . ." And he signs with the words: "From Annecy, the place of our pilgrimage and exile, where we sit, weeping at the memory of our Geneva."[132]

Francis de Sales's constant prayer for Geneva's recovery has been used by Protestant historians, such as Mr. Woolsey Bacon, as an example of his readiness to stick at nothing in order to defeat heretics and exalt the Catholic Church. Just before de Sales's consecration as bishop, the Duke of Savoy attempted to take Geneva by surprise, which he was entitled to do since they were still formally at war. The alarm, however, was given, and the attempt completely failed. It has been maintained that de Sales knew of the attempt and hoped to celebrate his first Christmas as bishop in Geneva's cathedral of Saint-Pierre. He might well have done so, but in fact there is no evidence that he knew of the abortive coup, and Mr. Bacon's argument that he did rests on his mistaken impression that de Sales made his pre-consecration retreat in Annecy, through which the troops passed. Actually, at that time, de Sales was in Thorens and cut off, by his retreat, from normal

[132] Ibid., 231-233.

communications with the outside world.[133] Before he was bishop, de Sales, as has been said, entered Geneva for his abortive conversations with Beza. He was to enter it only once again in his life.

It was in the year 1609, when he was suddenly called to Gex. He decided to go the quickest way — through Geneva. By that date, Catholics were allowed to do business in the Calvinist city, and a number lived there. But all open religious acts and all proselytism were forbidden. To the surprise of those with him, the bishop insisted on wearing his normal episcopal dress. He tells what happened in a letter to his old tutor, Possevino:

> Recently, while on my way to Gex, I got the inspiration, after saying Mass in a nearby village, to cross through Geneva. It was the quickest way. I was not at all apprehensive, perhaps because of a kind of boldness, more compounded of simplicity than prudence. As we reached the gates of the city, the official asked for my name. I told my vicar-general to answer and say I was 'Monsieur l'Evêque' ['the bishop']. To the response 'Which bishop?' I asked him to reply, 'Monsieur l'Evêque de ce diocèse' ['the bishop of this diocese']. The official then wrote in the register: 'Monsieur Francis de Sales, Evêque de ce diocèse.' I do not really know whether he knew what the word diocèse meant. Anyway, he let me go in, and so I rode on horseback through the town, saluted with great respect by most of the men and women.
>
> After I had left, the news that I had passed through spread among the people, and differing views of it all were taken. The seditious said that I ought to have been held so that I

---

[133] *Dublin Review*, Third Series, Vol. 7, 114.

could have been forced to deny my office; but the more sincere said that on the contrary, I should have been detained so that the proper courtesies could have been paid to me as a neighboring lord and friend. In general, my boldness in coolly passing through their midst, dressed as a bishop, was taken as a bad augury.

Although it took a Francis de Sales to break through all precedent in this way, the bishop had, of course, no hope of seeing the integrity of his diocese restored, and his only real personal concern was the souls of Geneva's inhabitants, not the worldly glory of a return to his true cathedral of Saint-Pierre.

Even more unexpected was the next strange incident in his life. It was to be the ex-student of Paris whose soul had been torn by the fear of predestination to eternal loss of God, to make what appears to have been the decisive contribution to the final ecclesiastical resolution of the conflict between the Dominicans and the Jesuits over the problem of God's efficacious grace and human free will.

On appeal to Rome, Clement VIII had in 1598 established the special Congregation *de Auxiliis* to settle the quarrel once and for all. Paul V was now determined to find a practical settlement to the impassioned theological discussion. It happened that de Sales gave his brother Jean-François, when he set out on his *ad limina* visit to Rome, a memorandum on the controverted subject. Jean-François passed the memorandum on to Msgr. Germonio — an old friend of the bishop — who held an official position. In a letter to de Sales of August 8, 1607, Germonio wrote, "I was most happy to receive Your Reverence's letter and to welcome your brother. . . . I have read your letter to His Holiness, and he appreciated it so much that he ordered me to show it to Cardinal Pinelli in his capacity of Prefect of the Sacred Congregation of the Holy Office and therefore of the Congregation *de Auxiliis*. He went further and asked me to make him a copy so that it could be read to the said congregation, as I did the day before yesterday."[134]

Although de Sales's memorandum was never published and has never been found, it is generally believed that it had a decisive effect on the views of the Pope, who made up his mind to bring the dispute to an end by allowing both parties to maintain their position and respect one another in doing so. Pius IX, in the brief proclaiming Francis de Sales a Doctor of the Church, accepted the tradition and said that it was "on his [de Sales's] advice that he [Paul V] imposed silence on both parties, believing that so delicate and dangerous a dispute should be allowed to rest."

In his *Treatise on the Love of God*, Francis de Sales wrote that God truly willed the salvation of all, "but in a way and by means suited to the condition of human nature with its gift of free will. In other words, He willed the salvation of all who were ready to consent to the graces and favors which He was to prepare, offer, and give for this purpose. So, among these favors, He willed that the call to salvation should be the first, and one so tempered to our freedom that we could accept it or reject it as we chose. And to those who, as He foresaw, would accept it, He willed to furnish the sacred movements of penitence; to those who would follow up these movements, He arranged to give holy charity; to those who received this charity, He decided to give what was necessary for perseverance; and

---

[134] *The Works of St. Francis de Sales*, Vol. 13, 406.

to those who made use of this divine help, He resolved to give final perseverance and the glorious bliss of His everlasting love."[135]

The truth is that only the subtlest theologians can hope to throw any glimmer of light on the relation between grace and human freedom, and the faithful may feel grateful to Francis de Sales for having been instrumental in the forming of a papal decision which leaves the field open to the theologians, while leaving the faithful to accept without worry, first, that in the work of salvation, *all* is from God, even our own cooperation in it, and second, that nevertheless man possesses what we call free will in the choice of good and bad.

Of the days, weeks, and months of these years, as Francis de Sales moved from his thirties (how young he still was after so much accomplished) to his forties, one sentence in a letter to Mme. de Chantal may stand as a permanent witness. He was preaching what he was calling his first Lent in Annecy in the spring of 1607, since, of the first, which he preached immediately after his consecration, he said in the letter that then "people just came to see what I looked like."

"For seven or eight days, I have not even been able to give a thought to myself. I can only get a superficial glimpse of myself. So many have come to me that I might see and serve them, thus leaving me no time for thinking of myself. For your consolation, however, I will assure you that I do feel deep down within me, God be praised. For the truth is that this kind of work is infinitely profitable to me."[136] This is interesting

---

[135] *Treatise on the Love of God*, Bk. 3, ch. 5.
[136] *The Works of St. Francis de Sales*, Vol. 13, 275-276.

evidence that active work to the point of utter exhaustion need not weaken a person's spiritual inner peace, but on the contrary strengthen it.

The Annecy Lent; a special two months' jubilee granted by the Pope for Thonon, to which pilgrims came from France as well as Savoy; the death of Anne d'Este, mother of the suzerain of Annecy (the Duke of Nemours), the princess for whose devotion the Holy Shroud had been brought from Chambéry to Annecy before Francis's birth, demanding of de Sales a funeral oration, a task he disliked because it meant mixing worldliness with spirituality — such were some of the outstanding events in the daily round of pastoral work and business, whether at Annecy or in the visitation of the diocese, to which he gave up time each year, completing it only in 1608.

But for Francis de Sales, so closely bound to his family, so fond of children, so tender in all personal relations, one event must have stood out — an event, the sorrow of which could be shared by even the humblest of his flock. It was the death of his youngest sister, Jeanne, news of which he received while on visitation high up in the mountain country of the Salève between Annecy and Geneva.

Jeanne, eleven years old, had been sent in the spring of 1605 to the Abbess of Puits-d'Orbe for her education, but, unhappy there and elsewhere, it was arranged in 1607 that she should go to Monthélon to live with Mme. de Chantal and her family. Francis took the closest interest in these arrangements. "I am rather worried about whether our abbess will be annoyed," he wrote to her, "but there is no help for it. It would not be reasonable to keep so long in a monastery a girl who does not wish to live there all her life." And he goes on to ask her to tell of all that is needed for the child. "You must tell me all that is needed for her in the way of equipment, and just as you yourself would wish it, like the princesses of Spain do when they are given noble girls as companions. I insist upon this, even to her having a cloth hood and cloak, if it suits your livery."[137]

For Jeanne de Sales, under the eye of Mme. de Chantal, they were happy times at Monthélon, as she worked and played with the boy Celse-Bénigne de Chantal, three years younger than Jeanne, and with his little sisters, Marie-Aimée, Françoise, and Charlotte. Alas, in the midst of this idyllic up-bringing for a girl, privileged to be the sister of a saint and un-der the guardianship of another saint, death came in the homely fashion of catching an autumn cold which would not yield to treatment. On October 8, 1607, Jeanne de Sales died at fourteen years of age. Jane de Chantal felt the tragedy al-most as keenly as she had felt the death of her husband. She had worn herself out striving in vain to save the child's life. She had eagerly offered up her own life if only God would take it and save Jeanne de Sales.

Francis interrupted the visitation on which he was engaged and returned to Thorens to console his mother. Writing on the feast of All Souls to Jane de Chantal, he poured forth his feelings in a moving letter:

> My dear daughter, is it not reasonable that God's holy will should be done, as well when it touches the things we cherish as otherwise? But I must first tell you that my good mother has drunk of this chalice with a wholly Christian fidelity. . . .

[137] Ibid., 189.

Last Sunday, she sent for my brother the canon [Jean-François], and noticing that he and his brothers were so unhappy, she said to him, "I dreamed all night that my daughter Jeanne was dead; tell me, is it true?" My brother, who was waiting for my arrival before breaking the news to her, for I was on visitation, seeing that this was a good opportunity, as she lay in bed, to offer her the chalice, said, "It is true, mother." He stopped there because he was too unhappy to say anything more. "God's will be done," said my mother, and she cried and cried for a time. Then she called to Nicole [a servant], "I want to get up and pray to God in the chapel for my poor daughter." At once she did so. . . .

I know that you want to ask me how I have borne the news and what I am doing. Alas, my daughter, I am a man and nothing if not a man. My heart has been broken in a way I could not have believed possible. . . . You well know, my dear daughter, how whole-heartedly I loved that little girl. I engendered her to the Lord, for it was I who baptized her with my own hands, about fourteen years ago. She was the first creature on whom I exercised my priestly orders. I was her spiritual father, and I was confident that one day I would make something good of her. Besides, what made her so dear to me (I must tell you the truth) was that she was yours. Still, my dear daughter, within my heart of flesh, which has suffered so much from this death, I very strongly feel a certain sweetness, tranquillity, and repose of spirit in Divine Providence which pours into my soul a great contentment even with its sorrows. . . .

I am sending you the coat of arms you ask for, and since you wish to have the service in the place where she rests in her body, I agree, but no pomp and ceremony, except for what Christian custom demands. Of what use is the rest? Afterward, please, make a list of all the costs, including those of her illness, and send them to me. I want it to be so. Meanwhile we shall pray from here for that soul and nicely carry out the little honors due to her. But we shall not send representatives to the forty-day anniversary. No, my daughter, there is no need for such mysteries in the case of a girl who has held no rank in the world. It would look ridiculous. You know me. I like simplicity whether in death or life. But I should like to know the name and the title of the church where she will lie.[138]

[138] Ibid., 329-333; see also St. Francis de Sales, *Thy Will Be Done*, 123-125, 127-128.

Putting Holiness
Within the Reach of All

1607-1609

With the turn of the century, as we have seen, peace had come to France and Savoy, and with peace, the beginnings of reconstruction and stability in all aspects of social life.

In particular, the insurgence of a harsh and defiant Protestantism — excusable, no doubt, in its origins, but often its own worst enemy in its combativeness and methods of proselytism — had been contained. In this connection, it is not easy to disregard the witness of Francis de Sales himself, whose constant insistence that the heretics should be approached and treated with nothing but Christian love was combined with his belief that so many of their ministers were "the most obstinate liars and sly fellows in the world."[139]

Reaction to the Protestant peril and the cruelty of much of its creed had been to give to the Counter-Reformation in France a fresh and most attractive spiritual quality. Where devout humanism under the enfeebled, sensation-loving Valois

---

[139] *The Works of St. Francis de Sales*, Vol. 14, 191.

had been a mixture of Renaissance skepticism, extravagant outward pieties, and first aid to the Church threatened in every field, under the tolerant peace of the easygoing, political convert Henry IV, there had been opportunity to take religious breath again and, with a new sense of assurance, to cultivate the inner strengths of Catholicism.

That was why the monarch was so deeply anxious to uproot de Sales from his rough mountains and give him a position of eminence in France and Paris. De Sales, gentleman, reformer, preacher, spiritual director, manifestly saint, seemed to the king to be exactly the kind of person who could do for religion in the new France what he wanted to do for his country in all other aspects of its life. Peace, prosperity, culture, a better deal for the poor: these should grow under the sun of a true human, as well as humanist, devotion.

De Sales himself, in one part of his complex personality, was certainly attracted by the idea, the more so in that he was apt to find the surveillance of his own ducal sovereign in Savoy rather oppressive. De Sales's friendship with Henry IV, his constant business with France over Gex and the French part of his diocese, his growing international reputation — such matters irritated Charles-Emmanuel as he grew older, and made him suspicious and jealous of a prelate who was in fact unusually faithful to the obscurity of his native land. Writing to his old friend des Hayes in 1609, de Sales said, "These obediences and mortifications which cause one not to dare to be free even though one is not a serf: are they so very different from the state of those who are not free because they are serfs? Still, we must put up with them, and as quietly as possible — that is what is important. How happy I was in that little shadow of hope of finding myself in Paris with you, as I so often dreamed."

Nor did the Savoy duke make things happier for him in taking umbrage at an incident like de Sales's famous adventure in riding through Geneva in his episcopal dress. The duke could not conceive how de Sales could have risked this without prior negotiations with the people of Geneva which had been kept secret from him.

Whatever de Sales's hopes of finding himself in his beloved Paris again and at the heart of the spiritual revival there, the prospect of a change in his fortunes, which he invariably saw as subject to the hand of God — "for my soul has no resting place but in God's Providence" — was brought to an end by Ravaillac's dagger plunged into the king's heart in 1610. It was not from a great See in France that Francis de Sales was called upon to play his part in the beginnings of the seventeenth-century revival of Catholic spirituality. He was called upon to do this in a humbler way, perhaps, but a far more subtle and enduring one. It was also the one which manifestly resulted from his own absolute obedience to the will of God, for it grew naturally from the kind of work which came his way and which he was brilliantly suited to carry out.

We have already had a glimpse of the Paris world in which a Madame Acarie and a Bérulle became the center of high mystical dedication in close association with the spiritual lead of St. Teresa and the Spanish Carmelites. The Carmelites had already spread from Paris to Pontoise and from Pontoise to Dijon, Jane de Chantal's country. From the Dijon Carmel, Mme. de Chantal had learned much of the teaching of St. Teresa and the methods of higher prayer from the prioress of the Dijon Carmel, Louise Gallois, known in religion as Louise of Jesus. She was the first Frenchwoman to hold this office.

From Annecy, de Sales's letters poured into Burgundy. He was watching from afar, encouraging, cautioning, and ex-changing spiritual experiences. "I only ask you to learn all you can about the foundations of all this, for, to speak clearly to you, last summer, having put myself into the presence of God without preparation and special intent, I found myself very close to His Majesty with a single very simple and continuous feeling of a love that was almost imperceptible, yet very sweet — but I would never leave the plain high road [of ordinary prayer] to look upon this as something normal. . . . I do not say that when one has made one's preparation and, in prayer, feels attracted to this kind of prayer, one should not go forward with it. But I find it hard to accept the view that prep-aration is not normally necessary, just as it is necessary not to come away from prayer without thanksgiving, offering, and actual normal praying. . . . Nevertheless (I speak in all sim-plicity before our Lord and to you, to whom I can speak quite simply and candidly) I do not pretend to know enough not to feel very, very happy to give up my feeling about this and to follow those who, in all reason, know more than I do. I do not only mean that Mother [Teresa], but many lesser people."[140]

Those Carmelites of Dijon were clearly strongly attracting the pious widow, but de Sales, who had other plans for her, kept her ardor for the mystical heights in check, while learn-ing all the time himself about the varieties of spiritual experi-ence which would be useful not only to him, but to the

[140] Ibid., 266.

growing number of very different souls whom he was guiding. For himself, he was content, slowly and quietly, to accept the will of God rather than to imagine himself called to any kind of spiritual pre-eminence in the way of religious austerity and mystical contemplation. These grew from within; they were not imagined and theoretical ideas to which he must live up.

In a sense, then, neither in his slow climb to the priesthood from the cultured world of his day nor in his episcopal rank did his vocation differ sharply in its spiritual quality from that of every Christian, priest, or layperson, to lead a truly Godly life. What he could do, as priest and bishop, in the way of living a holy and devout life, others, whether priests, bishops, or simple laity, could also do according to their state of life. Yet this logical, common-sense view of de Sales's that the way of Christian perfection was open to all, laypeople just as much as priests, was completely novel at the time. The way of perfection was then considered to be something for the few: those, whether clerical or lay, who had the clear vocation to enter monasteries and convents. And, alas, as we have seen, there were few of these which had emerged from the Middle Ages, the Renaissance, and through the Reformation in a state suited to the practice of self-dedication to God through continual prayer and penance.

Francis de Sales, as ordinary priest and overbusy, active, pastoral bishop of a difficult diocese, had steadily moved forward along the way of perfection, without theories or rare ambitions. He had found — to put it bluntly — in the hard, largely business job which God had allotted him the school of sanctity. What was there to prevent others from doing exactly the same within the secular and even worldly lives which God had allotted to them? Such, it would seem, is the perfectly simple basis of the spiritual direction he constantly gave to others. So simple — and yet at the time so revolutionary, because nearly everything that was written in the way of the practice of Christian perfection was written against the background that this ideal necessarily demanded great austerities and complete retirement from the evil world.

What de Sales could not foresee was the enormous response to something that seemed so natural and inevitable to him. What he had to offer was being offered at a moment of spiritual transition when so many people were looking for some genuine spiritual fulfillment after the quarrels, wars, abuses, controversies, and challenges of the Renaissance and the Reformation. They wanted religion, the relation of the individual soul to God, not just its abused and so often travestied name.

We have had occasion to quote from his letters to Mlle. de Soulfour, to Rose Bourgeoise, Abbess du Puits d'Orbe, and to her sister, Mme. Marie Brûlart. None of these women were much out of the ordinary. Mlle. de Soulfour did not persevere in her vocation. Rose Bourgeoise, to whom de Sales did not dare long entrust the care of his sister Jeanne, was a rather wayward religious of the old school, with poor health and much stubbornness. One is surprised to hear the bishop telling her that "you must keep the cloister and the dormitory closed to men"[141] and complaining of her not answering his letters. Yet just because she trod on low levels, while desiring to rise, we owe to her advice such as the following: "I am happy that

[141] Ibid., 146.

you do not often miss the spiritual exercises I have prescribed for you, for this shows that your faults do not come from infidelity, but weakness. Weakness is not a great evil so long as a faithful courage sets it right little by little."[142]

Her sister, Marie Brûlart, seems to have been an overly introspective, scrupulous soul, more troubled about the means and modes of prayer than its purpose. "What matter," he writes to her, "whether we are with God by one means or by another? In truth, since we seek Him and find Him as much in mortification as in prayer, especially in times of illness, the one way is as good as another. . . . Do not worry about not being able to serve God in your way, for in making the best of your troubles, you will serve Him in His way — and that is better than yours."[143]

In one of the letters to Mme. Brûlart, one finds the kind of sentiment so frequent in de Sales's correspondence which seems to jump the barriers of time altogether. Speaking of her son's First Communion, he approves an early date, "for the children of this age seem to know more at ten than we did at fifteen." How often must that have been said before and since!

But it was not the Bourgeoises and the Brûlarts who were destined, except indirectly, to make Francis de Sales a world figure as the apostle of perfection for people in the world. It was Louise du Chastel, wife of a cousin of de Sales, Claude de Charmoisy.

As a child, Louise had been a maid-of-honor of Catherine of Cleves, the widow of the third Duke of Guise. After her

---

[142] Ibid., 282.
[143] Ibid., 168.

marriage in 1600 at about the age of fourteen with Claude de Charmoisy, she settled in the grandeur — deadly dull as compared with the Paris of her childhood — of one or other of the Charmoisy residences in Savoy. She was not at that time a woman of any special piety, but one rather who pined for a livelier social life than Annecy and its surrounding mountain country could offer. Her husband and de Sales were old friends as well as cousins, the apostle of the Chablais having found refuge in the Charmoisy home near Thonon. But it was not for a year or two after Louise's marriage that she took special notice of the new Bishop de Sales.

As with Jane de Chantal later, the contact was made in church. The bishop was preaching in January 1603, and Mme. de Charmoisy, sitting among the congregation in front of him, strongly felt that the sermon was specially meant for her, a young woman of good will, but without spiritual zeal. After the sermon, she spoke with him in the confessional. From then on, they met socially and as relations, but there was no recurrence of the special spiritual contact.

It was not until May 1606 that an accident gave Francis de Sales the excuse to write to her at some length. He made little disguise of his marked spiritual interest in her, and he stated plainly that God desired something special in the way of devotion from her. Even so, nothing happened for nearly a year.

At last, in Lent of 1607, "the fish I have wanted for four years has come into our sacred nets," as de Sales expressed it in a letter to Mme. de Chantal. With so little to go on and so much to come, de Sales showed a remarkable power of discernment of spirits when he said in his letter of this latest fish:

"She is a lady, sterling throughout and infinitely suited for the service of our Savior. If she perseveres, she will do so with fruit."[144]

Mme. de Charmoisy had finally put herself in de Sales's hands because she would have to go to Chambéry in connection with a lengthy lawsuit and she feared the worldliness of the city and its court. The bishop wondered what he could do to help her in these circumstances. His spiritual direction to a number of different persons had to some extent been made easier by his writing little treatises or exercises on spiritual subjects, copies of which he could enclose, bidding the recipient pass it on to others. A piece of writing on "the perfection of life for all Christians" was enclosed in a letter to Mme. de Chantal "not for you, but for some others; nevertheless you will see if it is of any use to you."[145]

He was now also helping Mme. de Charmoisy with a similar exercise, as he told Mme. de Chantal in March 1608. "I want to send you an exercise which I have got ready and asked Mme. de Charmoisy to practice, as I do not want to do anything without telling you. . . . She is a good soul and admirable in the way she avoids being overeager. She has never written about her soul except these last days."

Rereading this letter, de Sales must have become worried at the thought that Jane de Chantal with her many letters might have taken this as a criticism of herself. He added, "I do not say this to praise her, for I like people to write to me and often. . . . I say this so that you will not think that you must

144 Ibid., Vol. 13, 275.
145 Ibid., Vol. 12, 266.

not write to me as often as possible in order to avoid too much eagerness."[146]

One way or another, then, Mme. de Charmoisy was able to take with her to Chambéry quite a number of the bishop's writings on the practical road toward spiritual perfection for people in the world (many of them hastily despatched while he was preaching the Lenten sermons). When she reached the Savoy capital, she showed them to Father Fourier, the rector of the Jesuit College and de Sales's own spiritual director, "my great friend to whom I often gave account of my actions," as de Sales wrote to the Archbishop of Vienne, his metropolitan. "It was he who pressed me hard to give publicity to this writing, and after having hastily revised and pieced them together with some little arrangements, I sent it to the printers."[147]

In fact, luck would have it that de Sales was preaching the Lenten sermons of 1608 in the peaceful little town of Rumilly, a few miles west of Annecy, when these papers were returned to him for revising and editing. With time for once on his hands and the ardor of the born writer who cannot waste a minute that might be devoted to writing, he would seem to have virtually rewritten at far greater length the substance of the notes he had given to Louise de Charmoisy, who, in the famous *Introduction to the Devout Life* has been immortalized as "Dearest Philothea." The little book was published by Pierre Rigaud in Lyons by the end of the year. The demand for the first spiritual book especially written "to instruct those who live in towns, in families, and at court . . . obliged to lead

[146] Ibid., Vol. 13, 366.
[147] Ibid., Vol. 14, 125.

outwardly at least an ordinary life" proved to be sensational. Rigaud had to reprint twice — and as quickly as he could. It was selling impelled by its own wings, as the Archbishop of Vienne said.

Within two months of publication, de Sales was explaining to the archbishop that he lacked the means for writing long books. "Perhaps there is no bishop within two or three hundred miles from here who is so much caught up in business affairs as I am. I live in a place where there are no books or the means of getting any. Because of this, leaving great plans to great writers, I have planned certain little books less heavy to undertake and yet suited to the condition of my life, which is vowed and consecrated to the service of my neighbor for the glory of God."[148]

Despite these protests, he was soon hard at work preparing the second edition of the *Introduction*. He wrote to Jane de Chantal for "all the letters and memoirs I have ever sent you, if you still have them." Now seventeen new sections or chapters were added and the whole divided into five, instead of three, parts. Alas, Rigaud accidentally forgot three of the original chapters and so the third and definitive edition of his lifetime had to be brought out before the end of 1609 to be finally revised in 1619.

Soon it was being read all over France, and pirate editions were being printed in half a dozen French towns. Translations followed quickly, the first English translation appearing in 1613. The queen, Marie de' Medici, sent a copy in a jeweled binding to James I, who carried it with him for six weeks, so

---

[148] Ibid., 125-126.

much did he relish it.[149] The delighted printer changed his sign from "*A l'Horloge*" to "*A la Fortune,*" and although the author would at first take no money, Rigaud did in the end persuade him to accept a sum to be used as a dowry for a suitable poor girl wishing to enter into a convent.

It is unnecessary in these pages to analyze or summarize a book of practical spiritual devotion which has proven to be one of the real "best-sellers" of devotional literature, not only among Catholics, but among Christian people of all Faiths. It is a book that is always in print and therefore always easily accessible. Hardly less important, it is a book that is extremely easy to read, for the author, in addressing an individual and real person, also personally addresses every fresh reader across the centuries, leading him by the hand as he gradually builds up the practice of a full Christian life within the conditions of normal lay life.

Nevertheless, certain observations about it may briefly, yet usefully, be made.

We have already shown in extracts from Francis de Sales's letters and other writings that one may easily get a very wrong

---

[149] The 1613 translation into English was by an anonymous translator, "I. Y." The initials have been identified with either John Yakesley or John Yarborough. According to Mr. A. F. Allison, of the British Museum Library, there is little substance in these attributions. "I have not yet succeeded in identifying the translator," he has written to the present writer, "but I can say definitely that Yakesley is very doubtful and Yarborough almost certainly a fiction. The 1637 English edition was called in by proclamation and publicly burned, on the grounds that certain passages, excised by the censor, has been reinserted.

picture of the type of person he was and of the nature of his spiritual teaching. Francis de Sales, we believe, was the most human of the saints — certainly the most consistently courteous and understanding in his personal relations, whether with his family, his friends, those whom he personally directed in their spiritual lives, those with whom he had to do business of every kind, and, not least, those of his own flock, whether powerful or weak, rich or poor, noble or peasant. So intimate could this personal relationship be, so clearly a relationship always of "I-thou," never "I-he," that one sometimes has to make a slight effort not to be shocked. How could a man of flesh and blood, one is tempted to ask oneself, attain such personal intimacy without some touch of baser emotion that seems inconsistent with the nature of his spirituality, of his vocation, and of his office? So much was he a man, so much was he a man of good sense, that his spiritual teaching constantly reflects a humanity and moral common sense that is enormously appealing to the ordinary reader who has no pretensions to being above the average. His are words of wisdom, not of spiritual fire, one feels.

Consider the following passage in the *Introduction*: "My advice, Philothea, therefore, is that we should either not utter words of humility, or else use them with a sincere interior sentiment, conformable to what we pronounce outwardly. Let us never cast down our eyes except when we humble our hearts. Let us not seem to desire to be the lowest, unless we desire it with all our heart. I hold this rule to be so general that I do not admit of any exception to it. . . . A man who is truly humble prefers that another should tell him that he is miserable and that he is nothing and that he accomplishes nothing than that he should say it himself."[150] Thus, in a few words, de Sales debunks nine-tenths of what passes as Christian humility. To read such words is to feel a tremendous sense of relief at truth penetrating through the current hypocrisies of respectable piety. Just because of this, de Sales seems not only an attractive, but an easy, teacher.

But the impression is totally false. De Sales, as we have said, was no theorist of spiritual teaching. Just as his personal character was a rare combination of immense natural toughness, of rushing activism, recalling the furious spate of the mountain torrents among which he was brought up, with a deceptive charm, slow methodicalness and contemplation as still and deep as the lake near which he lived, so his spiritual teaching combined deceptive common sense and ease with terrifyingly high ideals. He has been called the most mortifying of all the saints. The teaching simply reflected the man as he was and as he lived himself. That is why the *Introduction*, designed, as we have seen, to help the ordinary lay person toward spiritual perfection — and revolutionary at the time in so doing — may well strike us today as a strange combination of delightful and immensely appealing spiritual sense with, at times, a rigorous and frightening ideal, well out of the range of what we have grown accustomed to think of as a decent spiritual life for the man or woman of the world.

To some extent, we must allow for the change of period. De Sales, although writing for the layperson, was still probably thinking of the relatively few willing to face the struggle of personal reform in a Christian world of great anxiety,

---

[150] *Introduction to the Devout Life*, Part 3, ch. 5.

ignorance, and apathy. Today, not only have ascetic, moral, and spiritual values to some extent been modified in their application, but the Christian, if he takes his religion at all seriously, lives it more faithfully and more intelligently. From this level, we discern more readily than was possible in the seventeenth century a variety of stages along the upward path consonant with the great variety of people who, without being Philotheas in de Sales's sense, at least wish to live better and more fruitful Christian lives. But for these, too, the *Introduction* can offer the greatest help.

If the modern generation is apt to find some of the teaching too rigorous, some of de Sales's contemporaries thought it altogether too lax. One preacher tore the book to pieces in the pulpit in protest against the writer's tolerance of dancing as a pastime indifferent in itself and of "good conversation" which allows of "certain good-humored, jesting words, spoken by way of modest and innocent mirth. . . . We must be careful, however, not to pass from honest mirth to scoffing. Scoffing excites laughter in the way of scorn and contempt of our neighbor. Mirth and banter cause laughter by an unaffected liberty, confidence, and familiar freedom, joined to the sprightly wit of some conceit."

Two years before his death, Francis de Sales, in connection with the Italian translation of the book, wrote an amusing letter to the translator, the Jesuit father Antonio Antoniotti: "Some Italians say that the chapters in which I deal with games, dances, flirtations, and similar amusements and pastimes . . . suit the frivolity and freedom of the French people, whereas the reserve and natural gravity of the Italians have no need about such things. I leave the matter to Your Paternity's judgment, only adding that in certain parts of Italy, those nearest to Germany and France, like Piedmont, people do dance and people do play and people do make love. Besides, the little book has been translated without expurgations in Spain, even though there they make a great thing of outward gravity. The wise must be patient when one addresses in books like these the less wise. It is to the stupid as well as to the wise that I owe something when a work is addressed to people of the world, to courtiers and others."[151]

Another feature of the book which many modern readers find unattractive is one aspect of its style. This difficulty is the defect of de Sales's method: to write simply and easily for one individual person whose character and tastes he knew. The wife of a rich and highly placed nobleman of Savoy in the early seventeenth century was someone very different from any person alive 350 years later.

Francis de Sales was a painstaking person, never missing a chance of usefully spending the odd moment of leisure. Among the products of such moments was a list of similitudes, gathered from his reading, in this imitating Pliny the Elder[152] himself, whose *Natural History* was a favorite source for de Sales. And just as Pliny searched nature to support his own Stoicism, so de Sales searched it as the rich exemplar of the ways of God, every journey and walk in the hills and valleys of his beautiful country offering him endless examples and object-lessons which he could put to good use in his sermons and in his writings.

---

[151] *The Works of St. Francis de Sales*, Vol. 19, 319-320.

[152] Pliny the Elder (23-79), Roman naturalist and writer.

Writing almost pedagogically for Mme. de Charmoisy, he wanted to illustrate every point by examples and similitudes from God's revealed word in Scripture, from natural reason as echoed in pagan writers and from God's creative fertility in the endlessly changing pattern of nature. In doing this, de Sales may have made his book more tedious to read for later and more sophisticated generations, but he earned an immortal place in the evolution of French literature as a transition writer from the desultory and unformed charm of Montaigne's *Essays* to the regular, self-conscious classical periods of the age of Louis XIV.

The *Introduction* was clearly an unpremeditated and unprepared book, the casual consequence of his delight, as well as spiritual zeal, in writing long letters of spiritual direction, and it was an accident of time and place that Mme. de Charmoisy, to whom he wrote little and with whom he would have little to do later, should have been the occasion for the few weeks of concentration which, at Father Fourier's instance, he gave to the rewriting and shaping of his spiritual advice.

But de Sales, whose facility in writing was in marked contrast with his self-consciousness and shyness in speaking, could not but have at the back of his mind the serious preparation for what he would have thought a very different kind of book. The trouble was to find the time. Talking to Jane de Chantal of his writing plans months before he dreamed of the *Introduction*, he gave himself away, saying that he did it "to enjoy himself and to spin his thread also on the distaff." Two years earlier, in 1605, when he had been preaching the Lenten sermons in La Roche, the bishop had been deeply struck by the holiness of a local shopkeeper, called Pernette Bouthey, who was to die that same summer. We know little about this short spiritual friendship, but it reminds us that although the famous Philotheas were women of birth and culture, de Sales was no pastoral snob. One recalls Jacqueline Coste at Geneva.

It was the memory of the life and death of Pernette Bouthey in 1607 which was inspiring him to write a real book. He had arranged for the facts of her life to be recorded, and he himself would turn them into a book. From this village saint, filled with the love of God, to sanctity itself which is the love of God — such was the theme. "When I have a quarter of an hour's rest I spend it writing a life, admirable indeed, of a saint of whom you have never heard, and I beg you not to breathe a word about it," he wrote to Jane. "But it is a long-term project which I would not have dared undertake if some of my closest friends had not urged me on. I will show some substantial parts of it when you come here. And within it I can find a little place for our village saint, for it will be twice as long at least as the life of Mother Teresa [Ribera's]."[153]

Lack of leisure, however, made it impossible for him to carry out this rather ambitious plan, for it was exactly two years later, just after the appearance of the *Introduction*, that he wrote to the Archbishop of Vienne that he could not undertake major works. "That is why I am thinking of writing a booklet on the *Lamb of God*. I shall not treat the subject speculatively, but just to show how that love is put into practice in obeying the first table of the Commandments. After this I will write another booklet dealing in the same way with the second table. The two could be published together in a handy

---

[153] *The Works of St. Francis de Sales*, Vol. 13, 265.

volume. I am thinking also of bringing out a little calendar and daily guide for the way of life of a devout soul in which I will show Philothea how to fill the weeks of the year with devout occupations."[154] And he goes on to describe projects of an introduction to preaching and a book on how to preach to heretics.

Such were the writer de Sales's plans just before and just after the startling success of a book which was given to the world almost by accident. But de Sales, the writer, continued to be thrust aside into the rare quarter of an hour of leisure by the pastoral and business activities of the bishop and the spiritual direction of the father-in-God which was to yield such rich fruits. It would be many months before Francis de Sales's next and greatest book, the *Treatise on the Love of God*, would be written, nor would it have much in common, save the name, with the first of the booklets which he was planning at the beginning of the year, 1609.

[154] Ibid., Vol. 14, 126.

Chapter Eleven

A Unique
Religious Order

1607-1612

How often the bishop's letters contain sad, although resigned, complaints of the mountain of work which each day brought him. And we know, too, that although physically a well-built and strong man, he was easily exhausted. Twice illness had brought him to death's door, although, as with so many people, he enjoyed rather better health in his middle years. Those years, however, brought a certain degree of corpulence which must have increased the strain on a physique always affected by a bad circulation and, one must suppose, a prematurely early hardening of the arteries and high blood pressure. Yet his intense activity under such physical handicaps was less than half the story, for the most important part of Francis de Sales's busy days was the part which he devoted to prayer.

In the early years of his episcopate, he had felt obliged to cut down on the time of prayer that he had planned, and in his last years, mounting pressure of work and weakened health forced him once again to desist from a regular timetable of prayer, and this all the more readily in that he had acquired a contemplative habit of continuously attending to God, which, as he himself realized quite well, was equal to formal prayer. "I do something which is as good," he told his first biographer, the Feuillant superior-general Dom Jean de Saint-François.

But in his middle life, he allowed no day to pass without a full hour's morning meditation. "You gave me great pleasure in one of your letters in asking if I made a meditation," he wrote to Jane de Chantal in 1607. "My daughter, do so and ask me always about the state of my soul, for I know well that your curiosity in this comes from the great love you have for me. Yes, my daughter, by God's grace, I can say that now, better than before, I make my mental prayer, for I never miss a day, unless it be on a Sunday because of confessions. God gives me the strength to rise sometimes before daylight to do this, especially when I foresee the heavy weight of business during the day. And it all goes happily. I feel I enjoy it more and more and would willingly do it twice a day, but this is not possible."[155]

To this had to be added, of course, an hour and more of daily Office, his Mass, and his daily Rosary, which he had vowed never to miss. Intensely spiritual, too, was the part of the day which he devoted to hearing confessions and to his regular visits in Annecy to the poor, the sick, and the prisoners. How all this was compatible with the twenty to thirty letters in his own hand which he wrote daily, with the morning hours spent visiting officials, and the afternoon hours, when he held open house for all who wished to see him personally, is a mystery, but it reminds us that behind the intense activity there went a prolonged daily communion with God from

[155] *The Works of St. Francis de Sales*, Vol. 13, 318.

which he derived the peculiarly sure insight he possessed in making the great decisions of his life.

These decisions were never more mysterious and striking, and yet never more definite and decisive, than in the case of his relations with the Baroness de Chantal. We recall the unhurried and deliberate decision in regard to the vows she had taken to her first spiritual director, a matter that had led to the dramatic meeting at Sainte-Claude, the pilgrimage town where the roads from Dijon and Annecy met. That had taken place in August 1604. Each year since then, Jane de Chantal had made the journey from Monthélon to Thorens at her own request in order to disclose personally the state of her soul to a bishop who welcomed her, yet confessed how hard it was for him to find time to give her. "The place I suggest is with my mother at Thorens, because in this town, I could not promise you a single moment of my time. . . . I cannot tell you if we shall need many days to make the balance of your interior state; a little more, a little less: we shall work it out."[156]

In the spring of 1607, de Sales welcomed her with greater solemnity: "God will be glorified in your journey and your arrival, in that He alone has arranged it and freed me from the business which I thought a little time ago would prevent so early a date."

This time Annecy was the rendezvous. "You will be consoled to see in how small a way we live here in my house, in the daily round, in everything, and to see also our beautiful Office, for in this my chapter excels."[157]

[156] Ibid., 40.
[157] Ibid., 287.

As at Sainte-Claude, this pentecostal meeting at Annecy was to mark a decisive step for them both. Francis de Sales had once again made up his mind, it seemed out of the blue, yet in fact out of his long hours of prayer and meditation. It was Whit-Monday,[158] and Mother de Chaugy has given the story to posterity:

> Having taken her aside after Mass, he [de Sales] said to her, his demeanor grave and serious and as if rapt in God: "Well, my daughter, I have made up my mind what to do with you."
>
> "And I," she answered, "am resolved to obey."
>
> She then fell to her knees. The saint did not tell her to rise, but stood two steps away from her: "You must enter Sainte-Claire [the Poor Clares of Annecy]," he answered.
>
> "Father," she said, "I am ready."
>
> "No, you are not strong enough; I want you to be a sister in the hospital of Beaune."
>
> "Just as you please."
>
> "No, this is not what I really want," he went on. "You must become a Carmelite."
>
> "I am ready to obey."
>
> Then he made various other suggestions to try her, and he saw that she was like wax softened by the divine warmth, ready to be shaped to any form of religious life that he wanted her to accept.

After this little testing litany, the bishop was ready to disclose his real decision and explain to her his plan to found in Annecy itself a new religious congregation. Jane de Chantal later confessed that only when he explained this plan did she feel in harmony with him. Yet to both at the time it seemed a

---

[158] The Monday following Pentecost.

hopeless proposition which could not possibly be realized for six or seven years. How could this widowed mother of four children — the youngest only six years old — living with her irascible father-in-law more than two hundred miles away, hope to enclose herself in a new religious order in Annecy? No wonder de Sales warned her that he saw great difficulties ahead and not a clue as to how any of them could be overcome, "yet I can give you my word that Divine Providence will see to it by ways hidden from His creatures." And the Savoisien bishop can hardly have done much to reassure her when he said that he was quite determined to plant this new tree in such a way that its roots should cling firmly to the mountains of his native land.

What many have taken to be the first sign of the providential removal of the immense obstacles to the realization of Francis de Sales's plan took place a few days later, before Jane de Chantal had left Annecy. Returning from the Corpus Christi procession, she was so tired that she could hardly climb the stairs to reach her room. A number of men went to help her, but she turned to the bishop's twenty-four-year-old brother, Bernard, and said to the others that she would like them to allow him to escort her upstairs. She later definitely asserted that this invitation had no deeper meaning and that what she had said she had said out of mere politeness. But the choice and the words caused tongues to wag, and soon the bishop's mother was convinced that the rich Baroness de Chantal had it in mind to marry one of her young daughters to the relatively poor Bernard.

Subtly, the strange intertwining of events, whose ultimate purpose no one seemed clearly to discern, continued. For when the little Jeanne de Sales died at Monthélon, Jane de Chantal for the first time had the real inspiration to make it up to the Sales family by the sacrifice to them of her eldest daughter, Marie-Aimée — a sacrifice, which at the time she only saw as demanding of her in Monthélon a deeply painful separation from her daughter, who would have to live near Annecy.

Only after making this unselfish decision did she begin to realize that a marriage between her young daughter and Bernard de Sales would pave the way for her own definitive settlement in Savoy. Even so, this was still a dim and distant prospect, for not only did her son and her two younger daughters hold her to France, but both her own father and her father-in-law would never give their consent to losing her. After all, Bernard was of an age to look after a wife older than his own mother had been at the time of her marriage. That mother still lived at Thorens and was perfectly capable of looking after the prospective young Chantal bride. The most that could be looked for was that Jane de Chantal would have an excellent excuse for long stays with her daughter and son-in-law in Savoy, near Francis de Sales. It looked very much as though the latter was not exaggerating when he had foreseen a six- or seven-year delay before Madame de Chantal's vocation could be realized.

Yet within two years the situation had completely changed, for Mme. de Chantal had found a way of getting her old father halfway at least on her side. The education of her younger daughters now had to be seriously envisaged, for the environment of her choleric father-in-law and his deplorable old servant at Monthélon was not suitable for them as they grew older. Her father, M. Frémyot, desirous in his old age of having his daughter near him, was delighted to hear of her anxiety. Why should she not leave Monthélon and come to live with him in Dijon? Her headstrong boy, Celse-Bénigne, in his teens, was already of an age to leave his family, as de Sales had done years before, and train himself for a man's career in Dijon, under her father's care. Marie-Aimée would be settled with her husband at Thorens — "that little Aimée will be '*des très mieux aimées*' sisters you can think of, for I shall be her brother," as de Sales put it.[159] And as for the little ones, it was time that they should be put in the hands of the Ursulines.[160]

The poor man, in making these suggestions, had dug his own grave. His daughter quickly pointed out that these excellent suggestions would also free her at last "to follow the divine vocation which for so many years has called me to leave the world and consecrate myself entirely to God's service." To get his consent to this terrible separation would take a little time, but the old man had inadvertently yielded what had seemed such solid ground for resistance to the determination of the widowed mother and daughter. By October 1609, the de Sales–de Chantal marriage had taken place, and Marie-Aimée had become the Baroness de Thorens, the title bestowed by the duke on Bernard, who, in the division of the de Sales land, had received the *seigneurie* and château of Thorens. Jane's father now had to give his consent.

These plans were all the easier to realize when, early in 1610, Francis de Sales's mother died and the presence of Mme.

---

[159] *The Works of St. Francis de Sales*, Vol. 14, 14.

[160] The Church's oldest teaching order of women, founded by St. Angela Merici in Brescia, Italy, in 1535.

de Chantal near her young married daughter in Savoy became all the more necessary and fitting.

Thus it came about that the six or seven years were most unexpectedly shortened to three. By then it had been decided, with the consent of M. Frémyot, his son the archbishop, and even the old father-in-law at Monthélon, that Jane should part with her son and take with her to Savoy her little daughter Françoise. Charlotte, the youngest, had unhappily died, like Jeanne de Sales, only a few weeks before the solemn day of departure, March 29, 1610.

It was on this day that took place the famous heart-rending scene. Jane's father, unable to endure the pain of separation, had retired to his study. The other friends and relations were saying the final goodbyes. Jane then turned to enter her father's study and embrace him for the last time when her boy, Celse-Bénigne, threw himself at her feet to prevent her passing him. He said, "Mother, I am too weak and too unhappy to be able to stop you leaving, but at least let it be said that you have trampled on your son at your feet." As Jane, in tears, stepped over her son, his tutor said to her, "Are not this young man's tears enough to break your resolution?" "No," she answered, trying to smile. "But what do you expect? I am a mother." M. Frémyot had by now steeled himself to accept the sacrifice, and the mother, with her two daughters and Bernard de Sales, mounted their horses to begin the journey from Dijon to Thorens.

Celse-Bénigne's action was so theatrical that it was thought that his relations had coached him in it as a final and rather heartless attempt to prevent Jane from burying herself in a convent. But some may feel that both Francis de Sales and

Jane de Chantal were cruel to plan this separation from a fifteen-year-old boy, the even younger married daughter, and the little Françoise. Jane de Chantal, however, was not going into an enclosed convent, and indeed in a year or two, she would return to Dijon to see to the family business.

Celse-Bénigne was at an age when, in those days, a nobleman was beginning to make his own career. But he was destined to live a very short life. He was to be nearly executed through being involved in the conspiracy of the Comte de Chalais against Richelieu in 1626, and he died the next year fighting the English on the Ile de Ré. His daughter, Marie, married Henri, Marquis of Sévigné, and earned her literary immortality.

Finally, the separation of mother from daughters was not to be physical. Where Jane was to go as a vowed nun, both Marie-Aimée and Françoise would always be welcome as the dearest and closest of guests and friends. Once again, the gentle spirit of Francis de Sales was to convert what in itself was an excruciating sacrifice for God into a unique idyll of austerity, as the little girl, "Françon," played among the nuns with her squirrel and her birds, while a smile of silent love would light up the superior's face as, about her spiritual business, she saw her married daughter and her youngest moving through the convent or its orchard.

While Mme. de Chantal was responding with such determination to Francis de Sales's declared certainty as to God's will for her and so successfully brushing aside the "great difficulties, the solution to which I cannot begin to see," as the bishop had described them, things were happening in Savoy that seemed not less providential.

One by one, the first little community of which Jane Frances was to be the head was appearing. "Mademoiselle Favre has at last made up her mind with the consent of her father to give herself entirely to our Lord and to be my daughter more than ever — I think with her we shall fashion something good," wrote de Sales to Mme. de Chantal a few weeks before she left for Annecy.[161] Marie-Jacqueline Favre was the daughter of de Sales's closest friend and not by nature, it seemed, the type to make a nun. There had once been hope that she would marry Louis de Sales, the brother to whom Francis felt closest. But the reading of the *Devout Life* caused Marie-Jacqueline to think again about life in the world. "I no longer need to look for the way of virtue," she wrote to the bishop. "Against that love of freedom which I feel so strongly I am struggling, seeking to make myself obedient, and I dare not be cowardly in such a resolve," she had written to him.[162]

An easier vocation was that of Marie-Aimée de Blonay, whom de Sales had known as a little girl in the Chablais days. Her mother was dead, and her father had become a priest. It was only a question of time, as Francis de Sales knew, but he waited for her to make the first move. For an hour they talked, and, as Marie-Aimée described it, "during this very holy and very happy conversation, my soul was filled with a new awareness of the divine presence and of God's angels." "Courage, my daughter," the bishop wrote to Mme. de Chantal, "God wishes to help us in our purpose, and He is preparing for us the best. Mlle. de Blonay, of whom I used to speak to you, has told me

---

[161] Ibid., 247.
[162] Ibid., 414.

of her desire to be a religious. God has marked her for our congregation."[163]

The third vocation was inspired in France, not Savoy, by Mme. de Chantal. Tragedy seemed to hover over this vocation — first, because Jeanne-Charlotte de Bréchard, who lost her mother in infancy, led the most miserable of lives under a neglectful father; and, second, because it was her close relationship to the man who killed Jane Frances's husband which, it would seem, drew them together. The Poor Clares, the Carmelites — Jeanne-Charlotte had tried them both, but her health could not stand their rule. De Sales, when at Monthélon for the marriage of Bernard to Marie-Aimée, at once realized that here was a woman specially suited for the foundation he was planning. "Yes, truly, I can well believe how much you suffered in leaving your dear mother [Mme. de Chantal]," the bishop wrote to her, "for she, too, on her side was deeply upset. But one day your life in company with hers will last eternally if it pleases the Eternal God."[164]

But of the first little company, none perhaps is more touching than Jacqueline Coste, the devoted Geneva inn servant so faithful to de Sales, who asked to be *tourière* in the new community.

Thus the community selected itself, but what of the convent itself? This problem seemed to resolve itself just as easily. Louis de Sales's father-in-law, Bérard de Pingon, and his wife, Charlotte, had both resolved a few years earlier to separate and enter into religious life. Their first plan to do so had not

[163] Ibid., 101-102.
[164] Ibid., 160.

proved a success. Now they proposed to start a Carmel in Annecy. The wife would live with the community, while the husband would live with the Capuchins of the town. Perfect for the Carmelites was a house which M. de Pingon had bought, but . . . Let us hear the account as de Sales described it in a letter to Mme. de Chantal:

> Here is something rather remarkable. On my arrival, I found that one half at least of our hopes about the erection of a monastery into which to draw our good Carmelites had crashed, for one of those who, we thought, would contribute cannot make up her mind to leave the world. After this, the person who runs the whole ship and on whom the other foundress depends proposed to me, without my having said anything to him and without knowing anything himself, that since the house had already been bought and practically got ready for a dozen nuns, it would be a good thing to use it for a congregation of pious ladies along the lines which he had formerly discussed with an Italian Capuchin. I gave him no answer, and now he has come back. We discussed the subject, and he cannot get it out of his mind.
>
> So I am waiting, and if it all seems suitable, I shall not refuse the offer. God will be with us, if He approves, in all this.[165]

In this way, while Mme. de Chantal, with Bernard and her children, was at Thorens, settling her business affairs in such a way as to be left with only a small annuity for the convent, the house, called the *Galerie*, was prepared for the new community. It was so called because it was linked with an orchard by a

---

[165] Ibid., 228-229.

little bridge crossing the road outside the town walls by the lake to Faverges.

After certain final difficulties, all was ready for the opening on Trinity Sunday, June 6, 1610, significantly the feast of St. Claude, under whose gates, years earlier, the pilgrimage toward Mme. de Chantal's contemplative life had begun.

Jane Frances, ever a prey in her spiritual life to severe temptations and desolations, spent hours in misery, before the final step, haunted by the memory of the parting scene in Dijon and the anguish of her father, her father-in-law, her children, and her relations. In the night, she could not have recourse to Francis, but with a great act of faith and abandonment to God's so clearly expressed will, she overcame the trial and, with a renewed joy, went to the bishop's house for the Mass and Holy Communion, with which her life of religion would start.

Alas, Marie-Aimée de Blonay was not of the little company, for at the last moment, her father had withdrawn his consent. She would have to wait eighteen months before joining. Her vacant place was, however, very shortly to be filled by four vocations: those of Péronne-Marie de Chastel, Claude-Françoise Roget, Marie Marguerite Milletot, and Marie-Adrienne Fichet, the last especially dear to de Sales because he had baptized her in the course of his Chablais apostolate.

Meanwhile, that Trinity Sunday, the first three Visitation nuns, Jane Frances de Chantal, Jeanne-Charlotte de Bréchard, and Marie-Jacqueline Favre, spent the day praying and visiting the poor. At nine o'clock in the evening, with the sun beginning to set on one of the longest days of the year, the three postulants, accompanied by relations and friends, walked down toward the lake, to be received at the *Galerie* by Jacqueline Coste, the *tourière*, who had got everything ready for them. The next morning, they put on their black novices' habit to await the bishop, who would say the first Mass in their little chapel. Incorrigibly, Francis de Sales, when he returned to his own residence, smiled and said, "Really, one can't say that our ladies have improved their appearance with their new headgear."

More seriously, but with the same delightful spontaneity which characterized him, Francis de Sales on the next day turned himself into a composer and gave the new community its simple, three-note chant. He also made up his mind to improve the Latin accent of Mother de Chantal, as she now was, for his view was that "no one pronounces that language as badly as the French."

Francis de Sales, as we have had more than one occasion to note, was never the kind of man who envisaged great horizons, already filled in his imagination with elaborate and complex structures one day to be realized. He was not a man of theories and ideas. Rather, he lived experimentally, slowly, filled with the sense of God guiding him and mysteriously showing him the next step. It was in doing things that his love of God and his rich, zealous, but practical, imagination showed him how things should be best and most generously done. The apostolate of the Chablais, his conception of a Catholic bishop's vocation, his spiritual guidance of so many along the road of perfection: none of these did he foresee and plan. Had he been able to do so, he could have done nothing but recoil from seeming impossibilities. He could only have accomplished them because they were, for him, with his generosity and imaginative insight, the line of duty inherent in the love and service of God.

It was exactly the same with the foundation of the Visitation. Describing the foundation in a letter written about six weeks after the little community had been established, he said, "As to rules . . . this congregation receives either widows or spinsters, but not children under seventeen. They do a year of probation or, if necessary, two or three. . . . After the novitiate, they are solemnly received, but not to vows, that is, solemn ones, but to the kind of establishment and dedication which the Blessed Charles Borromeo drew up for the Ursulines. . . . No men may enter the house for any reason, and women only with written permission. The younger members only leave the house very rarely, but the elder members leave it to serve the poor, but under safeguards of the same kind as for the Ladies of the Torre di Specchi [St. Frances of Rome's community]. They only sing the Office of Our Lady with a very devotional chant. In the summer, they rise at five and go to bed at ten; in the winter, at six and half past ten. They have an hour's mental prayer in the morning and another hour in the evening. For the rest, they have a discipline of work, silence, obedience, humility, and poverty as strict as in any monastery in the world. . . . They only keep the ordinary fasts of the Church, except for Fridays and the vigils of feasts of our Lady. It is founded under the name of the Visitation of our Lady."[166]

It was a rough-and-ready sketch to be filled out and made precise in rule and spirit, as experience and spontaneous

[166] Ibid., 329-331.

growth would suggest. Even now, the name was wrong. De Sales's feelings about the nature of the foundation were, no doubt, expressed as he wondered whether to call it *Filles de Sainte-Marthe* or *Soeurs Oblates de la Sainte Vierge,* for the ideals of Martha and Mary were to be blended in the lives of the nuns.[167] Then, on the feast of the Visitation of our Lady, he told the community that the Visitation was the name he wanted, not merely because the nuns were to serve the poor, but because it was in meditating on that event that he was obtaining light about the future of the congregation. But the name *Visitation de Notre Dame* gave way to the popular name given to the community, *les Saintes-Maries* in the final title: *la Visitation Sainte-Marie.*

What is amply clear from the whole mind and spirituality of the founder — especially in his relations with Mme. de Chantal — is that, from the start, the new congregation was to be contemplative rather than active. Its purpose was to enable women, unfit through health, temperament, or vocation to withstand the rigors of the Poor Clares or the Carmelites, to live nevertheless contemplative lives in a dedicated and approved religious community. In this, it was simply a special application of the general teaching of the *Introduction to the Devout Life* for a small minority of women who felt called to leave the world, but not called to lives of great external austerity. De Sales, who was very hard on himself, and ready to prescribe to others a degree of external penance, such as the use of

[167] Martha and Mary, friends of Christ, represent, respectively, the active and contemplative sides of the Christian life; see Luke 10:38-42.

the discipline, was nevertheless very moderate in this regard for the times. His real emphasis was always on mortification of the mind, will, and senses.

There has been a good deal of speculation as to why he broke with tradition in not insisting on the enclosure of his community and in prescribing the active work of ministering to the sick and poor in their own homes — this in lay dress. But these first rules correspond with his own common sense, his naturally experimental mind. He himself was not a set contemplative, but a man called by his work to the most active of lives — so active that to this day, one cannot imagine how he could have got through so much work. In him, an ever higher degree of contemplative prayer remained consistent with an ever more busy life. Why, then, should he not have thought it best that his new nuns should mingle active work with their first contemplative aim, not only because action does not necessarily interfere with contemplation, but because practical good works needed in Annecy should be the fruit of a life of Christian prayer, however high. This view corresponds with his own words in a letter to the Archbishop of Lyons, Msgr. de Marquemont, when the question was raised in connection with the foundation of a Visitation convent in that city. "As for visiting the sick, this was really something extra, suited to the devotion of those who founded this congregation and to the place where they lived, not a principal aim."[168]

The belief that the Visitation was really meant to be an anticipation of St. Vincent's Sisters of Charity seems to be due to a misreading of the title. This was meant by the founder to be

---

[168] *The Works of St. Francis de Sales*, Vol. 25, 338.

interpreted in a spiritual sense, but it was taken by others to mean literally visiting the sick and poor. The actual work of visiting the poor was, even in the first practice of the Visitation at Annecy, restricted to a rota of nuns which left the majority to lead a contemplative life in a virtual enclosure.

Inevitably, a number of people were scandalized by what seemed to them to be getting the best of both worlds. Was it not a waste of a bishop's time to bother himself in this way about a few pious women who could not face the traditional austerity of convent life and yet would not live in the world? He was severe enough when it came to reforming the old orders, but when he wasted his time creating a new one, it was all softness. There was no future in this kind of semi-convent.

But he had many friends who fully appreciated the potentialities of this new way of religious life "not too easy for the strong, nor too severe for the weak. . . . Who would not pity a virgin, her lighted lamp in hand and with plenty of oil,[169] prevented nevertheless from entering the cloister, just because her shoulders are not tough enough to endure a camel-skin habit and her stomach not strong enough to fast for half the year or to digest roots?" Thus the Jesuit Father Ignace Armand reassured de Sales when he was consulted about the complaints.

Whatever the critics, a small minority in a city devoted to its bishop and edified by its new romantic community, might say — some of them objected to marriageable young women being whisked off to easy convent life — the life of the Visitation itself continued along the lines envisaged by de Sales. Exactly a year after the first establishment, on June 6, Mother de

[169] Cf. Matt. 25:1-10.

Chantal, Sister de Bréchard, and Sister Favre made their first profession. Marie-Aimée and Françon were, of course, present.

Françon is a delightful creature in the early Visitation story, for it seemed obvious to the community that Mother de Chantal's daughter, being educated by them, would live to be her mother's successor. The girl, full of fun, yet ready as young children are to imitate those around them, was willing to play up to them, even whipping herself with nettles collected in the orchard. But she had no intention of becoming a nun, and Francis de Sales understood her perfectly. He was content gently to reprove her for her love of pretty clothes. Catching her one day preening herself with her curls and ribbons, he frowned at her and made her blush. "The dress comes from the world," he said, "but the blush, it seems, from Heaven." Françon was destined to marry and live until 1684.

Although the community, on the day of their first profession, consisted only of three, with five novices, the founder was full of optimism. He saw the ceremony of profession, as he said in his sermon, as grains of wheat that had fallen in a certain province, destined to multiply in a few years across the whole country. A friend writing to him a little later, said, "It seems to me, Monseigneur, that this congregation was something that the Church needed, so that God called you in these days to raise it up. Our Lord has surely visited His people, and we must believe that this first blessing will spread to an ever-widening circle. What, indeed, was wanting to the weak but this moderate rule, what to widows but this gentleness, what to the strong and fervent but this mortification?"[170]

[170] *The Works of St. Francis de Sales*, Vol. 15, 388-389.

Amid so much that could be written about these first days of the Visitation, but which cannot be fitted into these pages, one significant incident cannot be omitted. It suddenly struck de Sales that his foundation, like the great orders of the Church, should have its own coat of arms. This would not seem to us a prime necessity, and even the times and de Sales's reasonable pride in his own ancient family would hardly account for his excitement about his idea. "God," he said, "gave me the idea that our Visitation house is, through His grace, noble and important enough to have its arms, blazon, motto, and battle cry. I have thought, my dear Mother, that if you agree, we should take for our arms a single heart pierced by two arrows, the whole within a crown of thorns, this poor heart as a ground from which a cross would rise, engraved with the sacred names of Jesus and Mary. My daughter, when I see you, I will tell you all the thoughts that have come to me from this idea, for truly our little congregation is the work of the heart of Jesus and of Mary."[171]

It had been the night before the Friday after the octave of Corpus Christi when this idea had come to him — in other words, the night before the future feast day of the Sacred Heart, revealed later in the century to the Visitation nun of Paray-le-Monial, St. Margaret Mary Alacoque.[172] There was, of course, no question that the heart in the Visitation shield, as proposed by de Sales, was a human heart, symbolic of the

---

[171] Ibid., 63-64.

[172] St. Margaret Mary Alacoque (1647-1690) was the principal founder of devotion to the Sacred Heart. Paray-le-Monial is only a short distance from Monthélon, where Jane de Chantal stayed so long.

Visitation nun, not the Sacred Heart which at that time was not a symbol of Catholic devotion to our Lord, yet de Sales himself in a note to Mother de Chantal before the profession ceremony said that he would pray to the "royal heart of the Savior for ours."

Vocations to the Annecy Visitation would make it necessary within a short time to find a larger and more suitable house than the *Galerie*, but the matter had to be attended to within two years, for the damp and coldness of the house was ruining the health of the inmates — another sign that the bishop had selected for his community women who could not have borne the normal convent rigors. Mother de Chantal herself, after her return from Dijon at the beginning of 1612, fell gravely ill, and only after de Sales had given her a relic of St. Charles Borromeo and himself vowed a pilgrimage to his tomb in Milan did she quickly recover.

The bishop himself had recently changed residences, for when Antoine Favre was made president of the Savoy Senate, he made over his fine house in Annecy, reputedly the largest in the town, to the diocese. Its new owner, after spending the days in the vast apartments, was glad each night to retire to a humble little bedroom. As he said, he could walk about as Bishop of Geneva by day and sleep as Francis de Sales by night.

For the Visitation, exactly two years later, in June 1612, a new house was bought just within the walls of the town, near where the town hall stands today. Here there was room to build, and despite various kinds of opposition and legal difficulties, what came to be called the First Monastery and the Grande Visitation, with a fine baroque church, was finally built. A large garden and orchard surrounded by the waters of the lake belonged to it. Its community came to be known as the *Sainte Source*.

The *Sainte Source* flowed out of Annecy for the first time five years after the foundation with the establishment of the Visitation of Lyons, an event of decisive importance in settling the character of a congregation which its founder had begun in so experimental a fashion.

Strangely enough, this took place through a runaway nun. This Mme. Elisabeth des Gouffiers belonged to the monastery founded by Peter Abelard and of which Héloïse had been the first abbess. The Paraclete, as it was called, had virtually become a comfortable dwelling for rich ladies who, although without rule or enclosure, took vows. Mme. des Gouffiers was most unhappy in this travesty of a real convent. When she read the *Introduction to the Devout Life*, she made up her mind to see its author and join his own foundation. So she ran away from the Paraclete and arrived in Lyons. From there, advised by a friend of de Sales, she went to the Visitation of Annecy. As she had come with two friends from Lyons, the bishop and Mother de Chantal suggested their founding the second Visitation in Lyons itself.

But in Lyons, the archbishop was advised not to imitate the Visitation of obscure Annecy, but to start a new Lyons foundation to be called instead the "Presentation." This proved to be a complete failure, and the archbishop decided to change back to a Visitation convent with the help of de Sales and Mother de Chantal. By some extraordinary accident, which seemed only explicable by providential intervention, the royal permission, originally requested for the abortive Presentation, came back from Paris with the word *Visitation* written on it, the secretary being quite unable to account for his having written that word. "I like that kind of Providence," de Sales said when he was told.

Mother de Chantal, with three others, set out from Annecy in January 1615, and de Sales, always original in his ideas, gave them seven little spiritual notes for Mother de Chantal to open and read each evening of the seven-day journey. By the summer, the Lyons Visitation was in being, with Sister Favre being trained by the foundress as the future superior, and a little gathering of Lyonnaises asking to be admitted.

But a grave crisis was soon to develop. Msgr. de Marquemont, the Archbishop of Lyons, seems never to have really approved of de Sales's new and undefined constitution. Various practical objections could be raised against it, chiefly in regard to canonical security. Were the nuns truly religious or really lay women living a life of religion? Once the original fervor had passed, all kinds of difficulties might arise with such uncertainties, and would parents, once they realized the uncertainty of status, wish to see their daughters involved in a nebulous religious future? Why strive to reform the older foundations by returning to the former strict constitutions if you started innovations of uncloistered religious without solemn vows? De Sales had heard most of it in Annecy already and brushed it aside. De Marquemont had less faith.

There was danger that the archbishop might return to his idea of the Presentation instead of the Visitation so that the Lyons foundation would become an entirely different congregation, separated from the Annecy founders and completely under the jurisdiction of Msgr. de Marquemont. Indeed, it seemed that was inevitable, since any Visitation convent must be a purely episcopal foundation. Unless and until it received approval and a constitution from Rome, any bishop could change it as he willed.

Happily, Msgr. de Marquemont was a holy and humble man, and he assured de Sales that he would take no steps unless the latter agreed. De Sales, on his side, with a humility that amounted to a complete detachment and readiness to leave all to God, made no difficulties about de Marquemont's insistence on enclosure and the adoption of the Rule of St. Augustine, the more readily in that this germinal rule which so many religious orders had adopted was "gentler than ours both for enclosure and everything else" and consistent with innumerable variations in practice. All that he fought for was that the name should not be changed and that the nuns should not be held to the liturgical Office, but the Office of Our Lady. He was rightly confident that under any outward guise, the spirit which Mother de Chantal and the spirit which he himself had breathed into it would endure.

He was too shrewd, however, to leave it at that. The real solution was simple in principle, although it might prove difficult in practice. It was to obtain the solemn approval of his Visitation from the Pope himself. Then it would become a true religious order that could flow across the world from the Annecy *Sainte Source* under the Church's authority instead of merely under local diocesan authorities. A humble bishop of a humble diocese de Sales might be, but his life and his fame had earned him powerful friends. It was to Cardinal Bellarmine, whom he knew to be deeply sympathetic with his own views about the Visitation, that he applied. Bellarmine was not optimistic about quick results. But Paul V also knew and appreciated the Bishop of Geneva. Contrary to all expectations, the Holy See's approval was given early in 1618 to the Visitation with the Rule of St. Augustine, enclosure, and solemn vows. And before the end of the seventeenth century, 146 Visitations in half a dozen countries had been established.

The changes, for which the Archbishop of Lyons had pressed, sound important and decisive. Canonically, they are. They were the outward defenses of the inner spirit. It was that inner spirit which de Sales and de Chantal, two pre-eminent saints, had breathed into a religious order which made the contemplative life in community possible for women whose physical strength did not correspond with their spiritual vocation. For Francis de Sales, the means were always secondary. Only the end really mattered. If he had attached value to the original plan, it was only, as he himself confessed, because he wanted his daughters, dedicated to lives of love and prayer, to be as simple and unassuming as possible, serving the poor and sick, in the least pretentious of communities. But "God's will made itself known, and it was against my own personal taste. It is much better so, and I bless His adorable Majesty for having in His mercy turned our congregation, which was to have been but a nymph, into a queen bee."

Chapter Twelve

Bearing the
Troubles of This Life

1610-1617

Francis de Sales was now well into his forties, an age which in those days was considered much older than it is today. Bald and with his greying beard, as we see him in his portrait, he looked venerable, although we cannot but think that the light touch, often cheerful and smiling, which characterizes his writings and especially his letters, showed more than ever in his features and especially in his eyes, despite the slight deformity in one of them.

At his time of life, the death of those to whom a man has owed much in his younger years marks the passage of time. As we noted in passing, the death of his mother, toward the end practically blind, took place in 1610, just before the Visitation was established.

Always specially devoted to her eldest son, Mme. de Boisy found it ever more difficult to reconcile herself to the way in which her son's increasing occupations kept them too often separated from one another. She even suffered pangs of jealousy because he paid, she thought, more attention to the

women he spiritually directed than to her. Just before his own
death, de Sales, doubtless recalling these last weeks of his own
mother's life, wrote, "These mothers, they are altogether admirable. They feel that one never loves them enough and that
the love owed them can only be measured by what is beyond
measure. How can one deal with this? One must have patience
and do as far as one possibly can everything necessary to correspond with it."[173]

Having a premonition that she had little longer to live, although still under sixty, Mme. de Boisy went from Thorens to
Annecy to be as near her son as possible. Francis tells the story
of her death in a letter to Mme. de Chantal:

> You would wish to know how this good woman has ended her
> days. Here is a little account of it, for it is to you that I
> speak — you to whom I have given the place of my mother in
> my Memento in the Mass without taking away the place you
> had in it before, for I could not omit this, so close do I hold
> you in my heart. You are first and last in it.
>
> This mother of mine, then, came here this winter and,
> during the month she stayed here, she made a general review
> of the state of her soul, renewing with very deep feeling her
> purpose to live well. She left me as satisfied as anyone could
> be in my regard, saying that never before had she derived
> such help from me. In this happy state of mind she lived on
> until Ash Wednesday.
>
> That day she went to the parish church of Thorens, going
> to Confession and Communion with very great devotion and
> hearing three Masses as well as Vespers. The same evening,
> she could not sleep as she lay in bed. She asked her maid to

[173] *The Works of St. Francis de Sales*, Vol. 20, 54.

read to her three chapters of the *Introduction* so that her mind would be filled with good thoughts, and she had the chapter on the Protestation[174] marked so that she could make it the next morning. But God, accepting her good will, arranged otherwise.

Next morning, while rising and attending to her toilet, she suddenly collapsed and seemed to be dead. My poor brother, who was still asleep, was wakened. He ran to her in his nightshirt and helped her to rise and walk, giving her smelling salts and waters such as are used when such collapses take place. At length she regained consciousness and began to talk, although almost unintelligibly, seeing that her throat and tongue were paralyzed. Then they called for me here, and I went at once with the doctor and the chemist, who found her to be in a state of lethargy with her body half-paralyzed; yet she could be easily roused, and then her judgment was sound whether in what she tried to say or in her gesture with the one hand she could still use. She talked much to the point about God and her soul. Feeling for the crucifix (for she was now quite blind), she took it up and kissed it. Everything she touched she signed with the cross and so received the holy oils. Blind and half-conscious as she was, she caressed me saying, "This is my son and also my father." She kissed me, holding on to my arm, and first of all she kissed my hands. For two and a half days she remained like this. After that she could hardly be roused, and on March 1, she gave up her soul to our Lord gently, peacefully, and with a countenance and beauty more striking than in anyone else I have ever seen. It was one of the most beautiful deaths I have ever witnessed. And I must tell you that I had the courage to give her the last blessing, to close her eyes, and to give her the last kiss of

[174] *Introduction to the Devout Life*, Part 1, ch. 20.

peace as she died. Only after that did my heart melt, and I wept for so good a mother more than I have ever done since I became a churchman. But my sorrow was, thanks be to God, without any spiritual bitterness. This is all that happened.[175]

Another great break with the past took place when, only four months later, Francis de Sales's old tutor, Déage, died in Annecy. Déage seems always to have been a somewhat cantankerous person, but de Sales's loyalty to those nearest to him and to whom he felt he owed much was absolute. Déage remained with him all his life and was made a vicar-general of the diocese. During the requiem and funeral, the bishop was deeply moved and wept a great deal. Afterward he explained what it was that had so affected him, especially at the Our Father: "I was recalling the fact that it was that good priest who first taught me to say it."

In that same summer of 1610, Henry IV was assassinated by Ravaillac, as has already been mentioned. The young Francis de Sales had had little use for the broad-minded, ex-Calvinist monarch who showed such tolerance for the heretics whose heresy he had abjured to gain a kingdom. Nor could he but deeply deplore the private morals of the king. But he had come to know him better and to appreciate his great qualities as a ruler and as a man. He had welcomed, too, the personal friendship Henry IV had shown, a friendship in contrast with the suspicions of his own sovereign, Charles-Emmanuel, and recognized that Henry had been sincerely desirous of meeting his wishes, as bishop, about Gex and the French part of the diocese.

---

[175] *The Works of St. Francis de Sales*, Vol. 14, 261-262.

Only a year earlier, matters had been arranged so as to enable three more of the Gex parishes to return to their former Catholicity. To Jane Frances's father, so loyal in his life to his old master, Henry IV, he wrote:

How true it is, my friend, that Europe could witness no more lamentable death than that of the great Henry IV. How can we not wonder at the inconstancy, the vanity, and the perfidy of worldly greatness! This prince, so great in his family, so great in his warlike valor, so great in his victories, so great in his triumphs, so great in his reputation, so great in every sort of greatness — who would not have expected that such greatness would be inseparably bound to his life so that, held together by a bond of unbreakable fidelity, it would shine forth with the applause of all the world in his last days to end in a glorious death? One would have thought that so great a life would have ended amid the booty of the Orient after the final ruination of heresy and the Turks. The fifteen or eighteen years of life that he could still reasonably expect, given his strong constitution and health, given, too, the good wishes of France and many outside France: such years of continued vigor until the end would have sufficed for this.

And now this great career of greatness ends with a death that has only one thing great about it, the greatness of its fatality, its sorrow, its misery, and its pity. He whom one would have thought to be almost immortal, since he could not die among so many perils so long warded off to reach the happy peace that he has enjoyed these last ten years, now lies dead of a contemptible thrust of a small knife and by the hand of an unknown person in the middle of a road! . . .

As for me, I have prayed that the sovereign Goodness should be merciful to him who was merciful to so many and pardon him who pardoned so many enemies. . . . As for myself, I must confess that the favors toward myself of that great king seemed to be infinite. . . . I have been greatly consoled that that royal courage, once having shown me its benevolence, should have graciously continued it for so long and with such kindness, as a thousand examples on different occasions have proved.[176]

Francis de Sales, lamenting the death at the age of fifty-seven of a king with such good prospects of a long life of successful labor for his country, could not know that he himself would die even younger, overcome by the continuous intensity of his own spiritual labors.

Toward the end of March in 1609, de Sales answered a letter from a Msgr. Camus which had been written on St. Joseph's feast day. Referring to St. Joseph, de Sales wrote, "My imagination can perceive of nothing tenderer than the sight of that celestial little Jesus in the arms of the great saint, calling him a thousand times 'Papa!' in His childish language and with a filially loving heart."

And the letter went on to accept the invitation to consecrate Msgr. Camus bishop in September, for such a consecration created "a spiritual parentage which neither death nor the ashes of our bodies can destroy."[177]

---

[176] Ibid., 309-311. It is a curious thing that the famous saying attributed to Francis de Sales, "You catch more flies with a spoonful of honey than with twenty barrels of vinegar," has also been attributed to Henry IV. Totally dissimilar in spiritual and moral elevation as the bishop and the monarch were, there was an affinity of humanity, tolerance, kindliness, and common sense between them.

[177] *The Works of St. Francis de Sales*, Vol. 14, 140-141.

This letter was the prelude to a friendship and an association which has ever since linked together the names of Francis de Sales and Jean-Pierre Camus, Bishop of Belley. The friendship is somewhat puzzling, for it would be hard to think of two more different people. Camus, seventeen years younger than de Sales, was one of the oddest of prelates. Among other things, he wrote a vast quantity of stories or novels of a secular nature, although written to point the good moral — his pen, apparently, flowing on without pause or correction. He nursed a peculiar hatred of monks, although once he called himself "a Jesuit in heart and soul, in everything." Yet these external extravagances went with a personal life of great holiness and special dedication to the poor. Long outliving de Sales, he was to hold various ecclesiastical positions, having resigned the Belley diocese at the age of forty-five. He finally settled in the Paris Hospice of Incurables, where he lived with great austerity, only to be taken from what would seem to have been a suitable place for his incurable oddity in order to accept the See of Arras. Then he died before the Roman bull of appointment had reached him.

Henry IV, who relished his company, had nominated him for the See of Belley before he reached the canonical age, and a dispensation had to be obtained before de Sales could consecrate him.

Nearly twenty years after de Sales's death, Camus published the six volumes of the *Esprit de Saint François de Sales*, forever after to be used — and abused — as a rich source book of reminiscences for the character, way of living, and devotional teaching — not to mention its endless stories and anecdotes — of the saint. To inform himself the better about the man he so deeply reverenced, he went to the length of making a hole in the wall so that he could observe the saint off his guard, rather like a scientific specimen.

For many generations, Camus's highly readable living portrait of Francis de Sales was accepted as a faithful and close likeness, but modern historians are on their guard against the vivid imagination of the novelist bishop, who was recalling events that had happened so long before he described them. A letter from Mme. de Chantal, written ten years after de Sales's death, witnesses to the fact that the ex-bishop of Belley needed cautioning lest his feelings and his pen ran away with him and gave scandal.

De Sales undoubtedly came to feel deeply for his young episcopal neighbor, for the See of Belley, although in France, was only some thirty miles from Annecy. He could appreciate Camus's charm and lively humor, while discerning the deep piety and zeal that underlay the superficial oddities and prejudices of this very French-sounding character. Most of all, he was always ready to help so young a bishop with his own experience and sometimes with his criticisms and scoldings, the more so in that the Bishop of Belley was the only bishop he had consecrated.

Camus himself tells us that de Sales encouraged him to write his novels in order to offset the vulgar and sometimes pornographic writings of the time. It seems that, but for de Sales's insistence on his remaining at the post to which God had called him, Camus would have resigned his See very shortly after his appointment. Belley was a very small town a very long way from his native Paris and the more cultured world of northern France. That two such different men could have become so intimate may well be taken as another example of the way in which Francis de Sales was able to use his own austere and saintly spiritual anchorage with an immensely understanding and tolerant breadth of spirit.

Deaths and new friendships, as well as further souls to set along the spiritual paths described in the *Devout Life* or in the *Treatise on the Love of God* — for the writing of which, as we shall see in the next chapter, he gave every minute not otherwise engaged — could not alter the general tenor of his busy episcopal life during the years when his days seemed to move ever more rapidly toward his fifties.

The death of Henry IV did not cut him off from the royal and governmental circles of Paris where Marie de' Medici was regent for the young Louis XIII. On the contrary, in the French Pays de Gex, which de Sales constantly visited, he was so well able to turn to his advantage the Edict of Nantes that his work of reconversion there was, in the words of the editors of the Annecy edition of his collected works, second only to the apostolic labors of his youth in the Chablais. Among his new spiritual children was the considerable figure of the Duke of Bellegarde, "Grand Ecuyer" of the kingdom, and Governor of Gex. He had long known him, because of the denominational problems of Gex, but only in these years do we possess letters which, being addressed to a man, compare interestingly with the many we possess of spiritual direction to women.

> Blessed be God eternally for the goodness He shows to your soul, Monsieur, in so powerfully drawing it to devote the rest of your mortal life to the service of eternal life — that eternal life which is divinity itself, in that divinity itself will be the life of glory and happiness in our spirits. That is life, the only

true life for which alone we should live in this world, since any life which does not end in eternal life had best be called death, not life. . . .

Without doubt you are called to a virile, courageous, valiant, unchanging devotion — one that will mirror to many the truth of heavenly love, one that will worthily atone for any past faults if indeed you have attached yourself to the vanity of earthly loves. . . . The world will have a high regard for you, and, despite its perversity, it will honor you when it observes that in its palaces, its galleries, its cabinets, you carefully observe the ways of a wise, serious, strong, unchanging, noble, and easy-flowing devotion. So be it, my dear son. May God always be your greatness and the world ever spurned — I am your father who loves you as his Benjamin and honors you as his Joseph.[178]

Such relationships with the great of France, including Marie de' Medici and in a short time with Louis XIII himself, who used to refer to him as "my good Father, my saintly Bishop," were not calculated to ease his relations with the increasingly jealous Charles-Emmanuel.

We hear much of praise of the Bishop of Geneva, but so ardent a reformer of easygoing ways and customary abuses had many enemies, and not only among the Calvinists. These people were constantly denouncing not only Francis himself, but his relations and his friends, to the prince already far from happy about a subject with steadily growing international prestige. It was only the beginning of this campaign of detraction

---

[178] *The Works of St. Francis de Sales*, Vol. 16, 56-57, 194-195. Benjamin and Joseph were the sons of the Old Testament patriarch Jacob and his wife Rachel.

to which he was referring in a letter to Charles-Emmanuel in the summer of 1611: "Having been warned that I have been denounced to Your Highness for certain evil business of state with foreigners, I am in utter astonishment, for I cannot imagine on what ground at all such calumny can be founded. True, I have been obliged these days to go to Gex and remain there for some time, but neither there nor anywhere else have I done or said anything but what appertains to my profession, which is to preach, to argue, to reconcile churches, to consecrate altars, and to administer sacraments. . . . Neither I, my lord, nor those near me have, whether in deed or intention, the wish to do anything but within obedience to Your Highness. I cannot imagine, therefore, how calumny dares to charge me with special foreign interests. . . ."[179]

Charles-Emmanuel was even angered by his business with the Visitation in Lyons.

But such unpleasantness, now or later, could not touch his inner peace. It was only a month earlier that he had written from Gex to Mother de Chantal: "God's goodness enables me to experience quite extraordinary sweetness and consolations here where they arise. How good our Savior is and how kindly He treats my poor puny courage. How firmly am I resolved to remain deeply faithful to Him — and faithful especially to the service of our heart which, more strongly than ever, I see and feel to be something unique. Who but God, my dear daughter, could cause two spirits to mingle so perfectly that they have become one only spirit, indivisible, inseparable, for He only is one by His very essence. . . . A thousand times a day my heart

[179] Ibid., Vol. 15, 66-69.

finds itself near yours; a thousand times it pours out to God prayers for your consolation."[180]

Francis de Sales was invited by the Savoy Senate to preach the Lenten sermons for a second time in Chambéry in 1612, and the bishop, so much of whose life and correspondence was with great people of the world, was once again rather nervous of the society of provincial Savoy's capital. "Let me tell you what I think," he wrote to Favre's wife. "I fear that I shall come up against too much worldly wisdom there. You know how the Cross loves simple and humble hearts. Still, it is the Savior whom I preach, the Savior who fills the valleys and lowers and flattens the mountains."[181]

He began by taking special trouble to preach in a manner fitted to the pretensions of a provincial society, but soon reverted to his old, simple way, filled with the usual spontaneous felicities of expression, such as the beautiful phrase in reference to the Jews seeing our Lord weep over Lazarus: "They saw love weeping";[182] or the light-hearted reference to the Devil's tactics in making us believe that all preachers are spoilsports, when what preachers really say is, "Feed on joy and happiness — but as for sin, there is no joy in it, so do not sin."

He was right in anticipating resistance and disinterest among worldly congregations of Chambéry, and he did not hesitate to show the severe side of his nature in warning them that the God who did not spare the angels for a single guilty thought "will not forgive you, you who burst out here in shouts

[180] Ibid., 56-57.
[181] Ibid., 54.
[182] John 11:35-36.

of laughter." But it was not long before he had exerted his spiritual authority, in its strength and in its meekness, on the worldly people so that once again, the weeks of Lent were one long uninterrupted ministry in the confessional and the service of souls: the rich, the poor, the sick, the prisoners, and the dying.

As we have more than once pointed out, the genius of Francis de Sales was not that of the scholar, the learned man, the student, the planner; it was the genius of an intensely spiritual and intensely wise man of action who had the gift of being able to rise to every circumstance and opportunity.

We have a typical example of this special genius of his at about this time when he found himself drawn very much against his will into the current controversy about the mutual delimitations of the authority of the Church and the authority of the state. The Reformation was over, and the traditional authority of the universal Church was challenged, not only in parts of Europe that had rebelled against Catholicity altogether, but also because Catholic states themselves had developed a new consciousness of nationhood and sovereignty. Catholic rulers were, in the circumstances, not unnaturally anxious to claim powers over ecclesiastical affairs within their frontiers which, of course, automatically fell to Protestant princes.

Msgr. Germonio, now Archbishop of Tarentaise, who had enabled Francis de Sales to give his decisive view in the *De Auxiliis* controversy, was once again looking for de Sales's valuable opinion in the present discussion. In March 1612, de Sales wrote to Germonio: "From Paris and Dijon, advices which I have received, as well as from the booklets printed in those towns, it is obvious that the discussion about the authority of the Holy See over kings is spreading more and more. It is the same with the argument about the councils and the Sovereign Pontiffs. It is clear that most of the *Parlements* and statesmen, even though Catholic, are taking the least favorable view, or, to put it better, the view most contrary to papal authority, for they believe that this is in better accord with the royal authority and serves it best." De Sales went on to argue the danger of this, given the minority of Louis XIII, despite the latter's "excellent and most Christian disposition. But, to have the matter discussed by able theologians does not seem to be a good idea, for the more heated the debates become, the more men's spirits will become heated, so that disagreements will increase. . . . The best remedy would be that during the regency, friendly relations, on the part of His Holiness, should be maintained with the queen and the council."[183]

In other words, the bishop very wisely believed that this great question, which Bellarmine had recently sought to solve by the doctrine of the "indirect power" of the papacy, i.e., power over the spiritual and moral elements in political authority, could best be handled, not by a respective taking up of positions, but by tact and mutual understanding in meeting practical difficulties, as they arose.

He had occasion a little earlier to write sharply to the father of one of the first Visitation nuns, M. Bénigne Milletot, who had written a book which took the side of the state.

"I see two things in your book: the work of the writer on the one side and its subject matter on the other. Truly, I think that

[183] Ibid., 183-185.

the way you write is good and praiseworthy, even exquisite and rare, but the matter displeases me — and if I must say what is in my heart, I say: the matter displeases me very much. . . . By natural inclination, by the way in which I was brought up, by my ordinary experience, and, as I believe, by heavenly inspiration, I hate all contentions and disputes among Catholics. They are purposeless, and I hate even more those whose effects cannot be other than dissensions and quarrels especially in these times when spirits are only too disposed to controversy, backbiting, censoriousness, and the ruin of charity. I have not even found to my taste certain writings of a saintly and most excellent prelate [Bellarmine], in which he has treated of the indirect power of the Pope over princes — not that I have thought what he wrote not be to the point, but because in this age when we have so many enemies outside, I believe that we should not disturb anything within the body of the Church."[184]

But the most curious circumstance in regard to this vexed and highly important question with which de Sales had thus accidentally become involved was that he finally gave his full opinion on it, not in any book or in some public declaration, but in a private letter to Mme. Brûlart, of all people. Mme. Brûlart was indeed a person of influence in the world of the magistrates of Dijon, and de Sales was doubtless really writing for them, but one cannot but be moved by the reflection that the future Doctor of the Church and patron of writers thought so little of his own learning and writing that he was ready to treat of a vital, controversial question of the day between

[184] Ibid., 95-96.

Church and state in a private letter to one of the women whose spiritual director he was.

It was a "difficult" question, he told her, "not in itself — on the contrary, it is very easy to solve for those who seek the solution by the road of charity." But it was "difficult" in an age of hotheads when one can so easily offend "those who, being good servants either of the Pope or of princes, insist on holding to extreme views, forgetting that the worst thing one can do to a father is to deprive him of the love of his sons, or for the sons to deprive them of the respect they owe their fathers."

Furthermore, the question was a "useless" one, "for the Pope demands nothing from kings and princes in this matter. He loves them all tenderly, desiring only the strength and stability of their crowns. With them he lives in peace and friendliness, doing practically nothing within their states, even where purely ecclesiastical matters are in question, without their agreement and good will."

De Sales then set out in some length the nature of the respective authorities of "the Church or the Pope (for they come to the same thing)" — a significant bracket in view of much later clarifications of the papal position — and of the state. Summing up, he wrote of the "great but reciprocal obligation as between the Pope and the kings; an unchanging obligation, an obligation lasting until death inclusively, and a natural obligation, divine and human, by which the Pope and the Church put their spiritual powers at the service of kings and kingdoms, and the kings their temporal forces at the service of the Pope and the Church."

"The Pope and the Church," he explained, "serve the kings for spiritual nourishment, conservation, and defense toward all and against all. Kings and kingdoms serve the Church and the Pope for temporal nourishment, conservation, and defense toward all and against all; for the fathers are at the service of the children and the children of the fathers. Nevertheless, kings and all sovereign princes have a temporal sovereignty in which neither Pope nor Church has any part and where they ask for no sort of temporal recognition. In short, the Pope is sovereign pastor and spiritual father; the king is temporal prince and lord. The authority of the one is not against that of the other, but they mutually support one another, for the Pope and the Church excommunicate and hold for heretics those who deny the sovereign authority of kings and princes, and the kings strike with their swords those who deny the authority of the Pope or the Church, or, if they hold back their sword, it is to await amendment and avowal. Leave it at that. Be a humble spiritual daughter of the Church and the Pope and a humble subject and servant of the king. Pray for the one and the other, and be sure that in so doing, you will have God for Father and for King."[185]

Had Mme. Brûlart torn up or lost that letter, the Church would never have had the benefit of a brilliant exposition of the principles that were directly applicable then and that still hold in principle today, adapted in concordats and other agreements or traditions which interpret temporal sovereignty in new constitutional terms and recognize the practical limitations of Catholic ecclesiastical authority in purely secularist states. That he wrote this exposition only for private advice underlines de Sales's real feelings that such questions are

[185] Ibid., 191-194.

best left to work themselves out without dotting *i*s and crossing *t*s.

Francis de Sales had not, of course, forgotten the promise he had made to go in pilgrimage to the tomb of St. Charles Borromeo in Milan in thanksgiving for the recovery of Mother de Chantal during those first months of the Visitation life in the *Galerie*.

How he found the time to accomplish this journey after Easter in 1613 can only be guessed through what he said to Madeleine de Mouxy, an early Visitation nun who was to make her entry into the convent covered with scapulars, medals, sashes, and other outward signs of a multitude of other spiritual commitments, to be quickly deprived of them all by the founder as so much spiritual lumber. This worried soul was now getting the bishop's advice about how to live more simply. "My daughter, do as I do," he told her, as she testified later. "I am just about to start for Milan. Yet imagine how busy I am. I have more than fifty letters to answer. If I tried to hurry over it all, I would be lost. So I intend neither to hurry nor to worry. This evening I shall answer as many as I can. Tomorrow I shall do the same, and so I shall go on until I have finished. Do the same as I do, daughter, for time is ours."

Besides the vow, another pressing matter called for the journey which was to be made across the Mont-Cenis and via Turin. He had to see Charles-Emmanuel, for his friends, his family, as well as he himself, stood in the duke's special displeasure. They had been accused of being involved in a beating that had been given to the secretary of the Duke of Nemours in the forest of Sonnaz — the forest, it will be recalled, where the young de Sales had received the three signs of the sword-cross to indicate to him the urgency of taking up his priestly vocation.

In Turin, he found the Duke of Savoy in no mood to listen to his plea of the absurdity of such accusations, although the duke yielded sufficiently to propose his daughter, the Duchess of Mantua, as a protector for the Visitation. "We shall have the Duchess of Mantua, who is virtue itself, as our protector," he wrote to Mother de Chantal, "but do not say anything about it yet for a reason which I shall explain to you."[186]

He also wished to get his sovereign's permission to accept an invitation to preach the next Lent in Paris. "My hopes remained frustrated and useless," he wrote to des Hayes, "for His Highness will not allow me to leave to preach, using polite words, but nothing more and not favorable to my wishes. . . . If you knew why he refuses, you would admire the industry of the Devil, who opposes our desires."[187] Charles-Emmanuel, he went on to explain, thought that M. Charmoisy, under house arrest for alleged complicity in the beating, and des Hayes were in league to establish de Sales in Paris. No wonder the bishop took the view that princes had quite enough power in ecclesiastical affairs, such as where a bishop might preach.

On April 25, ten days after leaving Annecy, Francis de Sales reached Milan, to be greeted by St. Charles Borromeo's cousin and successor, Cardinal Frederick Borromeo. Never wasting an opportunity, the bishop declined the offer to stay with the cardinal and accepted instead the hospitality of the Barnabite Fathers, for he had discussed with Charles-Emmanuel the

---

[186] Ibid., Vol. 16, 6.
[187] Ibid., 7-8.

possibility of bringing a Barnabite community to Annecy to take charge of the college there, where he himself had once studied. This business he successfully accomplished. Francis de Sales's Mass in the cathedral crypt before the tomb of Saint Charles was celebrated with such fervor and so many outward signs of interior ecstasy that it was said in Milan that the saintly archbishop had himself come to return the visit of the Bishop of Geneva. During one whole night of his short stay, he remained in prayer by the tomb.

Certainly not less spiritually inspiring to Francis de Sales was the feast of the Holy Shroud on May 4, when the famous relic was exposed for veneration, the same relic before which his mother had prayed in Annecy before his conception and birth. He therefore left Milan in time to be in Turin for the feast, passing through Vercelli where rested the remains of Amadeus IX of Savoy,[188] for whose beatification de Sales had pleaded to Rome, asking that the canonization in 1610 of Charles Borromeo, a prince of the Church, might be coupled with the beatification of Amadeus, a prince of the world. Rome was less immediately interested in the Salesian symbol of lay devout life, and Amadeus was not to be beatified until 1667.

In Turin, the Bishop of Geneva was asked to preach before the immense crowd and then to help in the unwinding of the sacred relic. As he did so, his tears and some drops of sweat, due to the excessive heat, fell on to the winding sheet. Those near him expressed their alarm and indignation at this accident, as he wrote to Mother de Chantal: "The cardinal-prince

---

[188] Amadeus of Savoy (1435-1472), a duke of Savoy, led a very austere life, despite suffering from epilepsy.

was angry when my sweat dropped onto the Holy Shroud of
my Savior. I felt able, however, to say to him that our Lord was
not so touchy, and that He had not poured His sweat and
blood but that they should be mingled with ours, that these
might win us the price of eternal salvation. So may our sighs
mingle with His that they may rise like a sweet scent up to the
Eternal Father."[189] Francis de Sales, who wrongly believed
himself — if we are to accept Charles-Auguste — to have
been taken in his mother's womb before the Holy Shroud, always had a special devotion to this relic, which he called the
"shield of this country," and his residence had reproductions
of the Shroud in many of its rooms.

Once again he saw the duke, whom he now found to be
better disposed toward him and his family, but he would do no
more than refer the question of false accusations to the Duke of
Nemours, whose conduct in the matter was to earn from the
gentle de Sales the following rebuke: "Your Highness has heard
accusations against these poor afflicted people and against
my brothers. You have acted rightly in listening to them, so
long as your ears alone listened; but if your heart has listened
to them also, you will forgive me if I tell you, as your humble
and faithful servant, but also as your affectionate although unworthy pastor, that you have offended God and are called
upon to repent. If anyone tells you otherwise, he betrays your
soul."[190]

Charles-Emmanuel was far more ready to consent to his
Bishop of Geneva's leaving Savoy when an invitation came

[189] Ibid., 178.
[190] Ibid., 319.

from Grenoble, the capital of the Dauphiné, to preach the Advent sermons there in 1616. The reason was that the duke cherished hopes of seeing the Dauphiné united one day with Savoy to form a large sovereign state from the Rhone to Turin, for the Dauphiné at that time was virtually the possession of its Governor, Lesdiguières, one of the great French soldiers of his day who had long fought with Henry IV against the League. Lesdiguières, marshal of France and duke, attracted de Sales for a very different reason. As one of the chief Protestant figures of the kingdom, he was the object of the bishop's prayers, and he could become subject to his spiritual ministrations one day. It was likely that Lesdiguières would be curious to hear the sermons of the famous preacher and holy man who had been so successful in his apostolate among the Huguenots.

De Sales, we are told, prepared that course of sermons with special care and rested his arguments and exhortations, as never before, on the Bible, to which the Protestants appealed. He had not been deceived in his hopes, for the great Lesdiguières came to the Grenoble Chapel-Royal where he preached. Better still, Francis de Sales and Lesdiguières conferred together for four hours, although without any immediate results.

After Christmas and the New Year, de Sales returned to Grenoble, which is only sixty miles away from Annecy, for the Lent of 1617, for he felt that in this town, which contained many Protestants, apart from the governor, much spiritual work was to be done. Among those whose souls he touched, two are worth mentioning as showing the wide ambit of a saint's spiritual conquests.

The first was the strange figure of Claude Boucard, who became a Jesuit when Francis was still a student and taught at Clermont not long after Francis had left it. His success was such that it went to his head, and when his superiors called him to Rome for the good of his soul, he ran away from the order and became a Calvinist in Switzerland. Seven years before this Grenoble Lent, Boucard had come to de Sales in Thonon to be reconciled to the Catholic Church, only to be lured back to Calvinism by his ambition. Now at last in Grenoble this unhappy man, after hearing de Sales preaching on the Last Judgment, fell at the bishop's feet to be reconciled once more. One feels that it would take a de Sales to remain so patient with him. But this time he was truly reconciled, to the surprise of the city, and he lived the rest of his days piously in Annecy — and at de Sales's expense.

It was the second person, however, whose conversion most thrilled the people of Grenoble. This was a Mme. Armand, who sounds to us very like many a contemporary woman. The greater part of her day was spent at her dressing table, making her face, which she looked after with such care that it had to be protected even against the steam of the soup. A fashion leader of her time, she was the talk of everyone at the theater and at balls. Out of curiosity about de Sales's reputation as a preacher, she went to hear him. She was completely overcome, entirely changed her manner of life, and settled with her husband in Annecy to be near him.

The end of the story is both edifying and charming. The young daughter of the Armands was dying in Annecy and believed to be dead. A messenger from the bishop had just come, and he was sent back to the bishop's residence to tell him of the tragedy. De Sales hastened to his chapel, where he made a promise to God that if the little girl lived, she would one day wear the habit of the Visitation. When the messenger returned to the Armand home, carrying de Sales's instruction that they must put their trust in the Blessed Virgin, the little girl was alive and said, "The holy papa of Geneva came to bless me and make me well." Not only was the girl, thus raised from the dead, to become a Visitandine — she founded the Visitation of Bordeaux — but so was Mme. Armand, after she and her husband had decided to enter religion. M. Armand became a Jesuit and was to say the Mass at the religious profession of his wife. But even such spiritual conquests at Grenoble left the bishop sadly remarking, as so many preachers have remarked before and since, that "here, like everywhere else, men leave the care of the household and of devotion to the women."

Lesdiguières — although not converted — asked Charles-Emmanuel to allow the bishop to return to Grenoble that same year for a second Advent preaching. "If only God should be pleased to touch, attract, and win him," de Sales wrote in the summer. "It is often the habit of God's Providence to use humble and weak instruments for the great gifts of His goodness. But between you and me, this hope, if anyone heard it, would be construed as coming from someone with excessive ambition. Yet the truth is that I have as little ambition in the matter as hope because of our Savior's words: 'How difficult it is for the rich . . .' "[191]

Indeed it took a further course of preaching, in the Lent of 1618 — in other words, de Sales had done for Grenoble what

[191] Ibid., Vol. 18, 105; Matt. 19:23.

he had never done before: preached two consecutive Advents and Lents — to move Lesdiguières to decide to abjure the Faith he had learned as a young man under a Protestant tutor. Although his change of spiritual outlook had already lost him his influence over the Protestants, political reasons, it seems, delayed his actual return to the Catholic Church until 1621, a few months before the death of Francis de Sales.

A permanent fruit of de Sales's work in Grenoble was the foundation there of the fourth Visitation convent.

∞

Some modern readers may feel that the close relationship between Francis de Sales and Jane Frances de Chantal, while most edifying, must nevertheless have had many tender human compensations, not easily reconcilable with the spiritual denudation to which they ever more ardently aspired as they grew older. A poignant tragedy which occurred during this period and the way in which the two future saints accepted a blow which struck at that which, in the order of nature, was deepest in them both, exemplifies the depths of their common spirit of self-sacrifice and dedication to God's will.

Early in 1617, Bernard de Sales, beloved brother and son-in-law, died of fever, while on a local military operation. His nineteen-year-old wife, Marie-Aimée, beloved daughter and sister-in-law, was with child, expected toward the end of the year. The child was prematurely born four months later, and Marie-Aimée could not live. That same evening, the bishop and Mother de Chantal were at the bedside. Marie-Aimée, completely reconciled to the divine will, begged her mother to admit her before death as a novice into the Visitation. Shortly after, she begged to be professed and take the three vows, changing the white veil for the black. This was allowed — and so she died.

A year earlier, Mother de Chantal, reviewing the nature of her vocation, had sighed, "Oh, how deep the razor has penetrated!" and de Sales had written, "Think no more about friendship, nor about the oneness which God has fashioned between us; your children, your body, your soul, or anything whatsoever. For you have placed all in God's hands."[192]

The oneness which God had fashioned between them united them in this double tragedy, so sudden, so overwhelming. Their resignation could not diminish the tearing at their hearts in this unnatural double, triple loss. "It is true," wrote de Sales in a fragment of a letter to an unknown correspondent, "God has afflicted our house in the death of my brother and sister of Thorens. But His divinely fatherly hand calls me to adore that gentle goodness which has so softly touched us. Did not my brother die a holy death among soldiers, where saints are rare? Did not my sister, that dear wife and my only daughter, die holily with God's servants and in His cloister, which is the school of sanctity? She is buried in the Visitation habit. The doctor said that if angels die, so would they wish to die."[193]

---

[192] *The Works of St. Francis de Sales*, Vol. 17, 218.
[193] Ibid., Vol. 18, 111.

Chapter Thirteen

The Common-Sense Way of Perfection

1612-1616

We have moved rapidly along during the years which brought the Bishop of Geneva to the fifties of his life, for Francis de Sales's very devotion, day in and day out, to burdensome and continuous episcopal duties lent a certain sameness to the days, months, and years. Volumes of letters could indeed have been quarried for the story of these years, and these alone are more interesting than the subject matter of many a biography, not excluding those of saints. But a choice has to be made, and we can most usefully go back a little to take up again the story of his relations with Mother de Chantal and his Visitation sisters and, most interesting of all, the account of his writing the one work of his life which he planned and settled down to work out as a professional author, the *Treatise on the Love of God*.

But "settle down" remains in his case a very relative expression, for settling down usually meant not a month or a week or a day, or even half a day, but the odd hour or half-hour which he could manage to squeeze in among the endless litany of a bishop's day as he saw it.

We have already noted that in 1609, he thought he would have to give up his long-standing plan of writing a real book, in part inspired by the life and death of Pernette Bouthey, the La Roche shopkeeper. Booklets, he thought, would have to take the place of *the* book.

But a writer with something in his mind and heart that he must say is not so easily put off, and much more important, something new had happened. It had happened in the *Galerie*, where Mme. de Chantal and her companions were living the Martha-Mary lives which their founder had offered them. As Bremond has put it, "His [the founder's] ideas would have the force of law, but only so long as God Himself did not intervene. This divine intervention the Visitandines would reveal to their founder, not in telling him what *they* thought, a matter of no importance to him, but simply by living under his eyes. So he watched them living with that intensity of affectionate and piercing observation which was his genius." It was what de Sales saw that urged him on with his work on the love of God.

Mother de Chaugy has revealed to posterity what he saw: "By divine grace, many very soon were experiencing the prayer of quiet, the spiritual sleep of love, very high union with God. Others received extraordinary lights about the divine mysteries in which they found themselves absorbed. A few often experienced raptures and ecstasies so that they were joyfully fixed and held in God, receiving great gifts and graces from the divine bounty."

The love of God was being revealed before his eyes in terms very different from his original conception of treating the subject against the background of the Ten Commandments. His nuns would need guidance which his studies would help furnish, and so would many others, for there was no reason to suppose that the graces bestowed on those who had moved from the *Devout Life* to its logical end must be restricted to a community of nuns who had followed his teaching. The Philotheas, thank God, abounded, and for them he had had no need but to edit what he had so long been teaching. Now he must write for a sterner, higher race which he called the Theotimuses,[194] men as well as women, as he underlined. But it was the Theotimuses of the Visitation — Jane Frances de Chantal above all — whom he had watched and studied as he gently, wisely guided them, himself learning infinitely more from their living realization of his ideal than he had taught them. What had they learned from him and what had they *taught* him?

Mother de Chantal has told us: "I say that I realized that the quasi-universal *attrait* ["attraction"] of the daughters of the Visitation is of a very simple presence of God by an entire abandonment of themselves and by exercising the virtues which leads to this."

As with all the greatest mystics, the final revelation seems almost commonplace. What writer, what poet, can improve the beauty of the rose which displays itself before every passerby, evoking such an infinity of reactions? But in the end, the supreme as much as the vulgarest eulogy of the rose cannot alter, cannot but bow to, that which we see: it cannot describe in itself, save in scientific terms, the rose itself. In much the same way, the nearer man comes to God, the less does language

---

[194] Theotimus is the one whom St. Francis de Sales addresses in his *Treatise on the Love of God*.

matter. Whole worlds lie behind such expressions as the "simple presence of God," "entire abandonment," "mortifying themselves," and "exercising the virtues," and those worlds have to be traveled through; but finding new and grandiloquent terms for them will prove to be as meaningless as simple ones, compared with that which is experienced as the journey proceeds and when the journey is done. It was for Francis de Sales to map those worlds and guide souls across them, if grace beckoned them and courage measured up to the grace; but it was also Francis de Sales who described his own experiences during the journey as experiences "so simple and so delicate that one can say nothing when they are over."

But the simpler and the more indescribable the goal, where the authentic could so easily be confused with the counterfeit of every sort of self-delusion, the more necessary was it to explore the long, true, arduous path toward it. Under de Sales's incomparable direction and in the light of the years of experience of their mother — experience of frustration, desolation, temptation so fully revealed in Francis's guiding letters to her — the early Visitandines seem to have been wafted up toward mystical heights.

Here was the opportunity of cataloging, analyzing, and gathering together in their proper order the elements that went to make up the story of how God's love for us should enable us to grow to supreme indescribable heights in our love for God. It had been de Sales's own life to return, by his love for God, God's love for him, and this amid the infinite distractions of an active episcopal life. He had seen his spiritual daughter subtly growing into his teacher. He foresaw how so many souls, whether in the Visitation, in other forms of religious life, and in the world itself, would need to be guided from the state of Philothea to that of Theotimus. No wonder that from 1612 on, the busy bishop, despite the growing fatigue of a none-too-healthy middle-aged man, treasured the moments when he could return to his study, his library, and his pen, which neatly and elegantly filled the folios with the large, sloping handwriting along lines so straight that they might have been ruled. It was a transfer of a life of love — of God and of his neighbor for God's sake — with all the spiritual history, philosophy, and theology on which such a life would rest — to paper.

De Sales's letters occasionally give us a vivid glimpse of the way it was done.

"Bless God for the leisure He is giving me during these two days for higher prayer. His goodness has truly filled my mind with so much light and my poor heart with such desire to write in our dear book of holy love that I cannot imagine how I shall find words to express what I conceived unless the same God who gave me this experience enables me to bring it to birth."[195]

A year later: "Alas, I assure you, dear sir, that I am so overcome by business, or rather by hindrances, that I can scarcely steal here and there quarters of an hour for these spiritual writings."[196]

And on the next day, in a mood of aridity, or perhaps just the cold of a January day, he wrote to Mother de Chantal: "The fear and laziness of outer man must yield to the conquering

[195] *The Works of St. Francis de Sales*, Vol. 15, 330.
[196] Ibid., Vol. 16, 137.

will of our Master, who wishes that however cold and frozen I may feel, I should write of His holy love"; and a little later: "If you need good paper to write, obtain some from M. Rolland, but ask for it for yourself, because if you ask for it in my name, he will get angry, for I have used too much this last week."[197]

So much progress did he make in that year, 1614, that in November he was writing, "The book of the love of God is finished, but I shall have to transcribe it many times before I can send it away."[198]

His enthusiasm was making him excessively optimistic, for two and a half more years were to elapse before the manuscript could be sent to the printer Rigaud, and even then it would turn out to be, not so much a balanced and finished book, as the work of a born writer who never really had the leisure to write. Moreover, having at last as best he could got it off his chest, he could find no time to write the preface, so that poor Rigaud wrung his hands and threatened to go to Annecy to get it out of him. Finally, the *Treatise on the Love of God* was published at the beginning of August 1616.

This long book, Bremond maintains, although too little read nowadays when so much literature on prayer is available, must be classed "as one of the more beautiful books of religious philosophy which the seventeenth century has given us, the most beautiful perhaps." But even more important, he holds, is its historical significance. "It was indeed a departure whose importance could not be exaggerated when the wisest and most authorized theologian and director of his day thus so publicly

[197] Ibid., 140-141.
[198] Ibid., 261.

and strikingly adhered to the great mystical movement mani-
festing itself on all sides, not without causing anxiety to some
good people. . . . I am afraid that the originality and the boldness of such an undertaking are insufficiently realized."

What may seem to some the book's weakness was really its
strength. It was not a book on contemplative prayer, nor a
book written for one sort of reader only. It was, like the *Devout
Life,* a book for all, and it contained matter suitable for all in
that it reflected the author's own development and experience which, until a few years before it was written, shunned
the highest levels of prayer, hesitating to "leave the great
broad road." The higher mystical parts were therefore organi-
cally linked with "the great broad road" the author had so long
trod. Because of this, it could be safely offered to "men of the
world, men of the court," as well as to privileged religious.
There would be no danger of the reader imagining that the
simple way was also the easy way, the soft way, as was to happen later with the spate of *Moyens Courts.*

In the book, Bremond points out, "one never knows where
the ascetical part, properly so called, stops and where mysti-
cism, properly so called, begins. These elements, elsewhere so
clear-cut, seem with Francis de Sales to be mingled together,
and indeed are. His book has all the seduction of contemplative works without their danger. And so we see spiritual directors, the least suspect of giving rise to illusions, and religious
orders most on their guard, adopting without hesitation this
mystical book."

On the other hand, the book was to have the defects of its
merits. Just because it was not written in a formal scholastic
manner — "I have sought to soften and to avoid difficult

lines" — and because the mystical parts flowered, as it were, so splendidly from the tough, thorny plant, it would be possible later for Quietist leaders to quote Francis de Sales as their authority — and this despite the fact that the future Doctor of the Church, "whose admirable doctrine in mystical theology shines forth," as Pius IX's doctorate decree puts it, has himself never been suspected of any taint of Quietism.[199]

The *Love of God* was not destined to enjoy the "best-seller" success of the *Devout Life,* nor did its author for a moment expect that it would. "I much fear that it will not have the happy success of the former book, since I feel it to be written in a more taut and strong way."[200] He also recognized in his preface that some would think it too long and with too many of the roots showing. "The first four books, and some chapters of the others, could be omitted by souls who are only looking for the practice of holy love." To modern readers, with so much at their disposal written in a more contemporary idiom, this advice is specially relevant.

The book, in fact, considering its nature, proved to be a great success, both in the actual demand for it and in its effects. It had to be re-edited at least five times in the few years which were left to Francis de Sales to live. Through the medium of religious orders, such as the Jesuits, not — one would have thought — especially likely to appreciate a trend toward a wide expansion of the contemplative approach to prayer, it

---

[199] The heresy of Quietism holds that a person can be holy only by attaining complete passivity and annihilation of his will, to the point of caring neither for Heaven nor Hell nor his own salvation.

[200] *The Works of St. Francis de Sales,* Vol. 16, 266.

did its work in taking many the stage further after the *Devout Life;* and St. Vincent de Paul recommended it strongly to his Vincentians not only for aspirants to perfection, but as "a universal remedy for the weak and spur to the lazy." It pointed the right way, which, but for later seventeenth-century misunderstandings and excesses, would have guided Christian piety through the trials of the eighteenth and nineteenth centuries.

Angélique Arnauld, whose friendship with de Sales is described in the next chapter, reported a conversation she had with him about the *Treatise on the Love of God.* She had suggested that the Holy Spirit rather than the Bishop of Geneva had really written the book. He — according to her report — answered, "It is true that I often found myself writing the book as though unconscious of what I was doing, so much so that I took up my pen again without knowing what I had written. Nevertheless the writing followed on logically."

As with the *Introduction to the Devout Life*, the *Treatise on the Love of God* was soon translated into different languages. The first of these translations was into English in 1630, by Fr. Miles Car of Douay. Italy, Spain, Germany, and Poland followed suit. Crashaw[201] was much influenced by the book. "His mind was imbued with the language of *Le Traite de l'Amour de Dieu*," writes A. F. Allison.[202] "He caught its inflection and borrowed its metaphor. In an age when poetic ideas were common currency, he was one of the most derivative of poets, and he did not hesitate to rifle the rich store that St. Francis offered him."

---

[201] Probably Richard Crashaw (1613-1649), English poet. — ED.

[202] *Review of English Studies*, October 1948.

∞

In all the annals of the saints, there is perhaps no more delightful and unforgettable a picture than that of Francis de
Sales sitting of a summer's evening in the orchard of the
Visitation by the lakeside, surrounded by the little company of
eager sisters as they listened to him chatting to them of all that
in the life of a religious community or indeed in any human life
goes to make up a life of the love of God in response to God's
love of us. In these informal talks, wherein surely Francis was
personally happier than in any other of his manifold activities,
he would find endless parables and similitudes from the scene
in which the group was set: the distant heights; the lake at one
moment so smooth, at another ruffled and threatening danger; the flowers at their feet; the clucking hens; the gentle,
meditative dove; the bees and their hives so well ordered with
nature's own division of labor; the distracted and distracting
butterflies; the vine climbing the trellis which gave them
shade; the temptations of the golden apricots and swelling
plums; the heedless child playing at the water's edge and the
anxious eye of his mother watching lest harm come to him.

This scene, enacted again and again, especially in those
early days of the *Galerie*, when Francis forced himself to make
time to be with the infant community — first three, then eight,
then after two years, ten — insistently recalls to the imagination the scene in Galilee where our Lord taught the disciples
as they walked together through the fields, finding in the pastoral scene around Him the images that would strike home
with His followers and posterity ever since. Other founders of
religious orders must have taught their first companions in the
same intimate way, but has anyone come so near to Christ's

own way as the Prince-Bishop of Geneva with his gentle, intimate, spontaneous, simple homely way, so full nevertheless of wisdom and deep human spiritual love, talking of the love of God by the Annecy lakeside?

"Our holy founder," Mother de Chantal was to write much later, "used often to visit us, heard our confessions every fortnight, and gave us little spiritual conferences to teach us true perfection, allotting to each of us the practice of some virtue according to each one's need, so that in this way, that first year went by with much progress made in holy perfection. What consoled them was these frequent conferences given by our holy founder. Even when it rained and snowed, he always came two or three times a week and even oftener." On such occasions, the mother superior's room or the gallery that linked the house with the orchards served as the informal meeting place.

It was by this means that de Sales's experimental mind built many of the ways and customs of the Visitation sisters. A slight difference between two sisters, notified to the founder, would prove the basis for the custom for a sister to ask pardon of another on her knees. Custody of the eyes in the refectory, the breaking up of the day into a succession of short duties: such ways were in the long tradition of community religious life, but here they seemed to be born anew as they were taught by Francis de Sales from the intimacy of those early experiences.

At first rather against the founder's will, a sister began busily to take down his words, for the little community knew, as Mother de Chantal was soon to put it, "that holy soul always goes on sanctifying himself and moving forward toward his wished-for eternity — nor will he stop before he is ranged among those great and ancient Fathers and prelates of the

Church." Every word of his was precious to them, to the communities which would grow from the *Sainte Source,* and to posterity. Happily another of the early sisters had an exceptionally good memory, and she was able to record even a day or two after the founder had been speaking the words he had used. What he had to say to them in his conferences, he assured the sisters, would all be found in the book he was writing, his *Treatise on the Love of God.* Occasionally the conferences had to be suspended so that the poor *conférencier* could find time to continue his *magnum opus.* It is not therefore surprising that the same spirit and teaching expressed itself in his talks and in his more thought-out writings.

In both it is the evangelical spirit that dominates: inner strength, courage, and complete self-sacrifice within a gentle, sensible, fully human framework. Whether in regard to Francis de Sales himself or with the reputation of the Visitation order, so often regarded as the "easy" way out as compared with the Poor Clares or Carmelites, the mistake so often has been made of supposing that it was just a case of easy, soft religion, when it was in fact the crucifying means to the most dedicated form of sanctity: "Be ye perfect."[203]

Dom Mackey, in his long preface to the *Entretiens* ("conferences"),[204] has explained it in the following words: "A pupil of

---

[203] Matt. 5:48.

[204] *The Works of St. Francis de Sales,* Vols. 6, 31. See also Abbot Gasquet and Canon Mackey, trans., *The Spiritual Conferences* (London: Burns and Oates, Ltd., 1906); and St. Francis de Sales, *The Art of Loving God* (Manchester, New Hampshire: Sophia Institute Press, 1998), an abridged edition containing a selection of St. Francis de Sales's conferences.

the Jesuits, the founder of the Visitation knew and appreciated the dexterous strategy of St. Ignatius; but he did not introduce it into his institute. For him, the surest way of perfection was to destroy self-love, not by declaring open war on it, but in despising its attacks. It is less important to overthrow the obstacles to it than humbly and simply to turn away from them — less important to conquer one's enemies in battle formation than to infiltrate through their lines. This is what the saint means when he talks of disliking one's dislikes, contradicting one's contradictions, declining one's inclinations, and averting from one's aversion. In inner worries, his advice is to divert the mind from what troubles and pains it, to 'press nearer our Lord and talk to Him of something else.' Do we feel a dislike for our neighbor; 'the one remedy, as in every sort of temptation, is a simple diversion — that is, not to think of it.' "

This practice of avoiding the romantic, full-blooded spirituality that can lead to scruple and self-regard is carried by Francis de Sales to lengths that can seem at first sight almost contradictory. "We must never cease to make good resolutions, even though we know that as we are, we shall not keep them and even quite clearly see that we shall not be able to put them into practice when the time comes." We should do this because we should also be thinking that "although it is true that I shall not have the strength to do or stand that thing by myself, yet I am even glad of it because it will be God's strength which will do it within me."

On another occasion, surely on some warm spring day when the twittering, cooing, and chirping of birds filled the air around them, he explained how the dove sat on her nest, while her mate with marvelous patience attended to her needs, even bringing a drop of water in its beak to quench her thirst. "How pleasant and profitable the law which tells us to do nothing but for God and to leave to Him all the care that we need. . . . This is so true for the spiritual progress of our souls in perfection. Do you not see how the dove thinks only of her beloved and the wish to please him, never stirring from her eggs? Yet she lacks nothing, while he, rewarding her faith in him, completely looks after her? How happy we should be if we did the same for our beloved Dove, the Holy Spirit. He would take every care of us, and the greater our sense of confidence as we rested in His Providence, the more ample the care He would take of us in all our needs."

Talking to the nuns, he would constantly apply the practice of the love of God to the simplest aspects of their lives, and do it with a rare common sense. Speaking of their relations, the one with the other, he said, "The second reason why we should not show more friendship for one than for another is that we cannot judge as to which are the more perfect and virtuous. Outward appearances are often very deceptive. Often those who seem the more virtuous are not so in the eyes of God, who alone is in a position to recognize virtue. It can well be that a sister who always seems to be committing many imperfections is really more virtuous and more agreeable to God than another with many virtues, natural or acquired. It may be because the first is most courageous even amidst her imperfections and refuses to become worried and anxious, even though so subject to failing; it may be she is growing in humility and in love because of her failings. The apparently perfect one may have less trouble and less to do, needing therefore less courage and humility than the other, so subject to failing."

But common sense was always brought in to avoid mere acting and insincerity in the quest for perfection. "I have said that we must try to love the sisters equally, the same for one as for another — but only insofar as we can. For it is not in our power to have so much feeling of love for those with whom we have less natural sympathy. But this means nothing. The love of charity must be general, and the outward signs of our love must be the same, if we wish to be true servants of God."

This was said just after one of those lighter interpolations which must have so delighted the nuns. "You ask me, my daughter, whether you ought to laugh in choir or in the refectory when something odd happens and the others laugh? I must tell you that in choir there is no need to add to the amusement of others. It is not the place, and such a thing should be sternly corrected. But as for the refectory, if everyone were laughing, I would laugh with them. But if a dozen or so were not laughing, then I should not laugh and would not be worried by the thought that I should be accused of being too serious."

The spirit — and perfection — of Francis de Sales's spirituality is perhaps expressed as well as anywhere else at the beginning of the conference entitled "On Asking Nothing and Refusing Nothing."

"My Mother, I have already answered your request elsewhere. You asked whether one should ask leave to go to Communion and mortify oneself more than the community. I told you that if I were a religious, I would never ask for singularities — neither extra Communions, nor hair shirts, extraordinary fasts, and disciplines, being content to follow the community. If I were strong, I would not eat four times a day, but if I were told to eat four times a day, I would do so and say nothing. If I were weak and told to eat only once a day, I would do so without amusing myself thinking whether I should be so doing or not. I have very few desires, and those I have, I have for God. There is little I want, and if I were to be born again, I would like to have [no desires]. If God came to me to favor me by the sense of His presence, I would go to Him to accept and correspond with His grace. But if He did not wish to come to me, I would stay where I was and not go to Him — I mean that I would not seek out the sense of His presence, but would be perfectly happy with the simple apprehension of faith."

This is a classical expression of the fruits of the teaching of the great mystical tradition of "indifference" (Francis de Sales's word, as it is also St. Ignatius's) or "abandon" or "detachment" (the commoner words today) from self in order that nothing shall obstruct the will's blind clinging to God. As Dom John Chapman put it, "I pray that you may get the grace of not minding whether you feel the love of God or not, or whether you feel commotions or rebellious or not; but that you may feel that to cling to God in absolute detachment is all you care for in this life"; and again: "When we have no comfort in God, but want it more than everything, then we are probably more united to Him than at any other moment. St. John of the Cross's[205] doctrine is austere, but St. Francis de Sales teaches exactly the same in a more cheerful manner."

We began this chapter by suggesting that the scene of so many of the Annecy conferences, in which Francis de Sales's

[205] St. John of the Cross (1542-1591), mystical Doctor and joint founder of the Discalced Carmelites.

teaching reflected in a more homely way the doctrine of his greater works, vividly recalled in manner the teaching of our Lord. We may end it with two quotations — the first from Camus, the second from St. Vincent de Paul — which suggest the same as regards matter.

"Francis had a great idea of the blessing of a simple, common life, nor would he permit the sisters of the Visitation to practice any extraordinary austerities as to fasting, clothing, or sleep. He regulated these matters by the laws which are common to all who seek to lead a Christian life in the world. In this way, he considered that he could best teach his spiritual daughters to follow the example of Jesus Christ, His holy Mother, and His apostles. He always left latitude to their spiritual guides as to any extraordinary mortifications which might be beneficial to individual character or requirements. Not that Francis undervalued bodily austerities, but he thought that they needed to be judiciously used, so as to be the means of controlling the flesh without damaging health. In a word, he preferred following the life of our Lord rather than St. John the Baptist."

Very shortly, as we shall see in the next chapter, Francis de Sales was to meet in Paris the young "Monsieur Vincent," St. Vincent de Paul. For a few months, their contact was to be close. Nearly forty years later, St. Vincent would testify at the Paris beatification process in the following words: "Msgr. De Sales ardently wished to imitate the Son of God. So closely did he model his life on our Lord, as I myself saw, that many a time I asked myself with astonishment how a mere creature could reach so high a degree of perfection, given human frailty. . . . Recalling and meditating on his words, I felt them to be so admirable that I could only see in him the person who most nearly reproduced the Son of God living on earth. I recall how, when in the grip of six years' illness, the thought constantly came to me: 'How great is God's goodness. . . . How good you must be, O Lord, since there is so much of tenderness in your creature, Msgr. Francis de Sales!' "

The founder's most personal and intimate words to his daughters in religion were naturally copied, recopied, and distributed to the thirteen Visitation convents established during his lifetime. After his death, they were considered even more precious, and the question of giving them to the world in a version edited for that purpose was soon considered by Jane Frances de Chantal.

But before anything was done, the manuscripts were stolen by some unknown person and, six years after Francis's death, published without the consent of the order. When she read this edition, Mother de Chantal wrote: "We have had the false *Entretiens* read at table to find out what they are. We have all been much scandalized at discovering that the spirit of our holy founder and the questions asked him have been audaciously distorted. Because of this, I ask you to burn everything or to use the sheets to wrap up parcels or to stick the window panes. It is a book without merit and which should never be read."

Her view was, it seems, rather exaggerated and, apart from a mountain of deforming misprints, she was most irritated by the outside world's being given all the intimacies of the relationship between the founder and his daughters. The result was that in 1629 the *Vrais Entretiens* ("the real conferences") were published for the Visitation, although in fact this true version was only a shortened edition in which the *conférencier's* natural talking manner was improved for the edification of the general public. Soon editions were appearing all over France, and within three years, an English Benedictine nun of Cambrai translated them for a Douay edition. Today, in the Annecy edition of Francis de Sales's works, an incompatible respect both for Mother de Chantal and for textual accuracy has caused the Visitation version to be printed with the differences from the original given at the foot of the pages.

Chapter Fourteen

A Simple Holiness
1618-1619

Francis de Sales, nobleman, Provost, Coadjutor and then Bishop of Geneva, with an international reputation in his lifetime as a writer, a theologian, a preacher, and a saint, managed through fifty years of life to remain personally obscure and truly married to his poor diocese. It was a remarkable achievement, never very satisfactorily explained. Such a person in those days could hardly avoid the high promotions showered on the friend of popes, princes, and the highest clerical dignitaries.

It was not even due to any conscious will on his part absolutely to refuse promotion, however much he would have detested it. Being a bishop at all was bad enough. He was too detached, too conscious that only the will of God counted, to make an issue of the pursuit of humility and obscurity, however much he loved these and sought them. One can only conclude that, supernaturally, this was God's will for him and, on the natural plane, the quality of his desire not to be great in the eyes of the world held the hands of those who would otherwise have made such a fuss of him.

Now that his explanation of a short illness was simply "I imagine it is just because I am old," he was for the first time to be transferred for long periods to the kind of ecclesiastical life in the immediate service of the great people of the world which so far he had successfully avoided. Even so, he was to manage to escape the preferred coadjutorship of the See of Paris with its right of succession, which Louis XIII pressed on him. The change was due, strangely enough, to Charles-Emmanuel of Savoy, who had for so long been one of the causes of his fidelity to his poor wife of a diocese. "As for me, I am about to start at once on the service of the Most Serene Prince Cardinal, according to the will of His Highness," he wrote on October 16, 1618.[206]

Charles-Emmanuel's change of mind was simply due to the fact that he wanted to marry his son Victor-Amadeus, Prince of Piedmont, to Louis XIII's younger sister, Christine of France (the youngest sister was Henriette, to be Queen of England) and had appointed his son Cardinal Maurice of Savoy to be his ambassador in the accomplishment of the plan. What more imposing people to be in the cardinal's suite than the famous Francis de Sales and his friend Antoine Favre?

One may perhaps suitably mention that not long before de Sales was to start on this high mission, he had performed a miracle of the type that must be rare in the annals of the saints and somehow in tune with the ampler days to come. He had been on his way to the Abbey of Sixt in the mountains. The September day had been one of excessive heat, and the company felt obliged to halt and slake their thirst at an inn. Alas,

---

[206] *The Works of St. Francis de Sales*, Vol. 18, 296.

the innkeeper had to confess that his wine had gone sour, so much so that he was going to use it to make cement. "The only thing you can do is to drink water," he said. But the travelers — and one must suppose Francis himself — were not too happy at the prospect even of mountain water. The innkeeper was asked to draw a glass, which Francis tasted. "But it is excellent wine," he said, "do not hesitate to give it to our people." The incredulous innkeeper had to admit that it was "first-class and very strong wine." One naturally thinks of the marriage feast of Cana,[207] but there the need for wine was clear. This was very much a miracle of supererogation[208] — if one may use the theological term — and one wonders why Francis de Sales has not been acclaimed as the patron of wine-makers and sellers.

The ambassadorial journey to Paris started in mid-October 1618, and de Sales, having excused himself for not being able to write a life of his old friend, Juvenal Ancina, was happy to think that he would have the chance of visiting the new Visitations in France. He met Mother de Chantal, who was also on her way to Paris, in Lyons, but missed Moulins, where Mother de Bréchard was superior, because it had been arranged to travel by river from Roanne to Orléans.

After the journey, de Sales wrote from Paris:

> The journey has been excellent. Our most serene lord has been very happy. Everywhere he has been heartily welcomed by great and little people, each one of them blessing God and the Royal House and expressing an ardent wish for the projected marriage.

[207] John 2:1-10.
[208] That is, a good work not morally required.

During the five days of the river journey, I had time to enjoy the company of the most serene cardinal, and we talked together of many things. Twice a day, His Highness read French books so as to get to know the language better and initiate himself into the affairs of this kingdom. Sometimes His Highness rowed and made me row with him. He thought I did not know how to, but he discovered that I was already doctor in the art.

In Orléans, we spent two days resting ourselves. His Highness went to Holy Communion on All Saints' Day, and so by small stages we have reached here, where His Highness was received with unprecedented honors by an unprecedentedly large crowd. The king, the queen, Monsieur the king's brother, Madame *l'aînée* ["the oldest," Christine] and Madame *la cadette* ["the youngest," Henriette] gave a great feast for His Highness, and it was the king himself who, his people tell me, was extraordinary in his happiness.[209]

De Sales took it all, no doubt, with his usual restraint, but Favre, for once, indulged in the sense of worldly glory as he heard the crowds shouting, "There goes the illustrious Bishop of Geneva, the greatest theologian of our days! There goes the President Favre who has written so many books, and who has become another brother of Francis de Sales by the tender affection and incomparable love which unites them." Curious shouts from a crowd — it must be admitted.

The bishop was delighted by the royal family: the king, seventeen years old; his queen, Anne of Austria, the same age; Christine, thirteen; Gaston d'Orléans, ten; and Henriette, nine. "Madame *l'aînée* is accomplished, majesty and goodness

---

[209] *The Works of St. Francis de Sales*, Vol. 18, 307-309.

written on her face. . . . It is impossible to exaggerate the esteem in which our first prince is held: all call him the mirror of princes in his goodness toward the people, his piety, his courage — in a word, all the qualities he needs."[210] He noted, too, "a truly marvelous increase of piety in Paris" and the king's "high idea of the most holy Catholic religion."

The true value of a court, whose "novitiate" he said he was making, although he would never make his "profession" in it, was doubtless brought home to him by the great mansion where he was lodged, the former home of Concini, Louis XIII's favorite, assassinated a year earlier, while his wife, Galigai, was arrested as a sorceress and sent to the stake.

Paris was once again a field for preaching and apostolic work, as well as the place where he could meet the great men of religion. Sixteen years earlier, he had been a nobody of great promise and of a holiness that more and more had impressed all whom he had met. Now he was a great theologian, the author of the *Devout Life*, which everyone had to read, and the *Love of God* — a man of whom everyone had heard as bishop, as reformer, preacher, and saint.

Much was expected, and great crowds — the royal family above all — pressed to hear him in the pulpit. At first, they were disappointed, for, as he wrote to Mother de Chantal, "I preached this morning before the queen and all her fine world. But in truth, I preached with no more care, affection, and pleasure than in my poor little Visitation." And a day or two later after another sermon, he wrote, "I assure you I preached neither better nor in better heart before all those

---

[210] Ibid., 309-310.

princes and princesses than in our poor little Visitation of Nessy."[211]

The truth was that he could preach in only one way: simply, directly, from his heart, and of the love of God — the more so now that his personal spiritual life was being more and more lived on the mystical plane. It did not take him long to conquer congregations who had come to enjoy themselves and who went away moved as never before by the "orator of holy love," as a duchess put it.

Meanwhile the object of the embassy from Piedmont and Savoy was safely accomplished, although not without difficulties having been overcome which threatened to send the visitors home. Favre related that only de Sales kept up their courage and one morning after Mass assured them that God would ensure success.

"You have no further doubts about our marriage, I am sure, for you will have heard that the contract was solemnized nine days ago and that everything went an unprecedented success," he wrote to Mother de Chantal on January 19, 1619. "The ambassadors have visited our dear little Madame with the title 'Your Highness' and congratulations on the marriage: she is the finest princess that one can see. The king has written to the M. le Prince de Piedmont calling him brother-in-law. The King of Spain [one of whose sons was an alternative candidate] has given his agreement. In Piedmont and Savoy, extraordinary celebrations have been held over Christmas. . . . The prince ordered a general tournament to which he challenged all Italy to come and see dying at his feet anyone who

[211] Ibid., 318-320.

would maintain that amaranth is not the most beautiful of all colors, and the princess who favors it not the finest who has ever lived, and her knight, who is also her slave, not the happiest in the world. However, I do not really know much about the challenge — besides it is hardly suitable for reading in the refectory."[212]

Have two other saints in history, founders of a religious order, ever corresponded together quite so frivolously — and charmingly? *Ama et fac quod vis.*[213]

Correspondence with the different Visitations, as one sees, remained, in the midst of court and apostolic life in Paris, a regular task for the bishop, who was helping Mother de Chantal to found a Visitation in Paris, and it is at this period that de Sales sent to Mother de Chastel in Grenoble a remarkable letter warning her about the extraordinary spiritual habits of one of her community, Sister Marie-Constance. One might be tempted to suppose that in the early atmosphere of Visitation, appearances of supernatural extravagances could easily be confounded with the genuine article. If so, de Sales was not to be caught. "I find nothing that makes me think her to be an especially good woman, although we must love and cherish her with all our heart. But as for her visions, revelations, and prophecies, they are for me infinitely suspect as being useless, vain, and unworthy of consideration. On the one hand, they are so frequent that this alone makes them suspect. On the other, they involve manifestations of certain things that God

---

[212] Ibid., 347.

[213] "Love and do what you will," St. Augustine, *In Epistolam Joannis ad Parthos*, tractus 7, sect. 8.

very rarely reveals: assurance of eternal salvation, confirmation in grace, the degree of sanctity of different persons, and a hundred other useless things."[214]

The writer went on to tell the story of Nicole Tavernier, who among other marvels multiplied bread for the poor and caused a host to be carried by an angel. She took refuge with Barbe Acarie, who soon realized that although Nicole was innocent herself, she was, in fact, possessed by the Devil. Happily, as it turned out, this was far from true of Sister Marie-Constance who, pruned of her early extravagances, lived to become a most saintly person.

Alas, Barbe Acarie, who had brought Carmel to France and had become a Carmelite herself after her husband's death, was no more. She had died a few weeks before de Sales had arrived in Paris. Often he visited her tomb. But other old friends were there to renew the friendships made sixteen years earlier.

The great friend of Mme. Acarie, Pierre de Bérulle, the founder of the French Oratory and mystical writer of the Sulpician school, was one of the first of his old friends whom de Sales met again in Paris. De Sales always seems to have had a special affection for the idea of secular priests living together in a community according to a rule; he had hoped to solve the problems of the Sainte Maison in Thonon through the Oratorians, and he himself nursed the hope that when, through age or sickness, he could retire from the bishopric, he might live with an Oratorian community.

Shortly before his death, Francis de Sales was to bless Jean-Jacques, the wayward and troublesome son of Mme.

---

[214] Ibid., 323-327.

Olier, and prophesy that the boy would grow up to be a great servant of the Church. He even promised to take the boy with him into his retirement and teach him theology with his nephew Charles-Auguste. Jean-Jacques Olier, as the founder of the Sulpicians, would one day say that Francis de Sales had been called by God to carry through within the Church the work of St. Ignatius, St. Teresa, and St. Charles Borromeo — St. Ignatius in extirpating heresy; St. Teresa in renewing religious life in the Visitation; and St. Charles in reforming the clergy.

Of new friends made, the most important was "Monsieur Vincent," introduced to him by Bérulle. Of their relationship we know little, but the two men had much in common. It was not the gentleman and prince-prelate whom Monsieur Vincent admired, but the man who had been brought up in the rough Savoy country, where rank counted for little — the man who was neighbor to the humble Gascon, the slave of the Barbary pirates, the dedicated servant of the poor of Paris.

Both of them had found in the combination of apostolic and inner mystical life the same priestly path of imitation of Christ. It is false, as we have seen, to suppose that de Sales's Visitation had anything in common with Monsieur Vincent's Sisters of Charity, except the accident that the early Visitation nuns served the poor in ordinary clothes, as did the Sisters of Charity, but St. Vincent was to have no more enthusiastic helpers in his work in hospitals and among the poor than some of the Philotheas of Paris who were under Francis de Sales's spiritual direction. The aging bishop and the young priest at the height of his powers must have had much to talk about. The practical outcome was that de Sales made Monsieur Vincent the religious superior and chaplain of the Paris Visitation. Monsieur Vincent was to hold this charge until his death in 1660.

But by far the most unexpected and curious friendship Francis de Sales was to make in this his last visit to Paris was no other than that of Mother Angélique Arnauld, of Port Royal des Champs and Maubuisson, the future Jansenist rebel against everything, spiritual and ecclesiastical, for which the Bishop of Geneva had spent his life. It is difficult from all that we know of Angélique Arnauld to understand how this, sometimes called his last spiritual friendship, could have been established.

Angélique had been thrust against her will into religious life as a small child, and her influential father had been able, although not without falsifying the girl's age, to make her abbess of the spiritually and materially decayed Cistercian Abbey of Port Royal at the age of eleven. For some years, her position and her duties were little more than the game of a child — a stubborn, willful child thwarted of natural affections.

Tired of what she came to realize to be an inhuman prospect of living her years in the prison of even a much relaxed monastery, she planned to run away, when suddenly in her deep depression she felt herself converted to an ascetical ideal by hearing a sermon on the humiliation of Christ in becoming man preached by a young Cistercian monk who, as it happened, afterward was to apostatize. Her whole outlook changed, and she dedicated herself and her community — much to their surprise and annoyance — to a life of extreme, harsh, and even repulsive austerity. All the bitterness accumulated in her unnatural childhood came to express itself in this passion for denudation and severity. She owed much to the help of Father Archange of Pembroke, whom the young de Sales had probably met in Paris. Not very long before this reformer abbess was to meet Francis de Sales, she had gone to the Abbey of Maubuisson, near Pontoise, to reform and cleanse it after the years during which it had been under the rule of Angélique d'Estrées, the sister of Henry IV's famous mistress, Gabrielle d'Estrées. Angélique d'Estrées, although an abbess, was indeed no better than her sister, for she had had twelve children by twelve different men.

Angélique Arnauld, although herself living a life of extreme penance and poverty, both because these seemed to express her nature and in the hope of shaming the Maubuisson nuns, could make little real impression on so extraordinary a community. So she began to interest herself in new religious orders that she felt to be more suited to her spiritual ideals. The first was the Carmelites in nearby Pontoise, where the famous Mme. Acarie had just died, and the second, that new order which had been founded by the Bishop of Geneva about whom everyone was talking.

The two, seemingly so ill-consorted spirits — the first, all fierceness and self-centered; the other, all gentleness and self-detached — met for the first time on April 5, 1619. Angélique had planned the meeting, getting the father of a girl in her care who knew de Sales to persuade him to come to Maubuisson to confirm the girl. Francis de Sales, there is no doubt, was at once spiritually attracted by this twenty-seven-year old ascetical reformer of so much of the religious laxity that he hated. Within three weeks, he was writing to her and telling her that he could not but call her "my very dear daughter," but his spiritual advice showed that he had at once discerned her needs. "The child will not perish if he rests in the arms of a Father who is all-powerful. If our God does not grant us every day what we ask, it is because He wants to hold us near Him. . . . He is gracious and kindly natured, for the moment we are ready to be humble according to His will, He suits Himself to ours."[215]

Such advice seemed to drive straight against Angélique's self-reliance and fear. A few weeks later, he was telling her, "Do not burden yourself too much with vigils and austerities (believe me, my most dear daughter, I know what I am talking about in this). Proceed instead to the Port Royal of the religious life by the royal road of the love of God and of one's neighbor, of humility and kindliness."[216]

In another letter, de Sales, almost foreseeing the future Jansenist fear of frequent Communion, tells her to "go to Communion boldly in peace, with all humility, so as to correspond with the Spouse who, to unite Himself with us, has made Himself nothing and courteously abased Himself."[217]

We do not know how often de Sales managed to get to Maubuisson, but it is thought that because of his frequent visits to the Carmelites of nearby Pontoise, he must have sometimes called at Maubuisson. Angélique herself has described one visit in July. "He was ill for nine days staying here, but never ceased to work in helping souls. [He gave Angélique herself a retreat.] Noting that the high altar had not been consecrated, he said to me, 'I must not leave without doing you

[215] Ibid., 369.

[216] Ibid., 390.

[217] Ibid., 400.

some small service; would you like me to consecrate the altar?'
Ill as he was, he carried out that long ceremony with an incredible devotion. After it, he preached for an hour and a half,
explaining all the ceremonies of the consecration."

Under the direction of Francis de Sales — which lasted by
correspondence until shortly before his death — Angélique
seemed to blossom and change, losing her scruples and intro-
version to share something of her director's humility and confidence and his supreme trust in the love and will of God. She
grew also in friendship with Mother de Chantal, who remained in her poor Paris Visitation after Francis had returned
home.

More and more, Angélique grew desirous of entering the
Visitation, but Francis de Sales strongly discouraged her, os-
tensibly at least because he did not believe in changes of vocation and could appreciate how much she had done and how
much more she could do for the reform of her own Cistercian
order. As he wrote to a Jesuit, "I would never wish to turn away
the most excellent creature of the world from her right vocation, even if she were to become a canonized saint of the Visitation. . . . The inconstancy of women is to be feared . . . and
this one's constancy is something that one can reasonably
expect."[218]

Nevertheless Angélique appealed to Rome for permission;
but permission was not given. One cannot help feeling that
only Francis de Sales could have added humanity to the fierce,
dark, and proud spirituality of Angélique Arnauld and that
with Mother de Chantal in the Visitation, she would have

[218] Ibid., Vol. 20, 183-185.

found happiness as well as crucifixion in her earthly pilgrimage. "How human you still are," she said forty years later to a nun in tears by her deathbed. Francis and Jane Frances de Chantal would have inspired her to say, "Thank God, how very human I still am."

After Francis de Sales's death, Mother de Chantal would keep up relations with Angélique Arnauld and derive help from her in the days of continuing desolation which proved to be the lot of the saint who had obeyed her spiritual father's injunction to sacrifice everything — absolutely everything.

Francis de Sales, still attached to the suite of the Prince of Piedmont and his wife, Christine of France, had remained in Paris after the court's departure to Tours. He had to catch up with it and accompany the newly wedded couple back to Savoy. On September 11, 1619, after ten months in the capital, he wrote to Angélique, "At last I start tomorrow morning, my most dear daughter, for such is the will of Him 'in whom we live and move and have our being.'[219] . . . My dear daughter, I bid you goodbye and implore you in your heart to be sure that mine will never be separated from yours. That would be impossible, for what God has joined cannot be separated.[220] . . . I am off in something of a hurry, for the queen [Marie de' Medici] wishes that I should pay my respects to her before my return home."[221]

From Tours, where he had to pay court to the royal family, he wrote to Angélique telling her that "among these grandeurs

[219] Acts 17:28.

[220] Matt. 19:6; Mark 10:9.

[221] *The Works of St. Francis de Sales*, Vol. 19, 14-17.

of the court (wherein I must admit to you that I am being made much of), nothing consoles me more than our ecclesiastical state. O God, what a difference between a swarm of bees who work together to fill a hive with honey and a mass of wasps who greedily feed on a dead body — so I must put it to speak honestly."[222]

To Mother de Chantal he was to send a description of his stay: "There I saw the queen mother, paying my respects when I arrived and when I left. . . . I came to know many prelates and especially the Bishop of Luçon, who vowed all friendship for me and told me that he would come to my side and busy himself with nothing but God and the salvation of souls." The Bishop of Luçon was, of course, the great Richelieu, then thirty-four years old, ambitious but still uncertain of his political future. De Sales evidently caught the young prelate, who had begun his episcopal life with genuine religious zeal, in a somewhat depressed mood. It is ironic that when two men, great in such opposite ways, met, the one should have promised the other almost exactly the opposite of what his future greatness should realize. Few churchmen of repute disregarded more completely than Richelieu de Sales's warnings about the corruption of the ideals which too often govern the business of kings and great political figures.

De Sales's letter went on: "Finally I saw the Cardinal de Retz, who first invited me to remain in France with a proposition which, in the way it was put, came nearer to appealing to me than any that have been so far made to me. I discussed it with M. de Bérulle and my perfect friend, M. des Hayes, and

[222] Ibid., 21-22.

when the latter gets back to Paris, you may hear all about it from him. . . . The question is not yet ripe and will not be for some time. Meanwhile we shall wait to see what God ordains. . . . If God does not show that He wills it, I shall never wish for it myself nor do anything about it but to consent to God's Providence as I see it in my service to Him."[223]

All this referred to Cardinal de Retz's proposal that de Sales should be his coadjutor in the See of Paris with the right of succession. Early in the next year, de Sales was to refer again to the proposal in a further letter to Mother de Chantal: "Certainly I am very much obliged to that great cardinal for the high regard he has of me, seeing how undeserving I am of the least of his thoughts in my regard. But I made it clear enough to him in Tours that I would not wish to be unmarried [to his own diocese] except to remain afterward unmarried [in other words, to retire]. That I should myself choose to take on the wife of another just to oblige — that, I think, would be impossible for me."[224]

Strangely enough, it was stated in one of the depositions for de Sales's beatification that the only reason he hesitated to give a formal refusal to accept the flattering offer was that it might give him an opportunity of traveling to England and attempting the conversion of James I. The apostle of the Chablais had a longing to be an apostle in heretical England. Charles-Auguste wrote, "That good prelate used to deplore the misery of so great a kingdom, and often confessed that he felt a strong desire for its affection and salvation. Whenever

---

[223] Ibid., 37-40.
[224] Ibid., 152.

the conversation turned on such great personages and prelates as St. Anselm, St. Thomas, St. Edward, and others, he would contrast those days with the miserable state of heresy and schism, expressing his deep sorrow and his ardent wishes for the country's conversion." He knew that James I was an admirer of his books, and he wanted to meet him.

Soon he would be writing with deep sorrow to his brother Jean-François about an unfortunate member of his own chapter, the nephew of Bishop Granier, his predecessor, who had left the Catholic Church and joined the Protestants in England. "Now he is separated from the rest of the world by the sea," he said of him, "as well as by schism and error. God nevertheless will derive His glory from the sin. I have a special leaning for that great island and its king, never tiring of praying to the divine majesty for its conversion, feeling very confident that my prayer will be granted, since so many share it with me. For the future, I shall pray even harder, I think, remembering that man's soul. . . . Assure him that not all the seas of England will ever quench the fire of my love, so long as there be any hope of his return to the Church."[225]

Exhausted as Francis de Sales was by the endless social life and entertainment of the court and the ceremonial of the journey of prince and princess to Turin, he at least had the great consolation of visiting the convents of the Visitation on his way home: the one in Bourges, where he met Archbishop Frémyot, Jane Frances's brother — and would not allow the sisters to be distracted by seeing the Princess Christine — and the one in the attractive old town of Moulins. Near the end of

[225] Ibid., 383.

his journey, Christine laid the foundation stone of a Visitation convent in Chambéry. Such an event gave him far more happiness than the sudden notion which Christine had of being as grand as her mother, Marie de' Medici, in being spiritually served by her own "Grand Chaplain." Naturally, it would have to be the Bishop of Geneva whom she had grown to love and trust during the past months.

"Madame, Her Highness and M. le Prince want me to be grand chaplain to her," he wrote to Mother de Chantal. "You will have no difficulty in believing that neither directly nor indirectly have I coveted such a post. Certainly not, my very dear Mother, for I feel no sort of ambition save to be able to employ the rest of my days for the service and honor of our Lord. No indeed, I have an utter contempt for the court, since more and more do I abhor the ruling pleasures of the world, the world itself, its spirit, its maxims, its silliness."[226] The honor, however, could not be refused without discourtesy. But he was determined to get back to what he called his nest and asked his brother who accompanied the party to Turin to undertake the duties of the office in his place. Nor would he accept the emoluments of the office. His brother, he said, "must grow and I must diminish."[227]

How happy he must have felt after living for so long with the great world to find himself once again with the sisters of the Visitation, at the moment deprived of their mother, and, typically, to choose for his conference with them the subject of simplicity.

[226] Ibid., 49-50.
[227] Cf. John 3:30.

"This is a purely Christian virtue," he told them as they eagerly sat around him, listening to words they would soon hear no more, "for the pagans, even those who have spoken so well of other virtues — like Plato and Aristotle — never knew anything about it, any more than they knew about humility. Of magnificence, of liberality, of prudence, of constancy, they have written well — but of simplicity and humility, not a word. It needed our Lord Himself to come down from Heaven to make these virtues known to men. Had He not come, they would never have known them."

He ended his conference with the words: "We must have an entirely simple confidence which will enable us to rest peacefully within the arms of our Father and of our Mother, being assured, as we must be, that our Lady, as our dearest Mother, will always protect us with her motherly care, since we are united together in her honor and for the glory of her beloved Son, who is our . . . most sweet Savior."[228]

Such was his own real climate, his real happiness, and one he had never more deserved than after the worldly glory of his days in Paris and his journey home when, even in the piety of the courts of France and Savoy at that date, he could doubtless find only too little of the Christian virtue of simplicity.

---

[228] *The Works of St. Francis de Sales*, Vol. 6, 202-222. See also *The Spiritual Conferences* (London: Burns and Oates, Ltd., 1906), 213-214, 233; and St. Francis de Sales, *The Art of Loving God* (Manchester, New Hampshire: Sophia Institute Press, 1998), 106-107, 111.

Chapter Fifteen

Abandonment to God

1620-1622

Francis de Sales returned to Annecy that winter of 1619 to 1620 a prematurely aging and sick man. He had never been physically strong, and he would soon begin to show ever graver signs of the disease which, given the medical ignorance of the times, would bring him to the grave within a few years. Arteriosclerosis, high blood pressure, an overtaxed heart, and consequent dropsy, with a steady increase in his already considerable weight — all these were symptoms which at least demanded early retirement from the immense burden of the episcopate and public life. He himself knew it, and he longed to live in reclusion in a quiet place, where he could pray and write in peace.

His writing plans included a *Treatise on the Love of Our Neighbor* and a study of the life of Christ, as well as more directly theological works. Although he well realized that his writing plans were highly optimistic — "to keep one's mind in tune, one must plan more than one can undertake, as though one still had many years to live, while being ready to do no more than would be possible if one were to die the next day" — he does not seem, to go by his letters, to have envisaged dying as soon, in fact, as he did. Human judgment cannot but regret that de Sales's last years were not to be spent in writing for posterity. Instead they were to be a martyrdom of public duty.

However, he was relieved and consoled when his brother Jean-François was nominated by the Duke of Savoy as his coadjutor bishop, an appointment that resulted from his own inability to accept Princess Christine's request that he should be her grand chaplain. Jean-François accepted instead, as nothing less grand than a bishop would serve for the job.

"You will believe me," he wrote to Mother de Chantal, "when I tell you quite simply that the nomination of my brother to the coadjutorship is so clearly the work of God that I have never written a single word about it and neither begged nor procured any recommendation."[229] Better still, "it gives me some hope of retiring from pressure of work. This is worth a good deal more than any cardinal's hat."[230]

Jean-François was to be consecrated in Turin and to return in 1621 to Annecy to share with the bishop in the ceremonial and pastoral work of the diocese. Francis had great faith in his brother bishop and, with his usual humility, saw in him the man to repair his own mistakes. Their temperaments, however, were very different, Jean-François being inclined to an external severity and rigidity greatly in contrast with the ways, softened yet further by age and experience, of the now almost legendary Francis. Consequently, they had their little troubles,

[229] *The Works of St. Francis de Sales*, Vol. 19, 172.
[230] Ibid., 194.

examples of which have been handed down to posterity in delightful stories.

On one occasion, on the feast of St. Anthony, Francis lingered at his devotions to that popular saint. "You are like those good women who rush to light a candle to St. Anthony when they have lost their distaff," Jean-François said to him irritably when he returned. Francis explained to his brother that he was very devoted to St. Anthony, on whose behalf God had effected many miracles. "Why not let us both pray together to St. Anthony to ask him to find the things we lose every day: you, Christian simplicity; I, humility."

On another occasion, while the two bishops were dining together, Jean-François was surprised at his brother's silence. "What were you thinking about?" he suddenly asked. "Well," replied Francis, "if you want to know, I will tell you. I was thinking that there was one lucky woman in the world." Jean-François innocently asked whom he had in mind and suggested some names. "I'm afraid you don't understand," Francis said, smiling. "The lucky woman I am thinking of is the one you did not marry."

Although Francis was not to let up in the slightest in his normally overburdened pastoral work in his diocese, there is a certain feeling of peace and relative leisure in his correspondence during these months, even though he confessed in a letter that he had no idea what might happen to him and where he might go, "being no more certain of what I shall do as of when I shall die, so much am I now committed to others."[231] A journey to Rome; preaching in Chambéry: such possibilities

---

[231] Ibid., 192.

are mentioned in his letters, but in fact he remained where he was, taking special pleasure in helping to educate his young nephew Charles-Auguste, son of his brother Louis, and destined to be his first real biographer.

De Sales's correspondence continued to be very heavy, with Mother de Chantal in Paris and the many superiors of the Visitation convents now dotted over France. "I am reviewing the rules, the constitutions, and the formularies," he wrote to Mother Rosset in Bourges. "In them I found much that was wanting, both in the printing and the writing, and I am correcting it all. I shall express those blessed vows so clearly that everyone will be satisfied and remain in peace."[232]

He maintained the keenest interest in the relationship between Mother de Chantal and Mother Angélique Arnauld, and we have many letters to both of them. Referring to Angélique in a letter to Mother de Chantal, he wrote, "I am so happy that you find her so amiable. She is very much to my own taste despite the things she says against herself — true things, I know, but balanced by such good will and frankness that it does not matter, especially as she herself has no love for these faults and one day they will vanish before the grace of God. Believe me, my dear Mother, I should like to support her wish to live in greater retirement with us, and I agree with your idea that she might. She would gain much from this. But how accomplish it? The more I think about it, the less possibility I see. . . . God knows things we do not know. If it is expedient for His glory, He will make possible what seems impossible to us."[233]

[232] Ibid., 170.
[233] Ibid., 337.

A visit from Camus, the Bishop of Belley, and a return visit to Belley were agreeable distractions in the summer heat which, by now, was very difficult for him to bear. "For eight days our most friendly Msgr. de Belley has been with us. He has given us some marvelously devout exhortations and especially on the feast of the Visitation. I have found it a very great consolation seeing him and savoring the true goodness of his spirit."[234]

We can imagine the two bishops in the cool of the summer evening, chatting together about their lives and work, as they were rowed by a boatman along the lakeside. It was at such a time, no doubt, that the older man would gently pull the leg of the always excited, gesticulating younger one, his head crammed with ideas, hopes, fears, and scruples about his worthiness as bishop and whether he ought to give up the charge laid on him at too young an age and which he managed in so mediocre a way as compared with his saintly companion.

"You preached magnificently at the convent this morning," Francis would say. "Everyone is crying out *mirabilia* ["wonderful"] about it. I know only one person who was not satisfied." And Belley begged again and again for the name of his critic. At last, Francis smiled and said, "You are looking at him." Crestfallen, Belley said, "I would rather have had your praise than that of all the rest put together." And Francis would explain that his friend had been flattering his congregation and making them feel good with windy rhetoric and sounding brass. "You should never go up into the pulpit without a definite purpose to strengthen some special corner of the walls of Jerusalem, to inculcate some special virtue or to expose some

[234] Ibid., 267-268.

particular vice, for the end of all preaching is to uproot sin and guide men to the good life. It is always safer to keep your hearer humble than to excite him to climb slippery paths beyond his experience."

And he would pull his leg gently again: "I hear that you have taken a fancy to imitating the Bishop of Geneva in the pulpit." "Is he a bad example? Don't you think he preaches much better than I do?" Belley answered. And Francis, laughing outright, said, "You are only spoiling the Bishop of Belley and not succeeding in copying the Bishop of Geneva. But, joking apart, you are spoiling yourself by going against all the rules of nature and art. I am the kind of person who always has to drive himself on, but the more I try, the slower I go. I cannot find words, and I cannot utter them when I do. I am heavier than lead. I toil and sweat and make no headway, while you go forward under full sail. You fly, and I crawl and drag along like a tortoise; you have more fire in the tip of your finger than I in my whole body, and now they tell me that you are weighing each word and dragging out your sentences. No wonder you bore your listeners to death!"

And Belley would recall the time when he had consulted Francis about a scruple he had had in giving soldiers in the field permission to eat eggs and cheese in Lent. "Why do you want to consult me about what soldiers may eat in Lent, as though any serious need did not prevail over regulations? God grant that these good fellows may never do anything worse than eat eggs or beef, cheese or cows. We would not hear so many complaints if that were the case."

Then they might chat about the many journeys they had had to make by mountain paths in bitter cold or excessive heat and the curious adventures they had had. "I am very fond of innkeepers," Francis would say, "for few men have a better chance of serving God and their neighbor and showing kindness"; and he told the story of how a traveler cheated by an innkeeper angrily left the inn to cross the road and enter another. On the road was a crucifix, and the traveler, entering the second inn, drew the innkeeper's attention to it and said, "I see that as of old, our Lord was placed between two thieves."[235] The poor innkeeper, who had done no harm, protested. "Oh well," conceded the traveler, "you shall be the good thief."

Francis de Sales's interest in monastic life and its reform was maintained until the end of his life. The founder of the Visitation was, before he died, to institute two more orders. The first was the Hermits of Mont Voiron. A quarter of a century earlier, the apostle of the Chablais had renewed the pilgrimage to that sanctuary of our Lady on this mountain range between Annecy and Thonon, and barely escaped with his life when he was attacked by Calvinist toughs determined not to see the shrine re-erected. Since those days, the Black Virgin had been restored and pilgrimages were popular among the Catholics of the Chablais. To serve the pilgrims, a few men had devoted themselves to living eremitical lives without any rule. Francis thought they should have a rule, the more so in that his nephew Charles-Auguste felt a vocation to join the little community.

With hermits, de Sales took strict views: many fasts, no meat, sleeping on palliasses, and rising in the middle of the night. The only relaxation from the strictest rule was a daily

---

[235] Mark 15:27; Luke 23:33.

recreation of three-quarters of an hour. Ever practical, he added a regulation not always observed in pilgrimage centers even now. There must be no eating or drinking on the part of the pilgrims within two hundred feet of the shrine. The Hermits lasted as a religious institution into the second half of the eighteenth century. Charles-Auguste did not join. He was, in fact, to become the third de Sales Bishop of Geneva.

Despite his age and health, the bishop was forced once again to face in winter the arduous journey to the Abbey of Sixt, more than 2,500 feet up in the Faucigny mountains. The commendatory abbot had rebelled against the reform and the bishop. The arguments which could be put before the abbot were unanswerable and therefore hotly answered. It needed the goodness of de Sales in person to break down resistance and restore peace, piety, and order. But only a few weeks later, he had to return to help the abbot to die in peace and resignation.

Another and tougher problem faced the bishop in the case of the ancient convent of Bernardines of Sainte-Catherine, just south of Annecy. Like Port Royal, these nuns, daughters of the nobility, had lived under a very relaxed rule for many years. De Sales would long ago have changed all this, but the convent was exempt from the bishop's jurisdiction. There was nothing for it but to persuade the inmates to live in a manner more in accordance with their vocation. He could hope at least to make an impression on the younger nuns, but knew that there was little hope with the older ones, grown too used to their comfort and their visitors and their social gossip. Happily, one of the younger nuns, Bernarde de Vignod, although notorious for her worldly ways and love of fine clothes and jewelry, was deeply shocked to hear of a grave scandal affecting a relation of hers in another convent. This was enough to bring her to her religious senses and make up her mind to change her way of life. Four other younger members of the community took the lead from her — and from the delighted bishop. The only solution was to withdraw the five young nuns from Sainte-Catherine and set them up in a new reformed convent at Rumilly which he agreed to call the convent of Divine Providence, although the name of Reformed Bernardines continued to be used by the people.

To one of the nuns, still hesitating about joining the reform, he was to write shortly before his death: "If, like you, I hoped for a reform, I could not wish the hour to join it to be too early. Since you have the authority of your superiors, you have no excuse for delay in acting. So, start as soon as possible for Rumilly, and pay my respects on your arrival to my dear daughters already there."[236] This Cistercian reform became virtually a new order, and from Rumilly a number of other Bernardine convents were founded.

But by far the most touching incident of this period was Francis de Sales's hopeless plan for retirement. Now that the coadjutor was taking on more of the pastoral load, he felt that he could make his preparations. He, too, would become a hermit, and the spot he had chosen was the ancient hermitage of Saint-Germain up the hill above the Benedictine monastery of Talloires, halfway down the Lake of Annecy on the eastern side. For a son of Savoy, he had chosen well, for below the hermitage lay the lake at nearly its narrowest point, with the wooded slope of the Semnoz rising to a point opposite,

---

[236] *The Works of St. Francis de Sales*, Vol. 20, 365-366.

and, reflected in the lake, Annecy itself could be seen to the northwest.

On an autumn day of 1621, he and his brother made their way up from Talloires to consecrate a new altar, to open the tomb of Saint-Germain and venerate his bones, and to inspect the cells which he had had made for his retirement there with the company only of his nephew Charles-Auguste, whom he would teach. "How beautiful this place is," he exclaimed, as he turned around to look at the lake. "Here great and beautiful thoughts will come thick and fast like the snow which falls in winter. When we settle down here, we shall serve God with the breviary, the rosary, and the pen. Here I shall have the leisure to write out, for God's glory and the instruction of souls, all that has been turning around in my mind for thirty years — all that I have made use of in my sermons, instructions, and personal meditations. I have plenty of notes, and I hope that God will inspire me."

If we may so put it, this was Francis de Sales's one self-regarding moment in his life. And how he had deserved that moment! Tired, ill, ceaselessly working for others — the vision of peace, instead of war, for God's sake, of contemplation instead of incessant activity, had come to him. How God must have been tempted to answer this prayer and say at last, "Well done, good and faithful servant."[237]

But Francis de Sales had taught others the sublimest spiritual ideal of utter detachment from self-regard, of utter abandon, and he had never taught anyone anything that he had not first done himself. Across France, his daughters, under

[237] Matt. 25:21.

Mother de Chantal's inspiration, were being offered no respite. Their self-sacrifice in prayer, penance, and poverty was until death. Could he expect anything else? Could he expect to finish in the comfort of contemplation? He knew himself it was a mirage. He had already written in a letter: "Here is another worry. I do not know if His Highness will want me to reside for some months with Madame Christine while my brother takes my place here. In a word, unless God takes a hand, half my freedom is caught up with that court — that court in which at no time in my life have I wished to live, nor in any other court, my soul being wholly antipathetic to those ways. I hope, however, that one day during this mortal life I may sing, 'Thou hast broken the chains that bound me: I will sacrifice in Thy honor.' "

But the first call was not to come from a temporal prince, but from the Pope. And hardly had the Pope's commission been fulfilled than earthly princes again required his presence, and he would never again see Annecy, Talloires, and the hermitage of Saint-Germain. His last days were to be an exile and a living martyrdom. God wanted him to drink to the last drop the chalice which he had always held up for himself and offered to others.

In May 1622, Francis de Sales received the order from the Pope, Gregory XV, who had been elected fifteen months earlier, to preside over the chapter-general of the Feuillants (reformed Cistercians) in Pinerole, near Turin. It was an important commission because of the belief that the coming election of a superior-general of the order might lead to an unedifying and unsettling division of votes as between a Frenchman and an Italian. The Pope evidently believed that the

Savoisien Bishop of Geneva, with his great reputation for sanctity and learning, was the best person to ensure a happy outcome. Unfortunately, the Pope or his advisers had not informed themselves of the rapidly deteriorating state of the bishop's health and the likely effect on him of a journey on horseback across the Alps in the heat of summer. He was indeed feeling far from well, confessing to a friend one day, as he put his hand on his heart, that he wondered whether he had long to live.

The mission to Pinerole meant further attendance on the duke and his family in nearby Turin, and he had to excuse himself from going to court before presiding over the chapter.

The journey, during which the bishop's companions had to watch lest he fall from his horse through weakness, turned out to be unnecessary. There was no special difficulty about the election of the best superior-general. Dom Jean de Saint-François was virtually unanimously elected, and the bishop's twenty-day stay no doubt greatly helped the new general to write his *Vie du bienheureux Messire François de Sales*, two years after the latter's death. In that life, Dom Jean told of the impression which de Sales made on the community because of his "first-class mind, able to examine the gravest matters, duly weigh and wisely resolve them, and his incomparable goodness of soul with his deep learning and abundance of supernatural enlightenment."

From Turin, after the commission had been accomplished, de Sales wrote to Cardinal Caffarelli-Borghese: "As for the chapter-general which has been held, I can truthfully say that never have I seen a more modest and more religious assembly, nor one in which peace shone with greater brightness. They elected a general gifted with eminent learning, rare prudence, and singular piety. Besides, he was elected with a virtual unanimity of votes. I feel sure that your illustrious lordship will greatly enjoy seeing him and view him with favor when he journeys to Rome in the autumn, for he is a person of great merit who has served and will continue to serve Holy Church by his learned writings, and, besides, seeing that he has been created general of your illustrious excellency's monastery, he greatly looks forward to your protection."[238]

The meetings of the chapter-general had covered, besides the election of the general, a great many matters concerning the organization of the order and its work, with liturgical questions, and with the election of lesser offices. The bishop had closely concerned himself with all this business, as well as preaching, hearing confessions, and doing other pastoral work in the town. No wonder he collapsed on two occasions, once having to retire from the business meeting and the second time in the crowded church when those around him thought he would never recover.

Once this ecclesiastical business was finished, Francis de Sales had no choice but to fulfill his obligations to the court in Turin and to Princess Christine whose grand chaplain he still was. He was naturally offered accommodation suited to his rank and function, but as he had come from Pinerole to Turin with the superior of the Feuillants in Turin, he asked that he might remain with him and have some humble accommodation in his convent. He seems to have been taken rather too literally at his word, for he was given a tiny cell exposed to the

[238] *The Works of St. Francis de Sales*, Vol. 20, 316.

midsummer sun. Once more, he was to collapse, and this time he had to remain in bed for two or three weeks.

Finally in August, he took leave of Christine, who presented him with a beautiful diamond ring in token of her gratitude. Shortly after leaving Turin, the attendant who had the ring was unable to find it. De Sales had, anyway, made up his mind to sell it and give the money to the poor of Annecy. When he was told that it was lost, his only comment was that perhaps some poor man would find it, sell it, and live happily ever after. He was content that it should be so. However, as so often happens, the attendant discovered the ring in a fold of his dress.

The return journey across the Alps was a terrible affair. Mother de Chantal was to give an account of it. Referring to the effects of the heat and the bad and filthy accommodation in Turin, she went on: "Overcome by all this, he crossed the mountains, affected by unbearable pain and inconvenience, because of the piles from which he was suffering and the consequent loss of blood. So ill was he that the attendants did not think that he would live to see his home again."

It seems difficult to explain this unnecessary journey to Piedmont with the peculiar horror of the tiny, dirty cell, turned into an oven by the Italian sun, save in terms of Francis de Sales's bargain with God. After all, he was a very great man even in the worldly sense, and it is hard to believe that pressure could not have been put on him to live in at least the modest comfort which befitted his state and office, the more so in that he was not a man to insist fanatically on external penance and degradation. He preferred to take what came without fuss, whatever it might be. One can only conclude that God had specially called him to complete his life of abandonment and dedication to the love of God and detachment from himself by following to his last hour that same way of the Cross of which his Master had given the supreme example.

In the next and last chapter, we shall see how this otherwise inexplicable way of the Cross was to be followed right up to his last breath.

Chapter Sixteen

In the Steps of Christ
to the Very End

1622

In October 1622, the Bishop of Geneva received the second summons to leave Annecy, and all hope of retirement to Talloires vanished. It came from Charles-Emmanuel, who commanded him to travel to Avignon to form part of the suite of the Duke and princes of Savoy who were there to meet Louis XIII and officially congratulate him on the successful ending of the recent Calvinist revolt in the west and south-west of France.

The presence of Francis de Sales at the meeting and triumphant celebration of the Catholic victory had, of course, been demanded by Princess Christine, her husband, and Cardinal Maurice of Savoy, and it was certainly fitting that the most eminent churchman of Savoy should be there. But the princes and Christine herself, who had so lately met the sick bishop, should surely have wished to spare him a commission that must inevitably endanger his life.

In Annecy, the summons deeply upset everyone, and de Sales was implored to make his excuses and inform the duke that he was quite beyond undertaking the fatigues of such a journey and of the ceremonial. He absolutely refused to do so, one reason being that he could never forget the unsatisfactory state of those parts of his diocese which were within France. Despite Henry IV, Marie de' Medici, and Louis XIII, all so devoted to him personally, he had never been able to obtain French consent to a free apostolate in Gex and the other affected parts. After this latest victory over the Protestants, he doubtless hoped to persuade the young king to grant him his wishes. "We must go wheresoever God calls us," he said. "We shall go on as far as we are able, and we shall stop when illness allows us to go no further."

In a letter, he does not seem to have anticipated that the journey would prove fatal, for he wrote to a friend on November 1: "I must start tomorrow for Provence, and I do not know when I shall return, but I hope that it will be very soon!"[239] On the other hand, he was ready to face the worst. With his brother, the coadjutor, he spent a long time settling his own affairs, making his will, and seeing to it that all the business of the diocese was in order. Having done all this, he spent many hours with his confessor. At the end of all the arrangements, spiritual and temporal, he said to his brother, "Now I really feel that, by God's grace, I am only attached to the earth by one foot, for the other is already off the ground and ready to fly away."

One cannot imagine him saying this without a chuckle. But whatever he may have thought himself, there is no doubt that everyone else was far from smiling and quite convinced

---

[239] *The Works of St. Francis de Sales*, Vol. 20, 387.

that their bishop would never be seen alive again. He did not contradict the many people who implored him not to go because if he did they would never see him again. At least, they would see him in Heaven, he insisted, and he declared that all this was "in the good pleasure of God."

The most moving farewell was with his daughters of the Visitation. The day before the party was due to start, he celebrated Mass in the convent, vested in a magnificent chasuble given by Princess Christine, and he preached to the sisters: "My dear daughters," he said, "ask for nothing and refuse nothing. Always be ready to do what God and obedience demand of you. Let your one and only desire be to love God — your only ambition to possess Him. Goodbye, my daughters, until eternity." And when the nuns protested that he would return, he simply said that if it was God's good pleasure not to allow him to return to them, they should not bless Him any the less. "Whatever His good pleasure, it is always equally loving."

It was characteristic of him that his last words were for the humble *tourière* of Geneva, Jacqueline Coste, who knelt at his feet, crying. He assured her that if he did not return, they would meet again sooner than she expected. In fact, she was to die on August 13, 1623, eight months after him.

And so the last journey started on the morning of November 9, the bishop being accompanied by nine companions, including the ever-faithful Georges Rolland of Chablais days, now a dignified canon, and his valet, François Favre. Many people from Annecy accompanied him the twenty miles or so to the frontier town of Seyssel, where the party was to take ship for the Rhone-river journey to Lyons. In Seyssel, Francis de Sales wrote his last letter to the great friend of his life, Antoine Favre. Typically, it was now a simple letter making a business request and ending, "Do this for me, Monsieur *mon frère*, while I go to Provence where Monseigneur the Prince Cardinal will pay his homage and where I, visiting the many places of devotion there, will pray God to keep you and Madame my sister [Favre's wife] and bless all whom you love."[240] Did he recall when writing this brief letter, with no mention of any premonition of death, those days long before when the two young amateurs of stylistic elegance vied with one another in the turning of the best Latin phrase?

In the face of an intensely cold November wind, the party sailed the short distance to Belley, where faithful Camus took de Sales to the most recently founded Visitation convent. There he said Mass. Here was another sad parting — de Sales from his Boswell-to-be, a man with many prejudices and faults, but with an unbounded love for his saintly colleague and a deep desire to imitate him; a man never to have remotely the balance of a saint, but as capable of spiritual heroism as of spiritual waywardness.

By the tenth of November, the party had reached Lyons. There, after three and a half years' separation, he met again the woman with whom his whole spiritual teaching and work had been most closely, most intimately, linked in surely the most remarkable of spiritual friendships between a man and a woman: Jane Frances de Chantal. He could not know that he would see her again, for she was traveling on the business of the order, and he at least could not be certain of any measurable

---

[240] Ibid., 389-390.

duration of life. Yet, heroically, he was content with a few words, for she had work to do and he had to press on.

Celebrated as he was, he had passport difficulties with the boatman on leaving Lyons — to his companions' anger but not to his, for he was content to remark that the man had his duties to perform. He made a point of making friends with him as they continued their river journey. At Vienne, he left a letter making his excuses to the archbishop "my superior," for the Archbishop of Vienne was the metropolitan of the Annecy diocese — "I can write no more for I haven't the time."[241]

At Valence, he had time to visit the Visitation convent, and to enable an old lady of eighty-eight to enter it as a nun. "You must appreciate the spirit of our institute," he told the superior. "It has been established for the young, for the old, for the healthy and the sickly and infirm." At Bourg-Saint-Andéol, some forty miles from Avignon, the bishop was received in triumph by the people, who insisted on taking him, willy-nilly, to their ancient church and singing a *Te Deum* just because he was there in their midst.

At last, by the middle of November, Francis de Sales reached the city of the Popes to be greeted by the vice-legate of Pope Gregory XV and the acclamations of the people, calling out, "the great Bishop of Geneva," "the apostle of the Chablais," "the author of the *Introduction to the Devout Life*." Such greetings followed him wherever he went as soon as he was recognized, so much so that he had to take refuge in the hostelry where he was staying or in some nearby shop. It was in a bookshop that he uttered the wise words about such public

---

[241] Ibid., 393.

praise. "Left to myself, I would be tempted to make a fool of myself so as to undeceive these people. But we must live with Christian sincerity, neither playing the fool nor the wise man, but simply and once and for all carry on serving God, our divine Master." All this, one might say, was his Palm Sunday.

So far as the record goes, Francis de Sales might just as well have never made this journey to Avignon. He avoided the great festivities associated with the entry of the victorious Louis XIII, staying in his hotel quietly writing, and although he had to give some of his time to official duties with the Savoy suite and to social functions with the French court, we have no details of them. All we know is that he remained at the beck and call of the churches, priests, and people all only too anxious to have the great bishop and already nearly canonized saint with them, saying Mass and preaching. He was asked to found a Visitation convent, and prophesied that one day the town would have two. The first was established two years later; the second, twenty.

The bishop had sufficient energy left to ask the Cardinal of Savoy for a leave of absence to make a pilgrimage to the shrine of the Sainte-Baume, high up to the east of Marseilles, where, according to the legend, St. Mary Magdalene ended her days. The shrine was sixty or seventy miles from Avignon and in mountain country likely to be very cold at that time of the year. Perhaps Francis secretly wanted to die there, if he could not die at Saint-Germain above Talloires. The cardinal, however, would not give permission, because duty on the court came first. "Anyway," he said, "your heart is at Sainte-Baume where you are always a solitary." Francis did, however, get as far as Tarascon to venerate the relics of St. Martha. Perhaps it was fitting that it should be so. The saint of the love of God, asking only to dedicate himself to "the one thing necessary," was chosen by God to find it in "the cares and troubles" of which Martha complained, but in which he could find "the better part."[242]

At last the celebrations and conversations were over, and Francis was able to leave Avignon, following the courts of France and Savoy traveling by land to Lyons. Francis de Sales's passion had begun.

It appears to have been nobody's fault, except perhaps his own refusal ever to look after himself. One must picture a very sick man, suffering all the time from severe inconveniences and pains, easily fatigued, and inevitably having to overcome the bad temper, restlessness, easy irritation that goes with the last stages of his disease. We must also remember that, however humble he might be, he was a bishop and already an almost legendary figure, not to mention his position in the princely suites. Yet somehow it happened that from now on, he was to live personally in extreme discomfort and in almost sordid circumstances — and so die. During the whole time, he manifested nothing but serenity, thought for others, and complete resignation to his strange lot. In fact, he welcomed it.

It began near Pont-Saint-Esprit, some thirty miles north of Avignon. There all the rooms in the inn were taken. He refused to allow anyone to say who he was, and he slept on straw in a loft. At Valence he was given a good room, but gave it up to a foreign lady who asked to have it. He himself had to share a single bedroom with Georges Rolland. Rolland slept on the

---

[242] Luke 10:41-42.

mattress with the bedclothes. De Sales slept in his clothes on the straw palliasse.

And when finally Lyons was reached, he refused many offers of hospitality because he wanted to stay near the sisters of the Visitation. All they could offer him — indeed, it was all they had — was the little upstairs room in what was scarcely more than the gardener's hut or shed. It was clean, but the fire smoked badly, and it was nearly December. At least, it would have to do for the night. The next day he could accept one or other of the many offers of accommodation suited to his rank and his only too visible infirmities. But he was adamant, although we cannot but believe that if a doctor had been called or if someone in authority had really insisted, he would have allowed himself to be persuaded by them.

At least, the poor sisters said, let him have a carriage for the carrying out of his duties. But he refused again, insisting on walking from one place to another on his badly swollen feet. For twenty-nine days he was to drag himself through the dirty streets and to sleep in that little smoke-filled room. In it he was to die.

There are penances and there are penances, but it is hard to think of a more unbearable martyrdom for a man in his state than the acceptance of such discomfort by night and by day until he inevitably collapsed. All that he had preached in the way of little and humble, unglamorous, unceasing mortification was being realized in those last days and most of all in the manner of his death.

All this discomfort can have meant little to him, however, in comparison with the pleasure of a day with Mother de Chantal again. She had come from Montferrand to discuss the accumulation of business which years of letters cannot cover. She had come, too, to obtain her father's advice on the state of her soul, more apt to worrying and self-questioning than was his. He was, of course, well used to speaking through the enclosure grille, and one wishes that it had been on the occasion of his many hours' conversation with her that he had been warned that the door of the room was half-open onto the road and letting in the cold. He got up to shut it when he saw some children outside gaping at the strange sight of a priest talking to a wall. Rather than disappoint them of their fascinating sight, he left the door untouched.

Mother de Chaugy has given an account of that last meeting between the cofounders. "Mother," he said, "we have some free hours together. Which of us shall start the conversation?" Mother de Chantal answered at once: "May I, please, Father? My heart is in great need of being looked over by you." "What, Mother," he answered, "have you still keen desires and a wish to choose? I expected to find you entirely angelic." And then he said, "We shall talk about ourselves in Annecy. Now it is our duty to talk of the business of our congregation."

Mother de Chantal immediately put away the notes she had made about the state of her soul, and for four hours they discussed matters concerning the Visitation. Then at the end of the conversation, Francis gave her orders to leave Lyons at once and continue her visitation of the convents in Grenoble, Valence, and Relley, and to visit the reformed Bernardines in Rumilly. In this last conversation with the lady with the light brown hair who had sat under his pulpit in the Sainte-Chapelle in Dijon eighteen years earlier, he preached to her the final, the hardest lesson: utter self-forgetfulness, utter reliance on the God who had chosen to enter so closely into the *fine pointe* of her soul.

His days in Lyons were devoted wholly, when he was free from attendance at court, to his customary pastoral work, to preaching, to hearing confessions, and to begging alms of the great gentlemen and ladies with whom he had to spend too much of his short time, that he might distribute them to the poor. He saw the king, but we do not know whether it was possible for him to introduce the old subject of Gex and French territories under his care.

On December 19, he wrote two letters, the first to an unknown lady, the second to Mother de Chastellux, superior at Moulins. In the first he wrote, "O God, how happy are those who, free from the trammels of courts and their flatteries, live peacefully in a saintly solitude at the foot of the Crucifix. I have never, I must say, had a good opinion of any vanity, but the vanity which is the atmosphere of the feeble grandeurs of court is worse than I thought. My very dear daughter, the longer I walk the way of our mortality, the more I despise it and the more attractive, each day, seems that holy eternity to which we aspire and for the sake of which alone we should have regard for ourselves. Let us only live for that life, my very dear daughter, for it alone deserves the name of life. In comparison with it, the lives of the greatest of this world are but a very miserable death."[243] His second letter to Mother de Chastellux ended with the words: "I am not yet leaving this town, and I believe I shall have the consolation of writing to you again."[244]

---

[243] *The Works of St. Francis de Sales,* Vol. 20, 395.
[244] Ibid., 396.

Now Christmas was approaching, and on Christmas Eve, at the request of Marie de' Medici, Francis laid the foundation stone of a new church of the Recollets and preached. The ceremony lasted three hours. The day had been cold and foggy, and suddenly he felt very chilled and ill. Nevertheless, he did not flinch from singing Midnight Mass and preaching in the Visitation convent and then saying his second Mass for the court at the Dominican church, where he gave Holy Communion to Prince Victor-Amadeus and Princess Christine. One of those who went to Communion at that royal Mass was Robert Arnauld d'Andilly, the brother of Angélique. Later, the then Jansenist recalled in his memoirs how after the Mass, he went to the sacristy to see the bishop: "He received me with unbelievable joy and, embracing me, said, 'My son, I recognized you in the breaking of the bread.' "[245] It was as if he was again anticipating the Jansenist repugnance to the frequent Communion which he himself had always recommended, reminding his readers and those he spiritually directed of the custom of the early Christians to go to Communion daily.

After that second Mass, he had been obliged to return to the court and, because of this, had asked another priest to say the three Christmas Masses at the Visitation convent. When he himself reached the convent, the other priest was still saying his Masses, and patiently he waited and prayed in the chapel until he could say his own third Mass. Later that Christmas Day, he received two postulants and preached for the occasion. Then until late into the night he had to be at court again to bid Marie de' Medici farewell, as she was leaving the next day.

[245] Cf. Luke 24:35.

No wonder that, the next morning — St. Stephen's day — people noticed how very ill he looked "one side of his face drawn, the eye retreating into its socket and dull." His memory was also failing, and he had difficulty in recognizing people. Expecting to leave Lyons and return home, he arranged to spend the evening with the sisters and to give them a conference — "On Asking Nothing and Refusing Nothing."[246] They begged for some last advice before he started his journey home.

"What do you want me to say, my dear daughter," he said to the superior, as torches were held up to light him to the garden cottage. "I told you everything when I said, "Desire nothing and refuse nothing.' I cannot say anything else. Think of the Infant Jesus in the crib. He suffers all the trials of weather and cold — all that His Father allows to happen to Him. He does not refuse the little comforts His Mother gives Him. Nowhere do we read that He held out His hands to His Mother's breast. He left all that to her care and foresight. So we too should desire nothing and refuse nothing, accepting what God sends us, the cold and the troubles of the times." And his last words to his nuns were, characteristically, a simple concrete example. Asked if, then, one should never warm oneself — they must have been feeling the cold in that poor Visitation convent — he said, "When the fire is burning, obedience clearly means us to warm ourselves, but we need not get excited and rush over to do so."

---

[246] *The Works of St. Francis de Sales*, Vol. 6, 383-389. See also *The Spiritual Conferences*, 399-406; and *The Art of Loving God*, 141-143.

The next day, the feast of St. John, he had a heavy program before him, for he had to take formal leave of the Savoy princes. When he rose, he noticed that his sight seemed to be failing, and he said Mass late at the convent after going to Confession to the chaplain. Once again, the superior asked for a last word of advice. This time he gave her just one word, writing it on a piece of paper. Thrice in very large letters he wrote, "Humility."

As he was leaving the convent, as usual on foot, he met the Duke of Bellegarde, to whom he had written on Christmas Eve, asking his help in connection with a common friend seeking employment. De Sales stood in the cold and fog, his head uncovered, talking to the duke. Then he fulfilled his appointments with members of the court, which, as usual, meant much ceremony and standing up.

At last, tired out, he returned to the convent in the middle of the day. His servants noticed that after his very light midday meal, he seemed unable to rise, but sat on at table in a kind of torpor. He roused himself to meet a number of religious who had come to bid him farewell, and most uncharacteristically, he let them depart without accompanying them to the door. He tried to write some letters, while the attendants were wondering whether he could possibly travel in his state and whether the homeward journey had not better be deferred. As they watched him, he tried to rise from his chair. Just as he painfully got to his feet, he collapsed.

Quickly, the half-paralyzed man was undressed and put to bed, and a priest and doctor sent for. The diagnosis of apoplexy through a rupture of a cerebral artery was quickly made. For this, the treatment in those days was to do anything and everything to rouse the patient from his stupor and from fall-ing back into sleep. He was given the Anointing of the Sick, but he was unable to receive the Viaticum. He asked that his rosary should be twisted around his right wrist.

Then began those strange long hours of evening, night, and morning when the poor patient in his agony was delivered to the crude and cruel remedies of the doctors of those days, and the scarcely less trying personal and spiritual good will of a long procession of pious and curious visitors. Outside in the town the news had spread, and people flocked to the churches to pray for the bishop's recovery. However good-intentioned the spiritual and temporal ministrations, one cannot but think of the dying man reduced to a public exhibition, a mere *thing* in the hands of his friends and well-wishers. The doctors mal-treated the poor, paralyzed, swollen body, shaking and slap-ping it, pinching it and rubbing it, opening veins, and even tearing at the hair.

Even his friends thought it well to try to rouse him by say-ing things that would scandalize him. He was told that his brother, the coadjutor, was at the door, and they promised him that soon he would be enthroned in the cathedral of St. Peter in Geneva. Most of the time de Sales seemed to be con-scious, and such questions did rouse him to protest vehe-mently. He had never wanted his episcopal throne in Geneva; he had only wanted the salvation of the people of Geneva. People should not lie, his brother could not be near. To the pi-ous exhortations he answered mostly with apt quotations from Scripture.

Hour after hour the agony endured as the morning of the twenty-eighth, the feast of the Holy Innocents, came and passed to afternoon. Now it was clear to the doctors that their half-measures were not proving successful. If the bishop's life was to be saved, more desperate measures must be used. A plaster of cantharides, or blister beetles, was applied to his bald head, the effect of which is distressing, especially to a patient in public view, for there appears to have been no privacy during this unhappy scene. Then he was lifted out of bed and placed in a chair. The doctors asked him whether he would agree to being cauterized. "My body is in the doctors' hands; let them do what they think best," the saint replied. A surgeon meanwhile was heating the iron rods. A priest reminded the patient to unite his sufferings with the Crown of Thorns, and he protested, murmuring that there could be no comparison. The surgeon then approached and pressed the red-hot iron on the back of the skull, but doing it so clumsily as to make two burns. By now the blister-beetle plaster had done its work, and the skin under it was all blisters. It was torn off to lay bare the live flesh. Into it the red-hot iron was once more plunged, smoke rising from it with the smell of burning flesh. Francis de Sales bore this cruel treatment without murmur and only a reflex of the tautening of his shoulders. He cried quietly and murmured, "*Jesu, Maria.*"

He was then taken back to his bed, still mouthing the holy names. By eight o'clock of the evening, he was dead.

Surely no one could say that in that last month of humiliation and service to others despite grave discomforts and constant distressing illness until the moment of actual collapse, all to be followed by three days of public agony in the most literal sense of the word, Francis de Sales had not drunk to the last drop the chalice which was the secret and the whole meaning of his own spiritual life and of the teaching he had given to others and to the world.

The most human, cheerful, approachable, and encouraging of all the saints was also the least compromising in following his Master — supreme model of all that we mean by human attraction — to the very foot of the Cross.

In his will, Francis de Sales had asked that if his body could not be buried in the cathedral of St. Peter in Geneva, it should rest in the Visitation Convent of Annecy. Permission of Louis XIII was needed to take so venerable a relic from Lyons and France, and it was carried in a triumphant procession to Annecy. On the saint's future feast day, January 29,[247] the solemn funeral service was celebrated by his brother and successor, Jean-François de Sales, the coffin covered with white satin, and on it a shield with the name "Jesus" inscribed on it.

Mother Jane Frances de Chantal then received the body at the gates of the Visitation, where it rested near the grille of the sisters. Kneeling by the coffin, the future St. Jane Frances finished the conversation about the state of her soul which St. Francis de Sales in Lyons had promised her once they were together again in Annecy.

The solemn ceremonies of beautification took place in St. Peter's on January 8, 1662, but the brief was signed by Pope Alexander VII on December 28, 1661 — thirty-nine years to the day after St. Francis's death. He was canonized on April 19, 1665, which happened, appropriately enough, to be Good Shepherd Sunday.

---

[247] The feast of St. Francis is now celebrated on January 24.

In the Steps of Christ to the Very End

∞

O God, who willed that
Francis, your Confessor and Bishop,
should become all things to all men to save souls,
enable us also to be filled with your gentle love and so,
led aright by his advice and with the help of his prayers,
may we also attain to eternal joy.

Collect of the feast of
St. Francis de Sales

∞

Biographical Note

Michael de la Bedoyere

(1900-1973)

Michael de la Bedoyere was educated at the Jesuit Stonyhurst College and at Oxford University, where he received first-class honors in Modern Greats. After teaching philosophy at the University of Minnesota for a short time, he became the assistant editor of the *Dublin Review* and, in 1934, became the editor of *The Catholic Herald,* the London weekly whose modest circulation rose significantly under his editorship. Later, with his wife, Charlotte, he founded and launched the independent newsletter *Search,* which he published from 1962-1968. He became known as one of the foremost scholars and journalists of his time.

During his journalistic career, de la Bedoyere wrote more than thirty books — many of them biographies of both religious and secular subjects, including St. Catherine of Siena, St. Francis of Assisi, Baron von Hügel, Lafayette, and Washington. Skillfully weaving together historical events, personal accounts, eyewitness testimony, and writings by and about his subjects, de la Bedoyere brings these religious and historical

SaintMaker

figures alive for today's readers. His popular biographies of the saints offer practical, real-life examples of how Catholics can be active as Catholics in all aspects of their lives — a matter of great importance to de la Bedoyere and in today's largely secular world.